REDUNDANCY AND RECESSION

# Redundancy and Recession
## in South Wales

C. C. HARRIS

and
The Redundancy and Unemployment Research Group,
School of Social Studies, University College of Swansea

Basil Blackwell

First published 1987

Basil Blackwell Ltd
108 Cowley Road, Oxford, OX4 1JF, UK

Basil Blackwell Inc.
432 Park Avenue South, Suite 1503
New York, NY 10016, USA



*British Library Cataloguing in Publication Data*

Harris, C. C.
Redundancy and recession in South Wales.
1. Employees, Dismissal of—Wales, South
I. Title II. University College of
Swansea. *Redundancy and Unemployment*
*Research Group*
*331.13*'79429'4 HF5549.5.D55

ISBN 0-631-15106-0

*Library of Congress Cataloging in Publication Data*

Harris, C. C. (Christopher Charles)
Redundancy and recession in South Wales.
Bibliography: p.
Includes index.
1. Unemployed—Wales, South. 2. Unemployment—Wales, South. 3. Wales, South—Economic conditions.
I. University College of Swansea. School of Social Studies. Redundancy and Unemployment Research Group.
II. Title.
HD5766.A6H37 1987 331.13'794294 87-6301
ISBN 0-631-15106-0

Typeset in 10 on 11½ pt Garamond
by DMB Typesetting, Oxford
Printed in Great Britain by
Billing and Sons Ltd, Worcester

# Contents

# Preface

This book is the product of four years' research financed by the Economic and Social Research Council (Grant G00230023). The research team comprised Dr R. M. Lee and Dr L. D. Morris, whose work was augmented by the research of the ESRC 'linked' student attached to the project, Mrs G. Leaver. The research was immeasurably enriched by the parallel study conducted by Dr R. Fevre which centred on the Port Talbot labour market. This study was also financed by the ESRC (Grant G00230048). The main results of the study are not fully reported here, but in R. Fevre's *Wales is Closed* (1987). A full list of all the publications arising from these two projects is to be found in Appendix 2, together with the publications of a parallel study of the older redundant workers undertaken independently by Dr W. R. Bytheway. Dr Bytheway and the members of the team have also contributed to R. M. Lee, *Redundancy, Layoffs and Plant Closures: the Social Impact*, (1986a) which is, indirectly, a product of the research reported here.

Because of the need to redefine the aims and purposes of the study while it was in progress, the analysis on which we eventually embarked was unfinished when Dr Lee left the project. It was completed by Dr Brown and the writing and editing of this volume fell to me, as director of both projects and supervisor of Mrs Leaver. Lee and Brown, Morris, Leaver and Fevre constituted the University College of Swansea Redundancy and Unemployment Research Group which is treated as my 'co-author' of this volume.

We were not a team in the strict sense: we did not all start together or finish together, and Dr Fevre's and Mrs Leaver's studies were quite separate enterprises. The members of the team are not collectively responsible for the final product as a totality: contributors' names appear on the chapters they were responsible for. It is nonetheless true, in varying degrees, that none of the researchers could have completed his or her part of the research without the contribution of the others, and that the final product is a result of what Comte would have termed 'the combination of efforts'. There is therefore a sense in which we were, if not a team, with the high degree of functional integration which that term applies, then at least a group. At the time of writing we are no longer a group but a geographically dispersed network with Swansea as its nodal point, and even that degree of connectedness has doubtless been prolonged only by the production of this volume. This decline is regrettably an inevitable result of the social conditions of intellectual production in Britain in the late-twentieth century.

*Chris Harris*
Swansea

# Acknowledgements

Many people have helped in the production of this book. We wish to thank the ESRC for funding the research and for the sympathetic understanding of the then Sociology and Social Administration Committee of the difficulties we encountered. In particular we should like to thank the committee member directly concerned, Professor Bryan Roberts.

We are also indebted to the staff and interviewers of Social Surveys (Gallup Poll) Ltd, who undertook the three surveys of the redundant steelworkers with a complex survey instrument involving a great deal of data preparation. We are particularly grateful to Margaret Davies of Port Talbot, the field supervisor, for her tolerance and her energy.

The survey could not have taken place without a sampling frame, and this was supplied by the Manpower Services Commission (Wales). We wish to thank its chairman, Sir Melville Rosser, for his good offices and all those in MSC who helped to draw the sample, especially D. E. L. Jenkins without whose assistance and enthusiasm we would never have achieved a sample at all.

BSC (the British Steel Corporation) itself figured much more largely in our research than was ever intended or envisaged, and we wish to thank the Personnel Department of the Abbey Works at Margam for its willingness to comply with our repeated requests for information.

We have greatly appreciated the help afforded us by all the staff of the Computer Centre at the University College of Swansea, especially Mary Bodger and Mike Llewellyn, in solving the numerous computing problems that arose through the course of the work.

Perhaps the most important member of the research team is the research secretary. A good research secretary is worth more than a research assistant, and in Ethne Jeffreys we had an excellent secretary whose contribution to the success of the project was vital, and far greater than she probably realized.

Ethne Jeffreys did not, however, type the present work. That task fell in part to Carol Cook but chiefly to Glenys Bridges, who has typed so much of my work over the years that she has become almost as much part of the team as Ethne Jeffreys. We wish to thank all our secretarial assistants for their help and forbearance.

We are very grateful to Eddie Jenkins of the Department of Further and Continuing Education for his help in organizing the seminar in which we discussed our conclusions with the steelworkers themselves, for our research could not have been undertaken without the co-operation of these men. To them we wish to express our sincere thanks for the tolerance and help in successive and doubtless increasingly tedious interviews, often conducted at highly stressful and critical moments in their lives. Diolch yn fawr iawn.

# Abbreviations

| | |
|---|---|
| BOS | Basic Oxygen Steel |
| BSC | British Steel Corporation |
| DHSS | Department of Health and Social Security |
| EOA | Employment Office Area |
| ESRC | Economic and Social Research Council |
| GHS | General Household Survey |
| IMS | Institute of Manpower Studies |
| ISTC | Iron and Steel Trades Confederation |
| LIFO | last in, first out |
| MSC | Manpower Services Commission |
| NCB | National Coal Board |
| SSRC | Social Science Research Council |
| TTWA | travel-to-work-area |
| VLN | very low nitrogen (steel) |
| WMIS | Work Measurement Incentive Scheme |

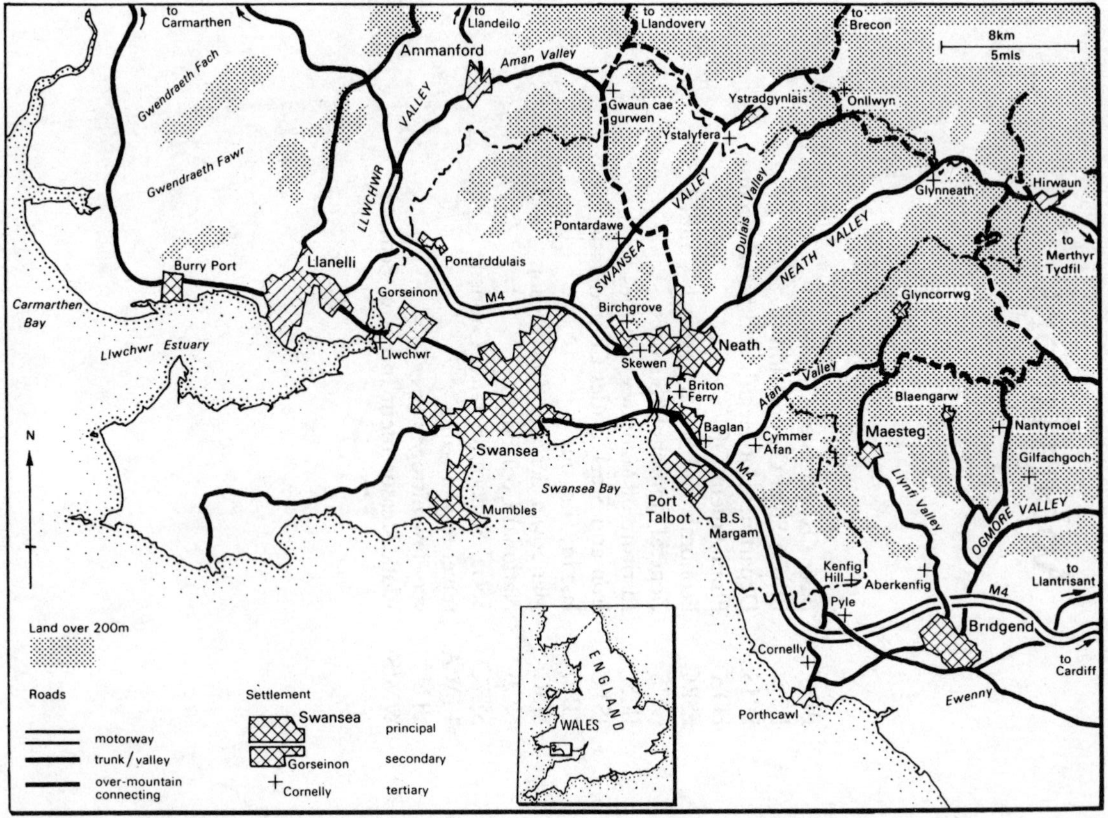


*Map of west Industrial South Wales copyright © T. Fearnside, cartographer, Department of Geography, University College of Swansea*

# Introduction

Some years ago Peter Laslett wrote a book entitled *The World We Have Lost* (Laslett, 1965; third edition 1984). Laslett's lost world was the world on the other side of that Great Divide so beloved of contemporary sociologists and other nineteenth-century thinkers: that profound transformation of social life which occurred in the late eighteenth and early nineteenth century which generations of school children have learnt to call by the name invented by economic historians in the 1880s: 'the industrial revolution'. That this period witnessed a profound transformation in European social life is not in dispute: what is less clear is how it should be characterized. 'Industrialization' is a term which emphasizes the rapid revolutionization of the means of production, leading to a quantum leap in the development of the forces of production and a profound acceleration in the rate of technological change. It was associated with a belief in the inevitability of human 'progress' and an extremely optimistic view of the human capacity to improve both the standard of living and the quality of life.

Nineteenth-century 'progress' seemed to provide the empirical warrant for the possibility of realizing the Enlightenment dream which Carl Becker has so elegantly described as *The Heavenly City of the Eighteenth-Century Philosophers* (1932). This dream-come-true provides the context of almost all political, economic and social thought since the mid nineteenth century, whether that of bourgeois thinkers like Comte and Spencer or of Marx, Engels and Lenin. If the Enlightenment boldly claimed the possibility of humanity creating its own Kingdom of Heaven on Earth, then this revolution of the means of production signalled the coming of the Kingdom of God with power: the power of steam, of electricity, internal combustion and atomic energy. For the first time in history, mankind could look a niggardly nature in the face and say: we are the masters now.

There is no question but that sociology as both an academic discipline and a wider, more diffuse intellectual movement is heir to this tradition. It shares with Enlightenment thought a concern with the realization on Earth of this Heavenly Kingdom by the exercise of human reason, and the post-

Enlightenment belief in the centrality of empirical enquiry in the production of the knowledge which was the basis of the great transformation. And yet sociological writers even at their most optimistic (Comte, Spencer, Durkheim) have sounded a note of warning, if not of outright despair. For sociology was born out of the conservative reaction to the Enlightenment, out of fear of the as yet unknown future to which industrial revolution pointed, whose profound difference from the known and familiar past was heralded by the transformation of social relations associated with the revolution of the technological means of production. Hence, although sociologists share in the nineteenth-century hope of glory, it remains for them an as yet unrealized potentiality whose actualization requires the development of new means of co-operation, which are themselves one of the chief means of production. The development of social relationships appropriate to the continually changing technological means of production remains problematic. And yet, if the relationships which come into being as the result of technological and industrial change are not appropriate, instead of becoming master of its destiny and captain of its fate, humanity falls into a new slavery in which it finds itself at the mercy of forces which it has brought into being but which it can no longer control.

For sociologists, therefore, our world differs from the world we have lost, not merely in terms of its levels of material production and consumption, but in terms of the character of the social relations into which people have to enter in order to produce and consume, and in terms of the way in which, by virtue of their participation in those relations, they come to have particular social identities, customary modes of thought and action, and characteristic types of sensibility. The sociologist draws attention to the fact, therefore, that the great transformation of the nineteenth century involved not merely the creation of a new technical system of production, but also a new way of life which eventually came to condition the operation of the system of production which originated it.

Hence, like Marxists, sociologists tend to emphasize not merely the quantitative development of the forces of production in the nineteenth century, but also the qualitative transformation of social relations. No economic historian, Marxist or not, would deny that an absolute precondition of using the new technology and new sources of power in production was the concentration of capital, and that the result was an extension of wage labour throughout the century until it became the dominant source of livelihood for the majority of the population. Nor would anyone deny that associated with these developments was the growth of an extensive division of labour within the workplace (the technical division of labour) and specialization by enterprises in the production of different goods for sale (the social division of labour). Both these processes had to be co-ordinated: in the first case by the entrepreneur, and later by an increasingly bureaucratized managerial administration; in the second case by the product market. Both these divisions of labour raise in acute form the problem of control: by entrepreneurs/managers over workers; by workers over their own labour; and by the members of society over the total productive process. The problem here is not, immediately, the control of nature by mankind, but the control of a process by those participating in it.

The problem of control constitutes an issue over which social and political thought has been divided. In sociological terms that division may be represented by the figures of Spencer, Durkheim and Marx. Spencer regarded the regulation of economic life as something that could be safely left to the market: the same competitive process that led to a progressive differentiation of society into different groups of producers would ensure naturally what Comte had termed 'the combination of efforts'. The system would be self-adjusting and equilibrating. What *we* still see as the hierarchical differentiation between employers and employed was for Spencer merely a form of functional differentiation whose utility provided its own legitimation. 'Rank' would wither in proportion to the growth of functional differentiation. For Durkheim, however, as for Comte, association in a highly differentiated society posed acutely the problem of the moral basis of such association, without which either contractual relations or their collective regulation was impossible. For Marx, no resolution of the problem was possible as long as the productive process required the co-operation of groups differentiated in terms of their economic functions and characterized by conflicting material interests in both production and exchange. Attempts to create the moral consensus sought by Durkheim appeared from this standpoint no more than the attempt by more powerful groups to impose a moral order favourable to their own interests on the less powerful.

Two world wars and numerous smaller conflicts have long since shattered the dream of an endless future of 'peace and prosperity' or 'order and progress' entertained in the nineteenth century, while the depression of the inter-war years destroyed the naive belief in the beneficence of 'natural', that is unplanned and unregulated, economic progress. The principle of intervention in natural social processes, both nationally and internationally, in both the 'economic' and 'social' spheres, is still widely accepted. However, such intervention continues to pose major problems with regard to the nature of the institutions of intervention, the technical means of so doing and the mobilization of popular support for the aims of such intervention. In so far as social and ideological conflict was largely absent in first world countries in the decades after the Second World War, that absence was due mainly to their enjoying a period of economic growth which masked their failure to tackle adequately the problem of the distribution of wealth. They were also characterized by the successful adoption of Keynesian or quasi-Keynesian interventionist policies to ensure full employment, combined with the development of social services and social security measures which mitigated the disadvantages of the least privileged. The problem of control was 'resolved' in favour of a mixed economy and, in Britain, steadily increasing state intervention and regulation.

## Unemployment, recession and transition

The 1960s saw the beginning of major changes in what, for the majority of the population of Britain, had become during the post-war period 'normal' life. The first was a change in consciousness which had two chief strands: a growing rejection of traditional authority reflected in a change in morals and manners, and demands for greater personal freedom and self-expression; and simultaneously an increased questioning of the existing social order and criticism of its materialism, its degradation of 'work', and 'society's' oppressive and inegalitarian structure. The second, though less remarked at the time, was a change in the behaviour of the economic system itself. Unemployment began to rise in the mid-1960s and attempts to reduce it by Keynesian reflationary measures became less and less effective. The 1970s became a decade of 'stagflation', a neologism coined to describe what was once popularly held to be economically impossible: not currency stability bought at the price of low levels of growth and significant unemployment, nor full employment and growth in the gross domestic product bought at the price of moderate or even severe inflation, but the worst of both these possible worlds.

The economic conjuncture of the 1970s had profound effects on social, political and economic thought, consciousness and action. In economic terms, the puzzle was why 'high' rates of unemployment remained resistant to attempts to expand demand. An initial response to this problem was to focus attention on the labour market, a relatively neglected area of enquiry in the academic disciplines of both sociology and economics. In conditions of full employment, when there was a rough equality between the numbers of unemployed and the number of vacancies and the problem facing the economy was labour shortage rather than surplus, labour problems were seen to lie with employers rather than with labour or the labour market. In those far-off days of 'overheating', labour shortages and 'wage drift', the problems of the economy were attributed to labour-hoarding by employers and their bidding up wage levels above the nationally agreed rates in order to 'steal' scarce labour. If unions were criticized, as indeed they were, it was for using their 'muscle' to enforce outdated and inefficient working practices which kept productivity low and endangered competitiveness. Unions were accused of 'living in the past' and clinging to practices born of the depression years whose purpose was to multiply jobs and spin out the available work as long as possible, practices which were, of course, irrelevant now that there were the means, political will and social consensus necessary to ensure full employment in perpetuity.

Persistent and rising rates of unemployment both in Britain and the USA in the 1970s provided a new perspective. Could we not have been witnessing a secular change in the 'natural' rate of unemployment? The natural rate of unemployment in a full employment economy is that rate which reflects the time it takes for workers coming on the market to find employment (plus, of course, that 'irreducible' number of persons who are deemed mentally, physically or morally unfit for employment).

If workers have cash reserves due to past high wages, redundancy payments, and unemployment benefits, they may well be more particular about the jobs they take and prefer to wait longer until a job they consider suitable and desirable turns up. Conversely, as the level of technical skills required and the degree of specialization increases, so the time taken to fit the right workers to the right job will also increase. If these are the causes of rising unemployment rates it is clearly absurd to attempt to reduce unemployment by increasing demand, which will not call forth an increased supply of goods and will simply bid up prices. The answer was thought to lie, rather, in reducing the *imperfections of the labour market* by improving employment services, and in an acceptance of the fact that a modern economy has a higher natural rate of unemployment.

An alternative or ancillary explanation of higher rates of unemployment denies the existence of a single market for labour and asserts the existence of a plurality of relatively closed markets. The first step in such an argument is to distinguish at least two distinct sectors of *employment*: primary and secondary; the first characterized by well-paid and secure jobs with relatively good conditions of service and the second by poorly paid and insecure employment. The second step is to claim that there are corresponding divisions in the labour force such that it is composed of two sub-categories of workers who find work in the different sectors, secondary sector workers being in some way ineligible for, or having low chances of obtaining, work in the primary sector. Unemployment is seen as concentrated in the secondary sector, while the primary sector is still suffering from labour shortage. Attempts to reflate the economy expand demand in the primary sector, create labour shortages there and bid up wages without affecting, except marginally, unemployment levels in the secondary sector. Once again, attempting to cure the problem by expanding demand will produce inflation without either growth or a reduction of unemployment. Instead the answer is thought to lie in programmes of government intervention to change the attributes of disadvantaged groups which lead to their constituting a secondary sector of the labour force.

Both these types of explanation shift the emphasis of economic policy away from political control and macro-economic variables to administrative attempts to alter the operation of economic mechanisms; in so doing they signal a renewed interest in the operations of economic *institutions* (and the social circumstances which condition their operation), of which the market is the chief. What is distinctive about these explanations, however, is that it is neither the productive process itself nor the product market but the *labour market* which becomes the focus of attention.

In contrast to such explanations are two other types which have considerable importance. The first is that unemployment is a consequence of the restructuring of industrial production in advanced capitalist societies, which results in a lack of demand for particular types of labour. Once again the answer is not reflation but retraining, and, of course, worker mobility in response to the re-negotiation of the spatial division of labour. The second explanation involves an atavistic return to the simplicities of classical economics: labour is a commodity like any other commodity. If there is a surplus of a commodity on a market, the market can be 'cleared' by lowering the price. There is a surplus of labour: *ergo* the price of labour must be too high. Since the price of a commodity will naturally fall to a level at which supply and demand are in equilibrium, the existence of a price of labour above the level at which the market 'clears' must be due to government intervention and more especially to union interference with the free play of market forces. The political force of this argument, especially in a period characterized by both rising unemployment and rising prices, should not be underestimated on the grounds of its simplicity; indeed it is one of its main strengths. It identifies a single enemy – the unions – responsible for both unemployment and inflation.

The effect of the preoccupation with the stagflation problem of the 1970s was to create a climate of economic thought which effectively severed the links forged in the 1940s between unemployment and deficiency of demand, and between full employment and government intervention. This had a profound effect on social consciousness: it weakened both the belief that the economy could be controlled and the will to control it. These had been cardinal features of the consensus politics of the 1950s and 1960s, dominated as they were by a generation who, having experienced the privations of the inter-war years, returned from the Second World War determined that the post-World War One experience would never be repeated. At the same time low rates of growth, combined with high levels of inflation, exacerbated conflicts between different sections of the labour force: conflicts emerged over the distribution problem at the very moment that the post-war consensus on the degree and nature of political intervention at the macro-economic level collapsed.

These two issues were, however, closely linked since the strikes of the winter of 1978–1979 were largely strikes of lower-paid public service workers. The attempt to control inflation by controlling wages led the government to attempt to hold down the wages of low-paid service workers as part of its policy of reducing public expenditure in the battle against inflation: workers whose demands were an attempt to restore living standards eroded by that very inflation which more strongly placed workers in the private sector had been able to withstand. As long as government intervention was required to increase demand it was possible, at least at home, to reconcile the imperatives of a macro-economic policy concerned with full employment with a moral commitment to alleviate the distribution problem. However, once it became necessary to reduce demand to control inflation the Labour Party, ideologically committed to both full employment and greater equality, found itself on the horns of a dilemma from which it was unable to escape.

By 1979 the historical and economic conditions necessary for the continuation of post-war politics had collapsed. The return of a new-style Conservative administration did not break the mould of post-war politics: like the division of the Labour Party which followed, it was the result of the emergence of a new set of social and economic conditions. The 1970s were, therefore, a time of a major economic transition, quite apart from successive increases in the price of oil and (in Britain) the effect on the economy of increasing North Sea oil revenues. This economic transition was signalled by disturbances in industrial and political life, which in turn had profound effects on social and political consciousness.

So far the economic transition has been characterized solely in terms of rising rates of unemployment increasingly resistant to demand-expansionary policies, and the association of those policies with rising inflation. The transition has, however, another aspect which requires exploration. The period 1960 to 1980 was characterized by a decline in the proportion of employment in the manufacturing and primacy (agricultural and extractive) sectors and a growth in the tertiary or service sector. At first this was understood in terms of 'affluence' and 'leisure'. At its simplest, the increased contribution to the national product by the service sector was understood in terms of what might be called the post-war historical paradigm. Social consciousness – which refers as much to the consciousness of politicians and academics in the social sciences as to the consciousness of 'ordinary people' – defined the present in terms of its difference from the past; the 'past' being the inter-war period. 'Unemployment then, full employment now' is perhaps the most obvious past–present contrast, but as full employment came to be increasingly taken for granted, it was replaced as a central feature of social consciousness by the contrast between working-class subsistence and affluence: a past in which work was characterized by long hours and low wages spent chiefly on housing, food, clothing and heating, had been replaced by a present in which shorter hours and higher wages meant that ordinary people had more of their income to spend on non-subsistence needs and the time to devote to non-work and non-subsistence activities. Given this type of historical understanding, the growth of service occupations is seen not as the result of the decline in manufacturing activity and/or employment, but as the result of the advance towards a new society characterized by 'leisure' and 'affluence'.

There is, however, an alternative conceptualization of this change in employment patterns, which emphasizes the growing role of the state in the provision of public services financed by taxation raised from those engaged in productive activity in the agricultural, extractive and manufacturing sectors of the economy. This is more 'powerful' than the affluence interpretation since it makes it possible to link the growth of the service sector with a perennial theme of political and economic thought since 1918, the declining competitiveness of British manufacturing industry. This is not the place to discuss the rival explanations of this decline, let alone evaluate them. It is sufficient to note three chief types of explanation. The first, or bourgeois, explanation is cultural and claims that, in contrast to our competitors, the management of British industry has been 'traditional' rather than 'rational', concerned with preservation rather than innovation, with sufficing rather than optimizing strategies. In class terms, the rising class of competitive, innovating manufacturers and traders which created the first industrial revolution has been assimilated to the pre-industrial middle class infected with the values of an upper class which stress tradition as opposed to change, co-operation rather than competition. English culture at first accommodated but finally absorbed and transformed 'the industrial spirit' which animated economic life in the first part of the nineteenth century. As a result, the consensus politics of the post-war era involved a tacit arrangement between the parties to improve the quality of life without altering its basic character, a determination reinforced by the rejection of the idea of indefinite material progress ('the worship of the GNP') by the individualist and existentialist ideologies of the 'cultural revolution' among the young in the late 1960s (Wiener, 1981).

The second explanation, much beloved of the left, centres on the claim that British economic life has been dominated by the City of London which has for the last 200 years persistently invested the profits of British industry abroad, thus improving the competitiveness of our rivals at the expense of British productivity.

The third explanation focuses not on capital, management and production, but on *labour and the market*. Competitiveness is the natural product of competition and lack of competitiveness is therefore the result of market imperfections. Poor productivity is the result of overmanning; as Saatchi and Saatchi's brilliant 1979 election campaign poster put it, 'Labour isn't working.' The restoration of competitiveness requires an increase in the level of competition and that in turn requires breaking the power of the unions to preserve jobs and archaic working practices. But it also requires an improvement in the motivation to work: that provided, on the one hand, by the fear of unemployment, and on the other by increasing the rewards for marginal increases in effort by reducing rates of taxation on wages and profits.

If we adopt the third explanation, the growth of the service sector appears in an entirely new light. In so far as it derives from a growth of leisure, this is a result of a preference for more leisure rather than more money, which is in turn the consequence of the poor monetary reward for marginal increments of effort. In so far as it is the result of tax financed services, the growing service sector is seen as an albatross hung around the neck of an ailing manufacturing industry, siphoning off profits which should be applied to modernization, and reducing the incentives to greater effort on the part of both capital and labour. Moreover, because public services are supplied by state monopolies they are by definition, uncompetitive and therefore overmanned.

During the 1970s, unemployment failed to rise at a rate proportional to the decline in manufacturing employment because jobs lost in manufacturing were partly replaced by the increase in service sector employment. In the 1980s, service employment too began to decline. However, according to the third explanation of decline, it would be a disastrous error to reduce unemployment by the expansion of public service sector employment. Rather, it is necessary to minimize such employment to make possible reductions in taxation which will improve productivity and increase incentives, even if this has the affect of diminishing the demand for services in the public sector thus decreasing employment in that sector also.

While the reconceptualization of the causes of unemployment which focused on labour market imperfections constituted a new departure in economic thought, it was a new departure *within* the paradigm of post-war political economy: 'full employment as opposed to inter-war unemployment', and the attempt to control employment levels by demand management. In contrast, the adoption of the third explanation of manufacturing decline constituted a major shift to a new paradigm. The meaning central to the new paradigm became the restructuring and revitalizing of manufacturing industry through increased competition and improved incentives. Within this paradigm unemployment ceased to be the central and became instead a subsidiary issue. Its solution lay in government action to improve competition in both the product and the labour markets, rather than in remedial action to reduce unemployment by increasing demand either generally, or by expenditure or public investment programmes. Such a policy could only be *initiated* by a party not ideologically committed to a resolution of the distribution problem; a party without what Bishop Sheppard has called a 'bias to the poor'. It could only be *persisted in* in the absence of a political opposition which could put forward a credible alternative policy. But we have seen that the economic transition of the 1970s deprived the Labour Party of its traditional platform of combining a full employment policy with a reformist programme designed to reduce equalities in distribution.

The 1980s would, therefore, have marked the beginning of a new era in economic, political and ideological terms, even without the advent of the world recession. In terms of historical consciousness it was marked by a redefinition of the past (always seen to be evil in a progressive culture). The bad old days ceased to be the 1930s and became instead the wasted post-war years when the 'wet' policies of successive administrations had allowed the growth of taxation and public expenditure and produced the decline in manufacturing industry which was the root cause of unemployment.

The outlines of this transition are only just beginning to emerge. They were certainly not clear even to the main protagonists in 1979, when the world appeared to be still the world of the 1960s, even though the basis of that world had already changed irrevocably to that of the 1980s. It was still assumed that any government which permitted major rises in unemployment would be courting electoral disaster or ejection from power by a revolt of its parliamentary supporters who *feared* electoral disaster. A sudden reversal by the new Tory administration was thought to be a matter of time. Equally, when the recession deepened, a return to levels of reasonably full employment was assumed to be assured once the recession had 'bottomed out'. People, whether politicians, social scientists or Welsh steelworkers expected, in good empiricist fashion, the future to be like the past. Intellectuals, such as those in the Marxist tradition, who do not regard history as a smooth progression but see it as punctuated by major discontinuities, and therefore live in the expectation or even hope that the future will be different, are no more capable of recognizing a major transition when they see one than progressivists. The historical discontinuities which they believe characterize social development are so rare and so profound that a vocabulary created to describe them fails to provide the conceptual means for the analysis and characterization of social transitions which do *not* amount to changes from one type of mode of production to another. They therefore leave the field wide open to idealist historians who, in Marx's words, characterize 'each age' in terms of an idea rather than by reference to changes in human praxis and relationships.

It is here, surely, that the sociologist must step boldly on to the stage, for the sociologist is, *par excellence*, the student of what some Marxists would term the 'superstructure', the ways of life erected on the basis of a given mode of production. It must, however, be admitted that contemporary sociology is little better equipped than Marxism to delineate the character of social transitions, since although sociology is at long last returning to its roots in history, and contemporary sociological work is increasingly informed by a historical dimension which much post-war sociology so signally lacked, it has yet to learn to think of social life in terms of a succession of societal situations, transitions between which pose new problems for human action. For within societies/formations of a given type, transitions occur which do not, like social transformations, involve the substitution of new structural elements, but the recombination of old elements to form new patterns.

Social transitions, being less profound than social transformations, are extremely difficult to recognize and characterize precisely because of their subtlety. They are also extremely difficult to live through. Social *transformations* destroy the very basis of the existing way of life which cannot therefore be carried on in any form. In contrast, those living through social *transitions* resemble 'cartoon cats' who walk blithely off the end of a plank and continue walking in the air only falling when they realize that their support has gone. People continue to behave as if the future was going to be like the past, and only fall into crisis when that assumption ceases to be tenable. Moreover, because transitions do not involve the abolition of structural elements but only their rearrangement, large segments of the population find their way of life not suddenly socially unsupported, but subtly changed; it is now an element in a different structure and living it comes to have an altered meaning, and different social consequences and new implications. The evils that befall the victims of structural transformations are intelligible after the manner of disasters. However, while plenty of people suffer personal disaster as a result of social transitions, the transition itself, because life continues to have a superficial appearance of normality, is intelligible after the manner of a nightmare, when everything is simultaneously familiar and alien and the connections between sequences of events, which ought to be obvious, are partially unintelligible.

It has been the privilege and misfortune, opportunity and challenge of those engaged upon the research on which this book is based to have undertaken that work during a period of social transition. It was conceived in the autumn of 1979 when the unemployment rate stood at 5.0 per cent (6.9 per cent in Wales) and Margaret Thatcher – elected chiefly as the result of the damage done to the Labour Party by Callaghan's ill-judged decision not to go to the country in the autumn of 1978, before the 1978/9 'winter of discontent' – had completed scarcely six months in office. The dole queue in the election poster referred to above seemed to have been a reference to the slow rise in unemployment under the Labour government and to signal that the new Conservative administration would operate within the post-war political paradigm. The more radical 'Thatcherite' ideas put forward during the campaign would either be quietly dropped or cause such an outcry from Conservative backwoodsmen that *she* would be quietly dropped. We were in for another spell of 'normal' rather than 'revolutionary' politics. Yet though the business of economic and political life continued as 'normal', the supports of that way of life had already gone. The realization that we were living through a major transition had to await the arrival of the recession of 1981/2, during which years manufacturing output fell by 14 per cent, unemployment rose to 12 per cent and whole sectors of the economy were devastated. It was the experience of living through that period (characterized as it was by the refusal of the government to react even verbally within the post-war paradigm and the ineffectiveness of the opposition parties) that made possible the *recognition* of the changes that had taken place in both the economy and political consciousness in the 1970s. It was only at this point that it became impossible for the opposition parties, the trade unions and those most directly affected by the recession to continue everyday life on the basis of the assumptions derived from the post-war economic and political situation.

The research on which this book is based was therefore undertaken during a period of major *social transition* as well as major *economic recession*. Its original design and aims derived from the social situation which existed before that transition from what we have termed post-war British society, apprehended, of course, through the type of social consciousness characteristic of that era. It follows that the research itself has had to go through a major transition in order to comprehend adequately the changed circumstances of those whom it set out to study, and our sociological consciousness has been transformed as a result.

## Was Wales closed?

The originator of the research and the author of this book teaches sociology in the University College of Swansea. Swansea is the 'capital' of the western part of the industrialized area of South Wales. Wales as a region has two predominant meanings in the British national context. The first meaning is contemporary: a largely unpopulated, beautiful, mountainous, coastal area, much favoured as a holiday and recreational location by the middle classes who live in the English conurbations. Its second meaning is historical and derives from the inter-war years: 'Wales' equals mining valleys; miners; slag heaps; Aberfan; socialism; chapels; Labour Party stronghold; rugby football; Dylan Thomas and nowadays, I suppose, Max Boyce. This second meaning derives from *Industrial* South Wales which is the part tourists used to avoid, before the completion of the M4, in order to get to the rest of Wales with which the first meaning is associated.

Historically, the connection of Industrial South Wales with mining is correct. If the Welsh valleys from Llanelli to Monmouth had not been rich in coal deposits, the present-day population, housing stock and infrastructure would not be there. The western part of Industrial South Wales differs substantially, however, from the east, since the origins of its nineteenth-century development and prosperity lie more with the metal manufacturing industries, zinc, nickel, copper, tinplate, and of course iron and steel, than with coal. The valleys of the eastern part of the coal field run south-east and centre on Cardiff, which was the coal capital of eastern Industrial South Wales. The valleys of the western part of the coal field run south-west and are linked by a string of settlements – Burry Port, Llanelli, Gorseinon, Swansea, Neath and Port Talbot – which lie on the narrow coastal plain situated between valleys and the sea. Historically, therefore, *west* Industrial South Wales depended on metal manufacture as well as on mining, and Swansea was both the centre of metal manufacturing and the chief port for the import of raw materials and the export of coal and finished metal products. Both metal manufacturing and coal were badly hit by the inter-war depression and the whole of Industrial South Wales experienced significant rates of out-migration.

Anyone who has lived in Wales becomes immediately aware of one of the distinguishing characteristics of the Welsh: their 'particularism' as sociologists call it, that is, their tendency to structure their social world in terms of relations between particular persons, places and events, which results in a strong attachment to the locations in which their relationships have been formed. The corresponding unwillingness of the Welsh to change their locality of residence is proverbial. As a redundant steelworker from Ebbw Vale commented in a television interview: 'I have been out [of work] now for two years. I'll give it another year, and if I don't get anything by then I'll have to start thinking about moving a bit further down the valley.' It is, however, difficult to square this attachment to locality with the South Walian diaspora of the inter-war years, and the willingness of the Welsh to forsake their native land to take up residence in the remotest parts of the earth. Everyone in South Wales knows the joke about the tombstone in the chapel cemetery inscribed 'Dai Jones, born 1898, not departed, but gone to Slough'. A way of reconciling these two contradictory aspects of Welsh behaviour immediately suggests itself to any weekend traveller on the line from Paddington to Swansea, which is extensively used by residents of 'Swansea' and 'Slough' to maintain that category of particular relationships most central to all our lives – family and kinship relations. The embeddedness of people in networks of particular relationships and the importance of those networks can have quite opposite effects. Local networks can retain members within a locality and geographically extended networks can facilitate mobility; past migration can facilitate current migration.

There must have been a point, however, when Welsh people lacked geographically extended networks. How was it they went to far-away places of which they knew little, such as Didcot, Banbury, Slough, Birmingham and the Great Wen itself, London? It is here that the difference between the present and the inter-war depression needs to be remarked. It was one of the characteristics of the inter-war years that unemployment was highly concentrated in what were then termed 'the depressed areas' and nineteenth-century industries. Other parts of the country were much less severely affected and the manufacturing industries of the second industrial revolution, associated with electricity, plastics and the internal combustion engine, were both labour-intensive and expanding. Hence a proportion of the unemployed left their 'depressed areas' for areas where they knew they had a good chance of obtaining employment in the sunrise industries of the 1930s, just as the affluent workers in Goldthorpe et al.'s study (1969) left their areas of origination in the reasonable expectation of improving their standard of living in Luton. Unemployment today is much more evenly distributed (though certain industries have been severely hit, leading to marked regional variation); the sunrise industries are not labour intensive and they require the labour they do employ to have specialized skills. One could not advise an unemployed steelworker from South Wales to move, for example, to Reading, capital of the 'M4 sunrise belt', even though it lies in one of the traditional routes of South Wales out migration.

In December 1979, the British Steel Company announced major reductions in production and manning which, delayed by the steel strike in the spring of 1980, began to be implemented in mid-May. These reductions were not seen at the time as the harbingers of the great recession which was to come, but as the result of the familiar problems of the steel industry. In west Industrial South Wales, the steel industry had been re-organized after the war, replacing the multitude of small plants (which in the previous hundred years had turned the beautiful Swansea Valley into the most extensive area of industrial dereliction in the country) by three major installations. A plant making steel strip was built at Port Talbot (seven miles east of Swansea) and two tinning plants, were established, one to the north of Swansea and one near Llanelli; in west Industrial South Wales it was at these plants that workforce and production were to be reduced. The reaction to the proposed cutbacks was extreme, for the plants symbolized, as nothing else could have done, the post-war era in (especially west) Industrial South Wales. They represented 'massive capital investment' in a previously depressed area which would ensure that South Wales would never return again to the privation of the inter-war years. They provided a very considerable amount of employment – the Port Talbot works employed at its peak in 1960 18,352 workers drawn from all over west Industrial South Wales. They represented stability of employment: 'I mean we thought once we were *in* [to employment with BSC], the only way we'd come *out* would be feet first.' They also represented high wages and good working conditions (see chapter 3) as the local name for the works, 'Treasure Island', implied. They generated a considerable amount of additional employment in firms working as suppliers and contractors, quite apart from that created by the expenditure of the wages of their employees. Small wonder then that the cutbacks, which affected Shotton in north-east Wales, the other major South Wales plants at Llanwern and the smaller works at East Moors in Cardiff, resulted in signs being posted on the Severn Bridge bearing the legend 'Wales is closed'.

Wales was not of course 'closed'. However salient coal and steel are as elements in the identity of South Wales in the minds of both its inhabitants and outsiders, and in spite of their undisputed importance in the historical *making* of South Wales, today they provide only 10 per cent of all employment in the sub-region. Continued employment in these industries is, however, the only basis on which the traditional settlement pattern and the way of life dependent on it can be maintained. Delete mining and the whole economic base of the South Wales valleys is undermined. Steelmaking and tinplate cannot be excised without profound effects on the economy of west

Industrial South Wales and upon the settlements of Llanelli, Port Talbot and Newport (Llanwern). Remove employment in heavy industry and mining and you sever the links of the working class with its own past and its present culture, and thus threaten the basis on which Industrial South Walian men construct and negotiate their identity as competent working-class people. Southern English middle-class readers, like the present writer, may have difficulty in grasping that to be working class (at any rate in South Wales) is not to belong to a residual category whose members lack, in the phrase of Sennett and Cobb (1972), the 'badges of achievement' which all others possess, but is, rather, to occupy an honourable status which gives you dignity and entitles you to respect. As one of our respondents who had been out of work for over a year put it: 'I used to be working class, but I can't claim that any more. I've fallen below that.'

'South Wales is closed' is a slogan that refers to a recognition of these facts and may be interpreted: 'without coal and steel, South Wales as we have known it and upon which we depend for our sources of social identity will be no more'. South Wales is not closed, however, even in that sense. The East Moors plant in Cardiff has closed; steelmaking at Shotton has ceased and the privately owned Duport steel plant in Llanelli has closed. Trostre and Velindre (tinplate) and Port Talbot and Llanwern remain open but have lost the majority of their jobs. Mining is continuing in the South Wales valleys even after the failure of the disastrous coal strike of 1984/5 and the closures which followed it. These circumstances created special problems for those made redundant: what they have lived through is not only personal disaster but social nightmare. In spite of the prophets of doom, social life has continued 'as normal'. Production at the Abbey works in Port Talbot goes on, and those who live in the town can still see their erstwhile work-mates returning home after their shifts. Video recorders continue to be bought and video libraries boom; working-class people continue to take holidays abroad. At the end of the year the shops continue to be thronged with shoppers buying Christmas presents and taking advantage of 'the sales'. The trappings of the affluent 1960s are still there. Yet two-and-a-half years after the redundancies, only 29 per cent of those made redundant in 1980 were either employed or self-employed. The market had not picked up; unemployment was still rising. Until 1984 the Abbey works endeavoured (successfully) to shrink its labour force even further.

## Studying labour market careers

The situation in which the redundants of 1980 found themselves was not one either they or the researchers predicted in 1979 when the cutbacks were announced. It had been assumed that a significant proportion would leave the area for work in more prosperous areas. In the event the proportion of redundants who left Industrial South Wales was under 6 per cent.

> What I say is this. Everybody on the news, the politicians, the government – everybody says it's going to get worse. Well, it can't get much bloody worse here than it is already, so it must be going to get worse somewhere else. If I was to go to Birmingham and get a job, chances after six months I'd be made redundant there too. What I say is this: if I'm going to be unemployed, I'd rather be unemployed here with my family and friends around me than away in Birmingham where I know nobody. (Steelworker, middle 30s, February 1981, 10 months into redundancy)

The redundant workers, many of whom had volunteered for redundancy, including younger men (under 45), assumed that redundancy pay, unemployment benefit (plus earnings-related benefit) and possibly some time on a retraining course would last them until they got another job, or (when the recession arrived) would last them through the recession. As a union officer put it: 'Remember we'd had redundancies at the Abbey before; in 1972. A lot of boys then took this redundancy money and within a year they got themselves taken back on. Some of the younger ones thought that would happen again. Nobody expected this.' A description of 'this' will be one of the themes of this book.

Both the researchers and ex-steelworkers entered 1980 with mistaken conceptions of the future, based on the erroneous assumption that the future would be like the past. The problems faced by the redundant steelworkers is another theme of this book. It is necessary, however, in this introductory chapter, to say something about the problems of the researchers. We had intended to interview the sample of redundant workers on 3 successive occasions at approximately 6 monthly intervals, that is to say (given the starting date of the research) at 9 months after redundancy (April 1981), at 15 months (October 1981) and finally at 21 months (April 1982). We were to compare the social and occupational characteristics of those who stayed and those who moved at each 'wave' of interviewing and monitor their employment fortunes. The purpose was to explore the way in which family and community ties assisted and impeded migration in search of work. The last year of the research was to be spent in analysis and writing up. Although we got into the field on schedule in April 1981 (Wave 1), the completion of the interviewing was held up (for reasons to do with the social transition through which we were unknowingly living). As a result the preliminary results were not available until February 1982, and they revealed that we had no 'movers'. We rushed back into the field in April 1982 to confirm this (Wave 2) while at the same time attempting to 'turn the study round', that is, design a new study which did not focus on out-migration.

'Turning the study round' is a significant phrase for we had, like the redundant workers themselves, advanced bravely into the future with our eyes firmly fixed on the past. But for us, as for them, 'turning around' wasn't enough, because (and here researchers' and respondents' problems coalesce), neither they nor we could discern what was happening to them; the significance of the present, like that of the future, was obscure.

The workers, many of whom had been with BSC for many years, had little experience of the labour market, of job search and of unemployment. This was not so in the case of the researchers, two of whom, living as they did on fixed-term research contracts, were familiar with both. But all of us were, like our respondents, ill-equipped to respond to the demands of the present, since the team had been selected (certain technical requirements apart) for its qualifications in the area of 'family-community-migration', rather than because of its knowledge of economic sociology, redundancy and labour markets. And yet it became clear halfway through the research period that it was in these areas that the research was henceforth to lie.

The original aim of monitoring our respondents' fortunes in the labour market was, however, still possible: we could therefore find out who was doing what at the time of each interview and investigate the social characteristics of those successful and unsuccessful in finding employment. This simple innocence was rudely shattered, as doubtless had been that of our respondents, when Morris's field investigation of the domestic circumstances of our respondents revealed that a significant proportion of them had had 'variegated' labour market histories. The implications of this were as profound for the research as they were for those affected. Our respondents would have to be distinguished, not in terms of their 'employment *status*' (employed, unemployed, retraining, sick, withdrawn), but in terms of their 'labour market *careers*' during the survey period. Collecting and analysing 'personal histories' is a time-consuming and difficult process; there is much debate in 'the literature' about how to do it, and none of us had ever done it. Moreover, in the relatively short space of time since redundancy, our respondents had had more complicated careers than those experienced over a whole lifetime by most workers in a society characterized by full employment. Yet career analysis clearly was what was required.

The fulfilment of that requirement raised yet another problem, however. A personal history study *begins* with the collection of the histories and spends the rest of the research period analysing them. We, in contrast, had to collect our histories at the end of the data collection period, two-thirds of the way through the research. The material was collected on the final 'wave' of interviewing (October–December 1982) and was not available to us until eight months before our research grant expired. The completion of our work has only been possible because of a number of extensions of both time and money granted by the SSRC (now ESRC).

It is appropriate at this point to say something about the notion of 'careers'. It is a truism that working-class people don't have 'careers', in the middle-class sense, except in the very early part of their lives. They obtain qualifications through schooling and apprenticeships and attain a given level and type of skill which they then attempt to sell to employers with varying degrees of success, involving varying degrees of mobility between different jobs. Over their working lives they do not acquire larger incomes, more skill, authority or social prestige, though they become more experienced and, as they do so, gain greater personal esteem in the eyes of their mates and employers. The notion of career is commonsensically applied to the 'middle class' that is, professional and business people who move from the position of law student to high court judge, from small proprietor to chairman of a group of companies, from trainee manager to the head of a division. The notion of a career in this sense involves the movement of a person through a set of statuses which are different from one another in kind or type and are hierarchically ranked. Working-class people, once established, move between statuses of the same type: they have 'work histories' rather than 'careers', and while they may be occupationally mobile they are not *upwardly* mobile. Neither of these two types of occupational mobility is, however, to be confused with social mobility which (in these terms) may be thought of as the movement of persons between that very broad category of occupations whose occupants have 'work histories' and that other equally broad category of occupations whose occupants have 'careers'.

Both notions, 'work history' and 'career' have, however, one thing in common: they imply that persons' biographies can be plotted on a grid of statuses which is fairly stable over time; the statuses and the relations between them, or to put it technically, the 'occupational structure', stays the same. The biographies of persons of whatever 'class' may be thought of as paths through a structure. Unfortunately, 'life', as T. S. Eliot once remarked, 'is very long', and over a lifetime the occupational structure changes significantly and thus raises enormous problems for the description of occupational biographies over whole lifetimes, or significant portions thereof, even when those lives do not involve passage through periods of social transition.

Description of movements between statuses when the status structures themselves are rapidly changing (as in periods of social transition), is even more problematic. Yet once again the problems of the researcher are but a pale reflection of the problems of those whose biographies are under study, since they face a situation which is not merely one of having to act in the light of inadequate information about the structure of opportunities which faces them, but in a situation where their knowledge of the types of opportunities available to them (based on past experience) is rapidly becoming redundant.

The biographies of the workers with which this study is concerned are not of course occupational biographies, but *labour market* biographies. A labour market may be thought of as the 'interface' (as the computer people have taught us to say) between two structures: first, a labour force composed of workers of different ages and sexes and ethnic groups, having different types and levels of skill, degrees of experience, and 'work records' of different degrees of 'satisfactoriness' from the standpoint of employers. Second, as a variety of employments requiring different types of technical skill and personal competence, recruitment to which is controlled by work-givers who may add all sorts of other requirements according to their past experience, cultural location and ideological beliefs.

A labour market is not, however, two structures but the *articulation* of these two types of structure: the *bringing together* of those who supply (the workforce) and those (the employers) who demand a commodity: labour. Demographic, cultural and educational changes are continually varying the supply of labour, thus forcing employers to restructure their operations, and hence the number and types of jobs they offer, to improve the match between the types of labour supplied and the labour requirements of their activities. Conversely, the competition between employers for shares of the product market forces them continually to introduce new techniques of production and hence to demand either new types of skill or worker behaviour or different proportions of existing skills and behaviour, or all of these. This in turn requires that the labour force continually adapts its skills and behaviour if it is to be successful in obtaining and retaining employment. The extent to which each side adapts to the other will vary widely depending on the extent to which product market competition requires a restructuring of the productive process, the nature of the restructuring and its relation to the existing stock of skills and behaviour in the labour force. These are historically variable *technical* factors. But who adapts to whom depends also on the *relative power* of the parties concerned: of employers relative to their competitors in the product market, and of employers and the workforce in the labour market. Market power depends in turn on 'market forces', that is on the relation between supply and demand for the commodity, whether product or labour.

In tight labour markets, such as those characteristic of the advanced capitalist societies after the Second World War, where the demand for labour has frequently exceeded supply, workers have to a degree been able to pick and choose and employers have been forced to adapt to the characteristics of the workforce. In a loose labour market, where the supply of labour exceeds demand (at the time of writing the excess of the unemployed over estimated vacancies is more than three million) employers can afford to pick and choose and workers are forced to adapt to the changed demands for labour occurring as a result of changes in methods of production, to secure an advantage in the search for work over *their* competitors – other workers.

In a loose labour market the term 'career' is simultaneously appropriate and problematic. Workers who, as a result of redundancy, come onto the market have suffered a loss, a bereavement: they are bereft of their previous secure employment. A movement through a succession of labour market statuses (for example, unemployment, retraining, part-time temporary employment, self employment, unemployment, full-time permanent employment) would constitute not merely a 'variegated labour market history' but also a successful labour market '*career*' – in the conventional sense. A worker with such a career would have re-established him- or herself as once again 'a member of the working class' in the sense used by the steelworker cited above. The term 'career' is however *problematic* because if it is a path *through* something, then *what* it runs through has been changing with startling rapidity during the period in which (in more than one sense of the phrase) the redundant steelworkers who are the subjects of this study have been 'going through it'.

In the first place, large-scale redundancy in a relatively small labour market of its self changes the balance of market forces. If a single person decides to sell shares, which constitute a tiny proportion of that type of share which is traded, he or she may expect to obtain the price ruling before putting them on the market. If, however, all the other holders of shares make the same decision at the same time, supply will exceed demand and 'the bottom will drop out of the market'. The redundancies of the 1980s were not like those of 1972: they were not sufficiently large to affect the price of labour, which is in the short term controlled by institutional factors, but large enough to affect massively the chances of early re-employment. The recession apart, the redundancies themselves had a profound effect on the *labour market chances* of most of those on the market, whether made redundant from BSC or not. To put this another way: the *labour market position* of these redundant workers was very different from what they expected on the basis of the experience of those who had left the works prior to the mass redundancies of 1980. The market itself underwent substantial change by the very fact of their arrival on it, for their arrival involved a massive increase in the supply of labour.

The labour market position of the redundants was affected also by the 'recession', that is, by the decline in the demand for goods and services of firms who might otherwise have employed them. The onset of the recession was marked by changes more profound and subtle than this, however: employers were not only not 'taking on' but 'laying off', desperately seeking more flexibility in their operations by attempting to obtain greater control over the number of their employees by converting 'full-time permanent' into 'fixed-term' or 'part-time' jobs, or both. This meant that what the workers were going through ('the market') was changing in terms of the types as well as the number of jobs offered by employers; or to put it another way, the type of demand for labour was not only falling but changing.

The transformation of the structure of what the redundant workers were passing through – the local labour market – posed problems for both us and them concerning our actions in that situation. Even those with previous labour market experience were at a loss, let alone those whose experience of labour selling or job getting was limited or remote. Understanding the behaviour of people in a situation which is new and unknown to them is extremely difficult, and understanding *outcomes* in terms of their *purposes and intentions* at the time they took particular actions is impossible.

In a stable situation careers can be understood in terms of the purposes of the subjects and the connections between the different actions, statuses and personal situations which go to make them up. It then becomes possible to ask questions such as, 'what motivated people to retrain?' and 'how successful was retraining?', answering the first in terms of the market situation which they entered and the second by examining the relation between different kinds of retraining and different types of trainee and the type of labour market status (for example, full-time employed; unemployed) occupied subsequent to retraining. In an unstable situation in which people have to act 'blind', the connections between situation, action and outcome are fortuitous: those who get jobs are those who happened to do not what was necessarily the right thing at the time, but what turned out in retrospect to have been right. For the workers concerned it's a matter of 'luck', a word which features frequently in worker accounts when explaining how they obtained work: ' . . . then I had a bit of luck. I was down the pub/met this chap . . . ' The market and its workings are as unfathomable as Calvin's 'God', whose inscrutability and arbitrary nature were, as any half-decent historical materialist will tell you, nothing but the reflection of the instability of the commodity markets of early capitalism.

There is danger that sociologists at this point are led up the same garden path as Calvinist theology and some applications of neo-classical economics, and produce a highly elaborate, formally rational, conceptual system for analysing and describing the fundamental unintelligibility of the world, in which the link between action and structure is severed so thoroughly that any relation between the two, as in Calvinist theology, disappears. The strings of labour market statuses constituting the labour market experiences of redundant steelworkers then seem to exhibit the configurations they do as the result of ineffective purposes and pure contingency. Thus we are presented with a situation characterized not by the randomness of the sort of 'ends' which Talcott Parsons found so objectionable, but by a randomness of outcomes.

It is not the purpose of this book to claim that we have achieved any final resolution of the conceptual problems, let alone the methodological niceties, of the analyses of careers (even in stable social contexts), since it requires that we apply one explanatory conceptual frame of reference which embraces both the sense in whose terms people's actions are intelligible and the structure which makes those actions effective. But we do wish to put forward a definitive conception of 'the economic' which sees it not as a sub-system of the social system (Parsons and Smelser, 1956) but as an aspect of social life (Marx, 1846) and of a labour market in which workers appear as 'people', that is, having a complex of social and natural attributes which amount to 'a social identity' to which reference has to be made in any attempt to *explain* labour market behaviour and outcomes, and hence 'careers'. That behaviour is of course economic: both behaviour and outcomes would be unintelligible without the specification of outcomes, in terms of the production, distribution and exchange of jobs and services, and reference to those sets of meanings which refer to them. But because, as Parsons would have said, of 'the primacy' – or better, the *centrality* – of those meanings, it does not follow that descriptions of what people do, let alone of the people themselves, can be couched in purely economic terms if economic behaviour and outcomes are adequately explained.

Once we recognize that people have social identities, which persist through time, through social transitions and even structural transformations, and which are derived from their past biography and the manifold of social relations in which they are currently embedded, then we are provided with a more stable structural context in whose terms to explain both labour market behaviour and outcomes than by reference to 'the changes and chances of this fleeting world'. The matter may be put this way. Labour market economists conducting redundancy studies are concerned with changes in aggregates: the proportion of redundants who met otherwise unfulfilled demands for labour, who displaced other less favourably situated workers or became themselves permanently unemployed, and the composition of each category of workers in terms of demographic and economic characteristics. But however elegantly such studies are able to describe the aggregate effects of redundancies by relating the numbers and type of redundancies to the character of the local labour market as a market in the economic sense, the practices, institutions and mechanisms which produce these effects necessarily remain unexplored. In order to find out how the market works it is necessary *not* to regard the actions of workers and employers as social actions *instead* of economic actions, *nor* individual and collective outcomes as social *instead* of economic, but rather to restore the economic *aspects* of the relations, actions, activities, institutions and outcomes under study to their social context, and then to ask again who experiences which sort of market outcome.

Such a move, we believe, is not only academically necessary to solve the 'career' problem, but is demanded of us by our role as witnesses to the local embodiment of a major social transition, and by the requirement of fidelity to our informants. They, as well as the general public and our fellow academics, need to understand what is happening to them and to their way of life, and we do not believe that this dual obligation can be discharged by the addition of ethnography to survey statistics with a generous mixture of 'wet' political sentiments. We wish to argue the centrality of social identity to any adequate understanding of local labour markets; but we emphasize it also because we believe that this is at the centre of what is at stake for our informants. It is to them that we dedicate this book.

# *Part I*

# The Redundancies and their Context

# 1

# Redundancy and Recession

## Redundancy under full employment

William Beveridge entitled his early work on unemployment *Unemployment: a problem for industry* (1909). In so doing he was deliberately and purposely redefining the meaning of unemployment which until then had been regarded primarily as an individual failing, and 'caused by the existence of large numbers of people who will not or cannot work steadily or strongly enough to make it possible that they should be employed regularly' (Marshall, 1925). Is unemployment necessarily a problem? If so, for whom is it a problem? The unemployed, industry, capitalism, the trade unions, the capitalist state, the working class, the labour market, the economy, labour economists . . . ? A similar question can be asked about redundancy. Is *it* a problem? For whom is it a problem?

If unemployment is a relatively modern concept (Ashton, 1986, chapter 1; Garraty, 1978: 4), redundancy is even more recent a term. Redundancy statistics have only been collected by the Department of Employment and its predecessors since 1965 and published monthly only since December 1983; the term only entered the popular consciousness after the Redundancy Payments Act of 1965.

When we began this study it was frequently assumed by other academics in our own or allied disciplines that we were studying *unemployment*, or *the unemployed*. Even if this has turned out to have had more than a grain of truth in it, that assumption was a bizarre one to make at the turn of the decade when the study was first mooted. As an early work pointed out: 'Redundancy is not necessarily the same thing as unemployment. Throughout this pamphlet it is assumed that a full employment policy in the sense of the maintenance of a general balance between supply and demand for labour is being successfully pursued. The problem of redundancy is isolated from that of depression, cyclical or other' (Acton Society Trust, 1958: 1–2). The term 'isolated' is a significant one. There is no reason to suppose that redundancy has been, is, or will be 'isolated' from 'depression' (or 'recession' as we say now). What the authors of the Acton Society study should have said was that unemployment and redundancy are analytically distinct phenomena, and that concern with the management of redundancy has only posed itself as a problem during the post-war era of full employment, when the general level of joblessness no longer masked that created by redundancy (Kahn, 1964: 19). As a result, the socially defined problems of recession or unemployment on the one hand and redundancy on the other have belonged to historically distinct economic eras. The present study took place at the beginning of a *new* era – at a time of profound economic, political and social transition. Since 1979 increased rates of redundancy have been, in contrast, one of the ways in which, throughout much of Britain, the recession has arrived.

The coming together of recession and redundancy in the early 1980s does not, of course, blur the distinction between them. In the post-war era redundancy was a phenomenon empirically associated with full employment and it was that very association that accounted for its problematic character. Hilda Kahn remarked in her study of redundancy in the 1950s (1964: 19) that 'with the event of labour shortage . . . it was the [worker's] propensity to bid adieu to his boss rather than the reverse which primarily attracted attention'. As a result, 'there was a tendency to ignore the fact that full employment does not mean an unchanging distribution of employment opportunities between undertakings' (Jeffrys with Moss, 1954: 11, cited by Kahn, 1964).

None the less, redundancies occurred. Queues of redundant men outside labour exchanges quite clearly constituted an anachronism in affluent Britain as the title of Richard Goodman's book *Redundancy in the Affluent Society* (1962) suggests; they belonged to a past which had been banished forever. During the 1950s, however, it came to be recognized that redundancies were necessary, in the present and the future. The Acton Society report notes as causes 'automation and mechanisation', 'rationalisation' and 'falls in demand'. Of the 200 firms surveyed in the study, no less than 150 had experienced redundancies in the preceding 8 years; 98 due to market shrinkage and 36 due to changes in production methods.

It was clear, therefore, that redundancies could not be treated as a relic of the past. On the contrary, they were the result of what Marx had termed, some years earlier, the continuous revolution of the means of *production* characteristic of capitalist societies and of the continuing redefinition and fulfilment of human needs through the *market*. At the same time the economic orthodoxy of the day understood the optimal distribution of labour to be that which equated the marginal productivity of labour between different concerns. This was a state of affairs which the labour shortage should have brought about. Workers should have moved from firms when marginal productivity, and therefore wages, were lower to other concerns where they were higher. The labour shortage tended not to bring about this optimal distribution since employers were willing to pay wages which were not proportional to the marginal productivity of their labour, in order to retain scarce manpower. The retention of workers whose productivity was sub-optimal was termed 'labour hoarding'; it was associated with the 'poaching' of skilled labour from one employer by another offering higher wages, leading to a third phenomenon termed 'wage drift', that is, a tendency for wages to move above nationally agreed minima. It may be said, therefore, that redundancy, as the shedding of labour, was thought to be an inevitable consequence of the development of the forces of production, change and fluctuation in product markets and a desideratum of any manpower policy which was concerned to optimize the distribution of labour and keep down its cost.

For these reasons, the price of keeping the *economy* at full employment was making *some* workers, albeit temporarily, unemployed. As a result, studies of redundant workers were the only studies of 'the unemployed' carried out during the full employment era, hence the confusion in many people's minds between studies of redundancy and studies of unemployment. The unemployment following redundancy was a new version of 'poverty in the midst of plenty'; but now it only involved a tiny minority of workers. The economic costs of remedying the disadvantages of the redundant were therefore small, however great the cost to those who were themselves made redundant. The *social* policy question was therefore not, 'how can we abolish redundancy' since *economic* policy was, frankly, interested in increasing rather than diminishing its incidence. The social policy question concerned the magnitude of the costs to those made redundant and the best means of mitigating the resultant hardship by some form of compensation.

W. W. Daniel expresses this point in a fashion characteristic of the majority of redundancy studies:

> We accept that rising living standards for the whole national community are dependent on industrial change, the efficient use of manpower and resources, the decline of some industries and the growth of others. This in turn inevitably means the creation of redundancy and occasionally the closure of whole plants and works. The critical point is that the costs of changes made in the name of general good should not be borne solely by those who are made redundant as a direct result. The whole community should share the costs and in particular be making provisions necessary to ease the transition from old jobs to new and from old skills to new that are demanded by structural change. (Daniel, 1972: 124)

The economic policy question was, in contrast, concerned with whether redundancies produced the desired economic results which the social policy point of view took for granted. If the total volume of enforced 'separations' (of workers from employment) occurred at such places and at such firms and involved workers whose characteristics were of such a kind that they were not 'redeployed' to the benefit of society and to the greater glory of the Expanding Gross Domestic Product, then redundancies did, after all, belong to the past, not to the Glorious Future: redundancies created pockets of *un*employment and were not occasions of successful *re*deployment. What measures could and should be taken to ensure the optimal redeployment of redundant workers?

The answer to both the social and economic policy questions centres on the labour market, and it is in this arena that the two policy areas may be seen in Klein and O'Higgins's words, 'to intertwine and interact' (1985 p: 2). Employment protection measures, redundancy payments and enhanced unemployment benefits have two aspects, functions and purposes, social and economic: to compensate the redundant for their loss of earnings and other costs which they incur, and to ensure the speedy redeployment of the redundant in a way which optimizes the utility of the available stock of manpower. These twin aspects come together in the labour market arena, since in a free market society it is the market that is the primary mechanism for the allocation of scarce resources between alternative uses.

In contemporary political ideology, the state and the market are seen as opposites and represent polar types of economic organization, characteristic of socialism and capitalism respectively. Western capitalist societies fall somewhere in the middle: the state intervenes to ensure that the market operates in the general interest as defined by those in control of the state apparatuses. Such intervention is seen to distort and impede the natural regulating and equilibrating tendencies of the market. State intervention needs to be either increased or diminished, according to whether or not the natural (that is, unintended) outcomes of market processes are judged to approximate those thought desirable in terms of a given set of political values.

This view is positively unhelpful. Even if it is held to be the case that the operation of free markets will, in principle, produce the optimum outcome, it is universally recognized that actual, concrete markets are, in practice, highly imperfect and actual outcomes distinctly sub-optimal. Thus state intervention may be required not to impede but to *facilitate* the operation of market processes. For example, it is perfectly 'rational' (in the theoretical economic sense) for workers not to move in the search for employment from areas of high unemployment if they own their own accommodation and find that it is virtually unsaleable. Absence of worker mobility is a market imperfection and state intervention in the form of substantial mobility allowances could help to overcome that imperfection.

State intervention may therefore be used as a means of improving as well as impeding the operation of market forces, and the manpower policy of the past, which included statutory redundancy provisions, has to be understood as designed to *facilitate*, not to impede, the operation of the labour market;

as an attempt to narrow the gap between actual and optimal market outcomes in the neo-classical economic sense. Such outcomes are optimal when the productivity of each labourer could not be increased by transferring him or her to other employment within the market at the national level.

It has to be recognized, therefore, that redundancy provisions can be simultaneously 'dry' and 'wet', that is, the same measure could be advocated on the technical grounds that it improved the effective working of the market, and on the social grounds that it compensated the worker for costs inflicted upon him or her by the redundancy. It is not self-evident that the provision of income after redundancy impedes the effectiveness of worker and employment. In so far as it extends the period of job search, it may well increase the level of frictional (that is, between jobs) or 'search' unemployment. If, however, the result is that the worker ends up in a job where his or her productivity is higher than it would have been had he or she been forced to snatch the first employment opportunity that came along, income provision may optimize the operation of the market rather than impede it.

It follows from this that the *redundancy studies* of the 1950s and 1960s were concerned to explore the extent to which redundancy events resulted in the speedy redeployment of manpower and to assess the adequacy of statutory provision, both in reducing the costs to the redundant and in maximizing the benefits to the economy. The redundancy studies of the post-war period lay very much within the British empirical tradition (Kent, 1981): they were written within the framework of a policy problematic, and the sort of data they collected and the questions they asked of it were much the same whether the investigator was a social administrator, sociologist or labour economist. The social significance of the event was taken to be self-evident, and not regarded as part of the phenomenon to be studied nor regarded as a determinant of the outcomes of redundancy events. Not until the 1970s did any critical literature appear which specified the meanings attached to redundancy or redundancy measures, and challenged their obviousness. (For an example see Fryer, 1973; Martin and Fryer, 1973.)

If it is the case that 'state' and 'market' are seen as polar opposites, then so are the processes of production and exchange, and this opposition is one of the principal dimensions along which the different locations of Marxian and neo-classical economics may be plotted. The redundancy study tradition is highly market-oriented in the sense that it has been very little concerned, as Wood has pointed out, with the manner in which redundancies are generated (Wood, 1977a, 1977b; Wood and Cohen, 1978). For Wood, that phrase implies the social processes whereby some workers are made redundant and not others, and which determine the timing of the separation and the consequent arrival of redundant workers on the labour market. Such a focus of interest takes us away from the market arena and back within the factory gates. It is, of course, not the case that the earlier redundancy studies were as uninterested in this process as Wood sometimes seems to imply. They were interested in it, however, very much from a manpower policy standpoint. The studies had demonstrated the predominance of what was confusingly called by the pre-1965 studies the 'seniority' principle, and was later referred to more intelligibly as LIFO (last in, first out). (See *Ministry of Labour Gazette*, 1963: 50; Kahn, 1964: 211–25; Wedderburn, 1964: 4–5, 1965: 30; Mackay and Reid, 1971: 380–1; Parker et al., 1971; Herron, 1975: 12–13.) The seniority (LIFO) principle once again had a double meaning. Its social meaning was that it protected those who were past their 'prime' (25–45) from redundancy and exposed prime workers who had a better chance of quickly securing a new job. LIFO was thus thought to be effective in reducing 'search' or 'frictional' unemployment following redundancy, protecting the weakest and rewarding 'company loyalty' as measured by 'length of service'. In economic terms it prevented the loss of senior and experienced workers to the redundancy firm, thus maintaining its viability in a way which would not have been possible if some other principle of allocation had been applied. It was perhaps because of the artificial separation of the economic and social meanings of this principle that the formal contradiction between elements of these two meanings was ignored.

The desirability of LIFO as a principle depended on two different categories of workers being differentially evaluated by their employer and the market. The redundancy firm apparently wanted to retain its senior workers, while 'the market' was thought to be hungry for its junior ones. Although convenient, this is extremely odd, since the market's demand is only the aggregate of the demand of the employers within it, and there is no reason to suppose *a priori* that the needs of the other employers in the market differ from those of the redundancy firm itself. Surely by no means all prime workers are ardently desired by the market, while many older workers are not necessary to the redundancy plant, and the value of their 'experience' may well be outweighed by declining physical and mental abilities, lack of adaptability and conservative attitudes. While it would be quite wrong to stereotype old workers in this way (as many employers appear to do) such considerations do suggest that the benefits of the LIFO principle for the redundancy firm are, to say the least, not self-evident. LIFO also discriminates against women (Callender, 1985) and ethnic minorities (Cornfield, in Lee, 1986).

Failure to consider these issues follows, of course, from the studies' focus on the market. Redundancies which released prime workers were obviously good, since they increased the supply of the sort of workers who were in demand. But the redundancy studies of the post-war era did not consider the other side: how effective the redundancy was from the standpoint of the firm concerned. The economic rationality, both formal and substantive, of the redundancy firm is taken for granted. There has been, that is to say, no investigation in this tradition of the generation of redundancy as understood, not as Wood does, in the interactional sense, but in the economic sense of managerial response to product or financial market pressures resulting in product changes or in the restructuring of the labour process. Once redundancy is seen as the outcome of a process which has to be understood in economic terms, and once that process is seen as one of production, then redundancy shifts its meaning. It becomes a moment in a dynamic process – production – rather than a temporary disequilibrium in an equilibrating *system*; it can also be seen as a moment in a *struggle* in which management fights for the enterprise's survival in the product market and its workers for their survival in the labour market.

The above statement will not commend itself to some Marxist sociologists on the grounds that it does not specify the struggle as being between management and workers. The formulation is, however, quite deliberate, since management may, under certain conditions, be struggling to avoid redundancies and workers, under other conditions, be queuing up to volunteer for them. Management and workers, on any given occasion, can be on the same or opposing sides on the issue of redundancy and it is precisely this fact that opens the way for a negotiation by members of both parties: negotiations which *define*, as much as express, the material interests of the parties in that specific situation.

The neglect of the study of redundancy situations, resulting from an exclusive focus on the *market* at the expense of changes in the organization of production, led, in the earlier studies, to an inadequate treatment of market phenomena themselves. Indeed it is true to say that until comparatively recently most studies of redundancy were chiefly concerned, in the terminology of this book, with redundant workers' *labour market outcomes*. The basic tables for any redundancy study consisted of a table showing the *current status* of the sample of redundant workers at the time of interview and then explaining that distribution in terms of the economic attributes and labour market behaviour of the sample's members. Distinctions were then made according to *when* the worker obtained the first post-redundancy job, so that the *speed* of *redeployment* could be measured, and this dependent variable, too, was related to attributes and behaviour. New jobs were then classified in terms of occupation scales, industrial classification and geographical location and compared with the redundancy job to yield measures of occupational, industrial and geographical mobility. These comparisons were then used to assess the degree of *successful redeployment*.

To this basic analysis was added such refinements as the distinction between single and multiple job holders (or job changers). Some redundants, it came to be recognized, only obtained work after short periods of unemployment (in the early studies many workers went *straight* into another job) because they 'traded down': that is, they took jobs which offered less favourable conditions and rewards than the redundancy job and did not fully utilize their skills and then proceeded to change jobs until they succeeded in replicating the redundancy job. This process was often associated with the rehiring of redundant workers by the redundancy firms when the product market or general demand in the economy picked up (Kahn, 1964; Mackay, 1972b). Single and multiple job holders were also referred to as 'stickers' and 'snatchers', terms originated by Hicks and popularized by Mackay (1972a). The stickers had relatively long post-redundancy unemployment durations but eventually achieved employment comparable to that lost, the snatchers trading down to obtain swift re-employment and then embarking on a 'career'.

The other refinement which came to be incorporated into the classic redundancy study involved more sophisticated measurement of respondent-evaluation of his or her current job in comparison with the redundancy job and the inclusion of attitudinal data on the redundancy process and the redundancy firm.

The classic research pattern resulted from the auspices, timing and funding of most redundancy studies and the implicit problematic which concerned the efficiency of 'the market' (see Lee in Lee, 1986) in redeploying redundant workers. Little attention was paid to the demand side of the market, which was effectively conceptualized as a demand curve or curves, since there was no investigation of the attitude of employers to redundant workers, or their recruitment and hiring practices, except what could be gleaned from data on the methods of *job acquisition*. At the same time little attempt was made to study either the effects of the redundancies on the market, that is, the way that the *labour market* was itself affected by a large flow onto it constituted by the redundant workers; or the effect of labour market conditions in determining the speed and effectiveness of redeployment.

In a full employment economy characterized by *labour shortage* the *labour* market was 'tight'. It was implicitly assumed when vacancy to unemployment ratios were at or above unity (that is, there were as many if not more vacancies than unemployed) that the chief factor affecting the effectiveness of redeployment was the skill of the redundant workers in finding an appropriate niche in the opportunity structure. Even where the unemployment generated by redundancies was the result of change in the opportunity structure, therefore, it was understood (in spite of being structural) as a type of frictional unemployment. Frictional (between jobs) unemployment could not be reduced by demand side factors since demand was, if anything, excessive. The only method of reducing it must be by improving supply side factors, specifically the efficiency of job search.

We can now summarize the chief defects of the classic early redundancy studies. In so doing it is important to remember that the inadequacies listed below refer to the *design and background assumptions* of these studies, not to their *results*. The results are a measure of the researchers' ability to transcend the limitations imposed upon them by the paradigm within which they operated.

The early studies are limited by their narrow policy-orientation, and by their uncritical acceptance of the contemporary significance of what they were studying. They ignore the social production of redundancy in both the economic and interactional senses, and do not set redundancy events in the context of wider economic and political processes and hence do not see them as occasions of various types of struggle. In spite of their concentration on the market they do not explore the demand side of the market, the effect of flows of redundants on to the market, or market conditions as determinants of the fate of the redundant. In spite of the fact that many redundancies generated structural unemployment, post-redundancy unemployment is always treated as frictional and the remedy seen to lie with the redundants and the employment services who together are responsible for improving the efficiency of the market by increasing the efficiency of job search.

## Redundancy and unemployment

The above remarks refer to the paradigm on which the early studies were based. In the late 1960s the character of redundancy studies changed in response to two new circumstances. After 1966, unemployment began to rise and regional differences in unemployment were more in evidence. In the next ten years unemployment, in both Britain and the US, came once again to be regarded as a problem; an economic policy problem. The nature of the problem was basically that there was a new type of unemployment which, like the latest 'bug', seemed to have developed a resistance to the measures traditionally used to control it. Unemployment responded to demand-expansionary policies ever more slowly so that bigger and bigger reflationary measures were needed to induce the same size fall in the rate of unemployment. Keynesian reflationary measures of demand stimulation did not seem to work as well as they had done in the previous two decades. The intellectual solution to this problem was to propose that the fault lay with the labour market. In broad terms, it was claimed that there was not one labour market but two, and when aggregate demand increased, so did firms' competition for scarce labour in what was termed the *primary sector* (made up of high-paid, scarce jobs, in large and prosperous concerns in production industries). This competition bid up wages and led to an inflationary spiral, but the increase in aggregate demand did not affect workers in the *secondary* sector of the labour market, made up as it was of poorly paid, insecure jobs occupied by categories of worker who found it difficult to get jobs in the primary sector: members of disadvantaged ethnic groups, women and the old.

The notion of a dual or segmented labour market (Doeringer and Piore, 1971, chapter 8; Gordon, 1972; Edwards et al., 1975; Piore, 1975) is an important one which we introduce here as an example of the way in which the rise in policy-resistant unemployment led to a greater interest in labour market studies, which in turn prompted a reorientation of *redundancy studies*. Clearly, labour market outcomes would differ between redundancies in terms of the relative importance of primary and secondary sectors in the labour market concerned. If the local labour market within which the redundancy occurred was composed chiefly of the secondary sector, and the redundants came from the primary sector, the chances of redundants replicating their redundancy job would be much lower than in a market with a large primary sector, which was *dynamic*, that is, experiencing a large number of flows on and off the market.

The second circumstance which affected the character of redundancy studies was the implementation of the 1965 Redundancy Payments Act and the consequent concern with its operation. This led to surveys of redundancies in addition to studies of specific redundancy events (Parker et al., 1971; British Institute of Management, 1974; Daniel and Stilgoe, 1978). As a result, more attention was given to the character of the redundancy event, however narrowly that was characterized. Parker et al. concluded that most redundancies did not spring from desirable organizational and technological changes, and this conclusion was confirmed by Daniel and Stilgoe's study. They found that over 60 per cent of the redundancies in their sample were due to deficient demand for the employers' product. Thus the function of the Act, whatever its purpose had been, was to 'ease' the laying-off of workers as a result of market failures, rather than to encourage employers to economize on labour and improve productivity.

The Redundancy Payments Act of 1965 became a landmark in the history of redundancy studies, not least by affecting the *redundancy process*. The Act provided for redundancy payments which were positively related to length of service and for higher rates of payment in respect of years of service after the age of 41 years. At the same time the Redundancy Fund, which paid a proportion of the cost of redundancy payments to the employer, paid a greater proportion of that cost in respect of redundants over 41. The net result was, in the words of a Department of Employment study (Jolly et al., 1980: 98), that although

> LIFO remained the most important criteria for redundancy selection . . . where the opportunity arose of accepting as *volunteers* for redundancy older workers who had long service but were considered, because of their age, to be less productive, [that opportunity] was taken. The size of the redundancy payment with its age premium was seen as sufficient to *cushion* a possibly long spell of unemployment, maybe until retirement. If the blow of redundancy could fall more softly on the older worker, his or her departure might mean it did not have to fall at all on a younger more productive recent recruit. As a result, for many older workers, the mobility that the Redundancy Payments Act facilitated was *mobility out of the active labour force*. (Emphasis added)

In spite of the fact that higher payments to employers in respect of older workers ceased in 1969, 'the movement in favour of older workers volunteering for redundancy as a prelude to retirement has grown and achieved a momentum independent of the minimum provisions laid down by the

Redundancy Payments Act' (Jolly et al.), so that as early as 1974 the British Institute of Management could conclude that age was the single most important mechanism for redundancy selection (see also *Employment Gazette*, 1978). By the time we commenced the present study, and before the full impact of recession had been felt, redundancy had ceased to be a measure whose primary function was redeployment and had become, especially in large enterprises, a means of shedding labour and slimming the workforce by encouraging early retirement. Redeployment affected, rather, a minority of *involuntary* redundant workers who were selected on the LIFO principle. A function of redundancy was, therefore, to reduce unemployment, not by ensuring greater efficiency within the redundancy plant or in job search, but by reducing (though not commensurately) the supply of labour at the same time as demand itself was reduced. 'Recession' redundancy rather than 'redeployment' redundancy had already become important before the recession itself arrived.

As we have seen, the rise in unemployment rates and the effects of the Redundancy Payments Act gave redundancy studies in the 1970s a different character from the early studies. They still, of course, contributed to our knowledge of the unemployed, in whom interest was already growing (Jones, 1972; Hill et al., 1973; Daniel, 1974; Marsden and Duff, 1975; Daniel and Stilgoe, 1977; Sinfield, 1978). But the chief characteristic of the new generation of studies was that much more attention was paid to the character of the labour market on to which the redundants came, so that redundancy studies came to be more and more *labour market studies*. Since the findings from all the redundancy studies emphasize the extent to which job search is limited geographically, and the unwillingness of redundant workers to move their homes, the focus on 'the market' was in effect a focus on the *local labour market*: on the labour market at a distinctly *sub*-regional level.

This new focus was initially the result of the work of Mackay and his colleagues (Mackay and Reid, 1971; Mackay et al., 1971; Mackay, 1972a, 1972b) and this approach is exemplified by the title of one of Mackay's publications: *Labour markets under different employment conditions* Mackay et al., 1971. It was followed by other studies: by F. Herron entitled *Labour market in crisis* (1975) and by R. Pearson and J. Greenwood: *Redundancy and displacement: a study of the Maidstone labour market* (1977). This emphasis on the labour market has continued into the 1980s (Mackay et al., 1980; Carmichael and Cook, 1981; Payne, 1984). The importance of Mackay's work does not lie simply in his explicit recognition of 'employment conditions' as a determinant of labour market outcomes, but in his implicit recognition that concrete labour markets depart significantly from the abstract models of labour economists. Mackay is centrally concerned with the tension between the classical economic model which 'predicts rational economic behaviour based on an evaluation of net advantages and previous empirical findings which suggest that imperfect information may prevent the comparison of alternatives upon which the classical theory rests' (1972a, p. 90). This, however, is an understatement given his citation of H. S. Parnes (1954). Parnes does claim that 'the average manual worker seems to have very limited knowledge of job opportunities' (p. 187), but he supports this claim by reference to his conclusions concerning *job search*:

> this search generally involves finding out from acquaintances where job openings exist, or even being 'spoken for' by friends currently employed in the companies that are hiring . . . it may involve applying more or less randomly at plants the worker happens to know about . . . the worker does not take the first job he finds; he will take the first one that appears to meet the standards he has subjectively established for a desirable job . . . [he does not] locate a number of desirable jobs and draw up mental balance sheets of their relative merits . . . (p. 188)

In other words 'the problem' is not merely that the worker lacks information, but that he does not behave rationally in the sense which 'rationality' has in economic theory. Though the primary meaning of employment is economic and workers do behave rationally (in the means-ends sense), their job search behaviour is not economically rational since employment has so many other meanings and employment decisions are therefore based on an evaluation of costs and benefits on a whole range of dimensions of which the economic is but one.

This issue is a central one if the effects of different labour market conditions (in the sense of vacancy/unemployment ratios, wage levels, relative levels of demand for different types of labour) are to be used to explain the labour market outcomes of the activities of redundant workers, since any simple inference from labour market conditions to aggregate outcomes of the job search activity of a population of redundant workers will depend on simplifying assumptions concerning the rationality of search behaviour. Underlying the Mackay enterprise is, therefore, a fundamental *theoretical* problem: how can we understand, in terms of economic theory, the labour market outcomes of different populations of redundant workers in relation to different economic conditions when the empirical evidence from all the redundancy studies suggests that job search behaviour is not economically rational? The difficulty of the studies of the 1970s was less that they were limited by paradigm and problematic than that their empirical findings, important as they were, were not susceptible to theoretical interpretation in the terms of classical economic theory, but demonstrated instead, the extent of its inapplicability.

It is not surprising, therefore, that Herron's concluding chapter (1975) makes little reference to the substance of preceding chapters and is really an essay on institutional provision and manpower policy. Nevertheless, Herron's work marks a major advance on previous studies. While still attempting to understand post-redundancy labour market experience in terms of job search 'strategy', the fact that redundancies took place under adverse labour market conditions leads to a recognition of the extent to which outcomes are adventitious in relation to the classical explanatory variables of age, labour market experience, skill and 'strategy'. There is also a recognition of the fact that labour market conditions are not static but changing, and are themselves changed by the redundancy event. Thus underlying Herron's study is an implicit model of the redundancy career in which worker motivation and the initial labour market context condition the worker's immediate post-redundancy response, but the outcome has to be understood in terms of that response and the subsequent labour market context.

Herron's is the first study which identifies the 'continuously unemployed' in its catalogue of labour market outcomes, and is therefore an ominous sign of the deterioration of the demand for labour, albeit in a geographically peripheral area (Clydeside) overly dependent on one old-fashioned industry (shipbuilding). Herron's study was the first to consider redundancy in a loose and falling labour market, but the redundancies differed from those described in later works because of the relative youth of the redundants. The continuously unemployed, though a significant category, constituted only 1 in 10 of the redundant population. Herron was therefore still able to carry out the conventional analysis of the factors affecting 'transitional' unemployment.

In marked contrast, Mackay's study of the Swan Hunter redundancies on Tyneside in 1978 (Mackay et al., 1980) found that 'the great majority of employees made redundant from Swan Hunter either withdrew from the labour market or were still unemployed a year after the redundancies occurred . . . this result flowed from the characteristics of the redundant employees and the characteristics of the local labour market' (p. 3). Only 22 per cent of those made redundant had ever worked since the redundancy and only 15 per cent were in work after 12 months; a further 10 per cent were retraining, 20 per cent were sick and 49 per cent were unemployed (p. 10). In these circumstances there was no question of conducting a conventional analysis of the determinants of the length of 'transitional' unemployment or of calculating unemployment durations and job acquisition rates for different categories of workers. A neo-classical redundancy study was not possible. Nor was it possible to study satisfactorily the labour market effects of the redundancy in the sense of estimating the amount of 'displacement' (that is, the extent to which the employment of Swan Hunter ex-employees filled jobs which would otherwise have been available to those already looking for work), a concern which was reflected in the labour market-orientated redundancy studies of the period.

Mackay's research agenda, set for him by the Department of Employment, was really that of the 1970s, not the 1980s: do redundancies create unemployment either directly or indirectly through displacement, or does the labour market adjust so that the market, albeit slowly in the case of mass redundancy, 'clears'? This problematic signals the shift from the 'redeployment' to the 'unemployment' conception of redundancy, but fails to take into account what was already known about age and redundancy (*Employment Gazette*, 1978). It also fails to consider whether the 'employment conditions', in Mackay's own phrase, were appropriate for such a study, since if at the point of redundancy the local market is extremely loose and demand is already unable to absorb the pre-redundancy supply, then the answer is, at least to the non-economist, patently obvious: the redundancy must create unemployment. Mackay appears to take the same view as the layman, but he covers it with a veneer of economic orthodoxy. Whether or not redundancy creates unemployment will depend on the match between the redundants' skills and attributes and those demanded locally; if demanded elsewhere, on their willingness to move. If there is a different pattern of demand then it will depend on the redundants' 'flexibility', their willingness to move geographically, occupationally and industrially, and possibly to accept lower rewards for work.

> The speed and ease of adjustment . . . will depend in part on the characteristics of the redundant men, but it will also be strongly influenced by the economic background to the redundancy . . . if the local economy is heavily dependent on a single activity and decline in that industry is severe, then transfer is likely to be difficult. The problem will be considerably exaggerated if unemployment is high not only in the local area, but also in the surrounding region and nation. *In such circumstances the degree of flexibility required if substantial unemployment is to be avoided, is considerable.* (Mackay et al., 1980: 8, emphasis added)

The last sentence must be one of the greatest understatements of all time. None the less, a complex statistical analysis was unable to provide any clear evidence that the redundancies were associated with a rise in local unemployment which would not have occurred anyway, given the regional and national trends.

## Redundancy and recession

The assumption which lies behind studies such as these is that redundancy events are essentially local events which can be *conceptually* isolated from aggregate trends at the regional and national level. The question posed is therefore, does the local event result in effective redeployment or cause unemployment? However, at the turn of the decade, the character of redundancy was changing yet again, from unemployment redundancy to recession redundancy. That is to say, redundancy was becoming a form of job loss and hence *the manner in which the recession arrived in particular local labour markets*. Redundancies, as such, ceased to be a local and became instead a national phenomenon: a component of job loss.

Employment in manufacturing industry declined by one-fifth between 1966 and 1979. By 1982 a further 1.5 million jobs were lost, reducing manufacturing employment to two-thirds of its 1966 level. 1980 also marked a turning-point in service industry employment which, having grown by 1.5 million jobs during the 1970s, began to decline in 1980, shedding 0.25 million jobs in that year alone.

There are only two ways in which a permanent job can disappear: its occupant can leave and not be replaced, or its occupant can be made redundant. Nationally much of the job loss during the 1970s was the result of the first type of disappearance, or natural wastage. One of the chief sources of natural wastage is retirement. We have already seen, however, that redundancy and retirement can go together since redundancy can be a form of forced early retirement. Ignoring this, however, and regarding wastage and redundancy as exclusive categories, it may be said that the majority of job disappearances in the 1970s were the result of wastage not redundancy: the redundancy curve remained fairly flat though showing a tendency to rise.

After July 1979 all the redundancy measures (Noble, 1981) started to rise. The figures for confirmed redundancies for 1980 were 2.8 times the 1978 level at 494,000, and remained high in 1981 at 532,000 before beginning to fall in subsequent years, so that by 1984 they approximated their pre-recession levels (*Employment Gazette*, 1983, 1985). In manufacturing alone, over one million jobs disappeared through redundancy in the recession years 1980 to 1982.

This does not mean that one million of the *net* job losses in these years were due to redundancy, chiefly because net job loss is the result of changes in the numbers of jobs created, as well as in jobs lost. Unfortunately, there are no statistics of disappearances and job creation, and therefore no simple ways of measuring the importance of redundancy in generating net job loss. This has led to some argument in the literature about the importance of redundancy in the current recession. The initial response was to assume that, in Townsend's words, 'redundancy does lie at the core of recession' (Townsend, 1982: 1392; see also Martin, 1982 and Jones, 1984). By 1984 there was a retreat from this position on the grounds that it had been implicitly assumed that severances were equivalent to gross job loss, thus ignoring the important part played by natural wastage (that is, non-replacement of workers) (Meager, 1984). What is not at issue is that redundancies played a far greater part in job loss in the recession years 1980 to 1982, than they had in the job loss of previous decades and that, therefore, increases in the redundancy rate were a major way in which the recession 'arrived'.

The work of Townsend, Martin and Jones is concerned with a new problematic: the importance of redundancy as opposed to wastage as a factor in net job loss. That is not our concern here. Our concern is with something that is more easily shown by the available statistics: that is, the increased importance of redundancy as a type of severance. In recession, workers hang on to the jobs they have so that voluntary separations fall, and flows *on to* the market are diminished. Employers do not expand their labour forces and do not replace workers who leave through natural causes (death, retirement, sickness), hence flows *off* the market are also diminished. In the absence of redundancy, therefore, the market stagnates in recession. If changes in flows on and off balance, the numbers of unemployed increase only through new entrants to the market being unable to find jobs. To this model must be added two further factors. The generation of new jobs through the development of new enterprises may compensate for the fall in the size of flows off. Redundancy increases the size of flows on to the market and thus compensates for the decline in the numbers of non-redundancy separations, that is, of voluntary quits. In recession, where engagements are falling already, redundancy therefore increases the tendency to higher rates of unemployment and affects the composition of the stock of unemployed by adding experienced workers to the new-entrant unemployed.

This is not to say that redundancy necessarily results in unemployment; if the redundancy flows on to the market are balanced by flows off, resulting from engagements in new firms, and/or by a net flow off resulting from non-redundancy separations having fallen more slowly than engagements by established firms, unemployment will not rise. However, it would be very difficult to create sharp rises to high levels of unemployment by relying on the excess of non-redundancy separations over engagements *alone*. Redundancy must, therefore, at the national level, be an important factor in 'achieving' large and rapid increases in unemployment, demographic factors apart.

Given a national recession and a rapid rise in redundancy, one would expect redundancy to be an important factor in job loss and rising unemployment at regional and sub-regional level. However, it is possible that, just as the level and size of increases in unemployment vary between regions, so will the incidence of redundancy and its importance in generating job loss and unemployment.

In their study of employment change in the three decades ending in 1979, Fothergill and Gudgin (1982) argued that differences in industrial structure and regional policy became *de*creasingly important in periods of recession and that the chief factors in terms of which the regions' different experiences of the recession are to be explained are 'urban structure' and 'size structure'. Manufacturing employment in the centres of large urban areas will continue to decline, but smaller towns dominated by small and medium-sized companies will continue to benefit from above-average rates of new firm formation, which in any case tend to increase in periods of recession. Though they predicted that peripheral regions (including Wales) will suffer greater loss of manufacturing jobs, they attribute this chiefly to the failure (in depression conditions) of regional policy to be effective: peripherality *minus* effective regional aid *equals* high rates of manufacturing decline (Fothergill and Gudgin, 1982, chapter 9).

Even on the basis of pre-1980s data, this judgement seems somewhat cavalier with respect to the peripheral regions and especially Wales. The whole of the Welsh principality cannot be discussed here, but confining ourselves to the sub-region with which this study is concerned, west Industrial South Wales, it is sufficient to note that the urban–rural shift and the concentration of services in erstwhile large industrial towns, which Fothergill and Gudgin predict, was characteristic of the post-war period and had already taken place by the 1970s. It is also the case that during that period the trend had been one of a movement of population from mining/industrial valleys to small coastal towns dominated by larger enterprises. This was a result of a distinctive industrial structure and settlement pattern which continued to differentiate Industrial South Wales from other sub-regions. *Industrial* structure remains an important factor in determining the fate of the region to which the generalizations of Fothergill and Gudgin cannot for that very reason be applied. The relevance of their analysis to South Wales becomes even more dubious when the impact of the recession is taken into account.

Townsend (1982) has demonstrated a major variation in the incidence of both net job loss and redundancy between the minimum list headings of the Standard Industrial Classification. This analysis suggests that industrial structure continues to be an important determinant of the local impact of the recession. He therefore examined whether the industrial distribution of job losses and redundancy (rather than urban structure) continues to be an important factor in explaining regional difference. He concluded that job loss at the regional level is what would be expected given the national level, and did not show important regional differences in terms of *either* urban structure *or* industrial structure. Wales is, however, an exception in the case of both net job loss and redundancies and this is a result of Wales' industrial structure, the importance of the steel industry, and her having had an above-average share of the redundancies in that industry. Both Wales and the West Midlands emerge from the analysis as exceptions to the conclusion that the incidence of misery in the regions is that to be expected from national data.

When we compare the regions in respect of the importance of redundancy as a means of job loss (Martin, 1984), Wales and the West Midlands once again stand out as distinctive, in two ways. First, while other labour markets behave properly, with severance *and* engagement rates both falling in spite of increases in the redundancy component of the severance rate, in Wales and the West Midlands severance actually rose markedly during the recession period. Second, in both regions redundancies equalled (and in the case of Wales substantially exceeded) the *engagement* rate: more people were being made redundant than were being taken on. Redundancy was therefore creating unemployment independently of any imbalance between flows off the market through engagement and flows on through other types of separation.

Just as Townsend found that inter-regional structural differences did not explain net job loss or redundancy variation between the regions, Martin demonstrates that differences in redundancy rates cannot explain inter-regional variation in separation rates (rates of flow on to the market). It is rather variations in 'natural turnover' (non-redundancy separations) that constitute the main explanatory factor. Martin suggests, moreover, that redundancy rates are explicable in terms of variations in the natural turnover rate and the unemployment rate. The higher the unemployment rate, the lower the natural turnover; the lower the turnover, the harder it is to contract the labour force through natural wastage and the more often employers will have to resort to redundancy as a means of slimming their labour forces. Townsend noted that Wales was already experiencing relatively high rates of unemployment in the late 1970s due to the consequences of its peripherality (closure of branch factories) and its dependence on steel (where jobs were already disappearing before the crisis of 1980). In Wales the recession inflated an already high level of unemployment and we would expect therefore a low natural turnover. This situation was compounded, however, by a relatively low engagement rate, which in Martin's words 'has itself contributed to a low rate of natural job turnover and has produced labour market conditions highly inimical to the task of relieving the high rate of redundancy there'.

Martin concluded his study with a plea that more attention be paid to the 'corporate and technical aspects of production in moulding the pace and pattern of employment adjustment and industrial restructuring in response to recession' (p. 455). In other words, to understand the behaviour of the market you have not merely to investigate the behaviour of workers, as most of the redundancy studies have done, but to follow the employer back into the place of production, and do this not simply to understand redundancy but to understand job loss of which redundancy is but one form. Why? Because, in Martin's words, 'differences in the forms of employment production are likely to generate different labour market policy problems'. Indeed, economic geographers are already taking up the challenge of trying to relate national and regional redundancy trends to industrial trends and exploring this relation by investigating the economic, social and political factors which predispose firms to resort to redundancy (Townsend and Peck, 1985).

If both the process of regional employment contraction is to be better understood, and labour market policies are to be more appropriately tailored to the needs of individual localities, research needs to be conducted at finer levels of spatial and sectoral disaggregation. As yet there have been few analyses of the dynamics of labour market adjustment and manpower strategies of individual firms in a local labour market context. Much greater emphasis should be accorded to such an employer based local labour market approach, however, because it focuses on the level at which labour market policies are intended to work. (Martin, 1984: 356)

This book is an attempt to make a contribution, however modest, to that endeavour, by reporting on a study of a major redundancy occurring early in the recession in one of the only two regions in Britain where redundancy is indisputably a major contributor to net job loss.

# 2

# The History of a Labour Market

Economic geographers and planners work with regions. People live in much more delimited areas: neighbourhoods, villages or small towns. Between the immediate locality in which people reside and the national region to which the locality belongs, there are yet other areas within which they travel to work. These are defined by the relative distributions over space of the housing stock and employment opportunities; they are also shaped by the communications pattern, which is in turn affected by the character of the terrain. Travel-to-work areas might appear difficult for the sociologist to handle: they are not formally defined and they are not the basis for any collectivity or institution peculiar to them. They can, however, be regarded as the physical sites of local labour markets, in so far as the workers living within a travel-to-work area are all potentially employees of the employers whose firms are located in that area and all employers are potentially employers of the workers who reside within it (Harris, 1984).

This is not a naïve empirical statement which ignores the existence of complex economic and social mechanisms, resulting in the 'allocation' of different types of workers to different industries or establishments. Indeed, it is the investigation of just such mechanisms with which the sociologist of labour markets and many labour economists are concerned. However, if it is highly unlikely that worker W will be employed by employer E, then the fact that E does not employ W is of little interest and needs no further explanation. The geographical definition of a local labour market therefore does not involve the claim that all workers from each and every location travel to employments at each and every other location, but only involves the claim that they could do so.

At the outset of the present study census data were used to define the boundaries of the travel-to-work area within which the BSC works at Port Talbot were located and which was therefore most affected by the redundancies of 1980. In very simple terms, the procedure used was designed to define an area such that movements to work between it and adjacent areas could not be reduced by including those adjacent areas within it, and such that movements between sub-areas were not smaller than those between the area and other adjacent areas. The result (Harris, 1982) approximates very closely to the area of the new (1974) County of West Glamorgan. West Glamorgan corresponds therefore to the local labour market area which was most immediately affected by the redundancies in the BSC works in Port Talbot with which this book is concerned. West Glamorgan is not, however, co-extensive with west Industrial South Wales, since it excludes that part of the South Wales coalfield which lies to its west in the old county of Carmarthenshire which is now part of the new county of Dyfed. Dyfed comprises the predominantly rural south-west corner of the Principality. Neither West Glamorgan, west Industrial South Wales, nor Industrial South Wales or South Wales as a whole, are *regions*, and this poses problems in connection with statistical data. In what follows reference will be made to areas other than West Glamorgan, areas which differ from it because they include industrial Carmarthenshire, centred on Llanelli.

West Glamorgan may be a relatively self-subsistent labour market, but its economy has to be understood as part of the economy of west Industrial South Wales, and this in turn cannot be understood outside the context of Industrial South Wales. It is to the character of the sub-region of Industrial South Wales that we turn first.

## Industrial South Wales

Industrial South Wales includes the old countries of Glamorgan, Monmouthshire and the part of Carmarthenshire within which the South Wales coalfield lies. Coal has been mined and metals worked in South Wales since the middle ages, but it was not until the eighteenth century that those activities began to make a significant impact on the economy of the sub-region (John, 1980; Roberts, 1980). The industrialization of South Wales began in west Industrial South Wales where the coal measures ran down to the sea, and through whose ports ores were imported from Devon and Cornwall. However, it was in Neath and Swansea that the smelting of both ferrous and non-ferrous ores grew up.

During the nineteenth century the whole of Industrial South Wales was opened up for the mining of coal (Williams, 1980). Once again, however, west Industrial South Wales was distinctive in supplying anthracite and higher grade coal rather than the steam coal produced by the majority of mining valleys to the east.

The nineteenth century was a period of almost continuous expansion for Industrial South Wales, an expansion which

> continued to be substantial into the twentieth century . . . the years immediately preceding the First World War [witnessing] the breaking of output records right

across the industrial board. However, this economic development had created an environment, and a physical and organisational infrastructure which were both overly narrow and largely inappropriate to the circumstances of the twentieth century. (Baber and Thomas, 1980)

As a result, after the short-lived post-war boom of the 1920s, South Wales experienced a severe depression quite distinct from the cyclical depression of the inter-war years. Coal was being rapidly displaced by other forms of energy, and the remaining supplies of Welsh coal were difficult to mine for geological reasons, and hence difficult to mechanize. As a result Welsh productivity fell and the competitive position of the industry declined. Employment in mining fell from 233,800 in Glamorgan in 1913 to 112,337 in 1944. The western anthracite part of the coalfield suffered less, however, and major contraction was delayed until the coming of the Second World War.

Nineteenth-century iron-works and steelmaking had been centred at the northern rim of the coalfield, especially at Merthyr and Dowlais. The exhaustion of local ore deposits imposed heavy transport costs and in the 1890s the first move was made to relocate metal manufacturing on the southern coast. By 1914 steelworks had been established in both Cardiff and Port Talbot. During the first war a new plant was built at Margam adjacent to the Port Talbot plant (established in 1903) and in the 1930s the East Moors plant at Cardiff was established and then expanded. Even so, by the end of the inter war period, Port Talbot had emerged as the main centre of steelmaking in Glamorgan. The building of large and accessible *basic* steelmaking plants between 1915 and 1935 ensured that the Welsh industry was able to take advantage of the increase in the demand for steel as the world moved out of recession in the mid 1930s.

This cannot be said of the western part of the county, however. Port Talbot apart, basic steel production in west Glamorgan was dispersed among 13 small firms carrying out different stages of production and supplying a multitude of small tinplate concerns. Consequently the 1920s saw substantial import penetration by foreign producers benefiting from the economies of scale and from the vertical and horizontal integration of production which large enterprise size made possible. With the arrival of the depression in world trade after 1929, the plight of steel and tinplate west of Port Talbot became desperate and was not eased until the Import Duties Act of 1932 provided some protection. However, it simultaneously reduced the pressures to consolidation and rationalization, with the result that it was only during the Second World War that the number of tinplate works were reduced by conversion to other purposes more suited to a wartime economy.

In 1913 coal, steel and tinplate production provided between them 70 per cent of total employment in Glamorgan; even in 1929 these accounted for 56 per cent. These figures bear striking witness to the lack of diversity of the Country's employment structure. This concentration manifested itself between the wars when the effects of the depression amplified structural unemployment in coal and steel so that the Glamorgan County unemployment rate reached 38 per cent in 1933 and three years later had fallen to only 32 per cent. These high county rates were the result of even higher rates in areas heavily dependent on the ***nineteenth century*** iron and steel industries and on steam coal production. Unemployment in Merthy Tydfil reached 62 per cent in 1932, though west Industrial South Wales and the coastal areas were in a more favourable position, if unemployment of between 20 per cent and 30 per cent as late as 1937 can be described as favourable – especially when compared with a British national rate of 13 per cent. Although unemployment fell rapidly thereafter, this was due to substantial out-migration of the young and to a small increase in demand for the products of basic industries. At the same time, however, the unemployment differential between South Wales and Britain worsened, the age of the unemployed and time spent unemployed increased, while gross rates started to rise again with the recession of 1938. South Wales was only saved from further calamity by increased government spending and positive regional policy (implemented for strategic reasons) as Britain prepared itself for war.

The Second World War, of course, increased the rate of out-migration of the young, thus accentuating the trend of the 1930s, and did much to increase the diversification of the region. At the same time, it reduced coal exports; large numbers of small collieries closed, and employment in the coal industry fell by over 25,000. For the same reasons, many of the small tinplate works in west Industrial South Wales closed between 1940 and 1943 with a loss of 14,000 jobs. In 1946 employment in coal was only 60 per cent of its 1939 level and the industry was unable to meet domestic demand. There were also major falls in employment and construction work and, as soon as the war ended, in the demand for dock labour. A return to the conditions of the 1930s was averted, after 1945, for a number of reasons: because of the wartime improvements in power supply and communications; because the war had increased the stock of manufacturing premises; because firms which had been 'relocated' in Glamorgan retained their Welsh premises as branch establishments; and because the incoming Labour government designated the whole of the South Wales coalfield as a development area and assisted it with public work schemes. At the same time, experience of working in a variety of industries had diversified the skills of the workforce and created a supply of semi-skilled female labour, while successful enterprises in Wales during the war had done much to improve the 'image' of the region in the minds of industrialists.

The post-war experience of the traditional industries, coal and metal manufacture, differed markedly. In coal, modernization – the closure of small inefficient collieries, capital investment in new mines and the mechanization of established ones – began slowly in the early 1950s. It only gathered speed at the end of that decade, when competition from other fuels placed a premium on productivity rather than total output and when, in the early 1960s, technological advances made possible the introduction of power-loading in the mining of narrow seams. The combination of increased productivity and falling total output necessarily led to manpower reductions, which generally took the form of voluntary redundancy, which the relatively tight labour market and the age structure of the workforce made possible, combined with transfers to other pits which involved an increase in commuting. However, some areas such as the Rhondda, where job loss was significant and alternative sources of employment were not available, suffered increased levels of unemployment as a result, while in others, where new pits were sunk near major urban centres, the National Coal Board experienced difficulty in recruiting labour, especially among the young, among whom mining had a negative image.

While a demand for Welsh coal is still assured because of its quality, the specialized nature of that demand renders it highly sensitive to fluctuations in the market price of competitive fuels, and the complex geology makes it extraordinarily difficult to estimate the ratio between investment and return, even in terms of output. It was predictable, therefore, that the closures associated with the period 1955 to 1970 would continue into the future and that such closures would be controversial. That they should generate high levels of emotion was also inevitable, since the majority of closures were in valley communities where collieries constitute the chief source of employment, and where commuting was difficult since the only lines of communication run along the valley floors and new major pits have been located elsewhere, on the coastal plain or at the mouths of the valleys. Even if total mining employment had not declined, the closure of valley collieries would still have eroded the economic base of the mining valleys and accelerated their depopulation as their inhabitants were forced to move south in the search for employment in the industries of the coastal plain, which were then still expanding.

The coastal plain was the site of the expansion of South Wales's other traditional industry: metal manufacture. Very briefly, though the inter-war years had seen a concentration of ownership in fewer hands, it had not seen a replacement of the multiplicity of small plants by modern integrated plants using continuous production processes which involve rolling hot metal into strip on the same site as the production of iron and steel; nor had the small tinning mills, half of which did not survive the war, been replaced by larger plants.

The first integrated metal manufacturing plant was built at Ebbw Vale in 1936 on the northern rim of the coalfield in response to the unemployment problem of that area. The site was difficult, communications poor, and it proved a blessing to Ebbw Vale that was of strictly limited duration: steelmaking at Ebbw Vale ceased in 1978. The only other pre-war innovation was the building of a continuous strip mill at Shotton in 1940. The main steel companies in Wales combined in 1947 to form the Steel Company of Wales which then built a massive integrated plant, the Abbey and Margam Works, on a greenfield site beside two existing steelworks at Port Talbot. The Abbey plant opened in 1952. With hindsight it is fairly clear that it should have included a tinplate works as well. However, in those days west Industrial South Wales was not a single local labour market, as transport between Port Talbot and Swansea, and Swansea and Llanelli was poor. It was in the Swansea and Llanelli travel-to-work areas that the majority of the obsolete tinplate works were or had been sited. As a result, 'for sociological reasons', the Company was persuaded to build two electrolytic tinning plants in 'west Wales', at Trostre near Llanelli and at Velindre, north of Swansea. These plants opened in 1953 and 1956 respectively. Some of the remaining tinplate works were closed and workers transferred to the new plants, but the major spate of closures did not occur until 1958, when 14 tinplate plants and 8 sheet handmills closed during the recession of that year. The remaining 2 handmills had closed by 1964 and the remaining cold steel plant in west Industrial South Wales closed in 1961.

By the early 1960s the re-structuring in the industry was complete. The one serious weakness of the whole western complex was, however, the absence of a deep water port. This was remedied by the decision of the National Ports Council to establish two deep water terminals in South Wales, one at Port Talbot to serve the Abbey Works, and the other at Newport to serve the new plant at Llanwern which came into full production in 1961. For complex political reasons this policy was not fully implemented and only the Port Talbot terminal was built, thus giving Port Talbot an advantage over a plant which was to become, in the 1980s, its competitor.

It will be clear from this account of the history of the South Wales economy in this century that its industrial experience has been a world away from that reflected by the redundancy studies reviewed in the previous chapter. Redundancy, resulting in structural unemployment after the massive reorganization of the coal and steel industries, has since the Second World War been a normal rather than an exceptional feature of the South Walian scene. Like those made redundant elsewhere, however, Welsh workers found themselves in a relatively buoyant, if not exactly tight, labour market with the result that, except in special circumstances, redundancies did not force up the local rates of unemployment.

## West Industrial South Wales after 1945

The preceding account gives the impression that Industrial South Wales *is* coal and steel. This impression must, however, on the evidence of that account be false, since the story is one of decline in coalmining and the closure of the whole of the pre-war steelmaking capacity and its replacement by more productive plant.

In west Industrial South Wales, in 1947, the coal industry employed 30,000 men in 77 collieries which produced 6 million tons of coal a year. By 1970 only 17 active collieries remained and they employed only 10,000 men and produced only 3.5 million tons a year (Humphrys, 1971b).

No comparable change had taken place during this period in the steel industry. In 1959 employment in metal manufacturing had reached 44,800 and had fallen only to 44,200 in 1968. Major falls in steel employment had yet to come.

Table 2.1 traces the decline of the basic industries traditional to west Industrial South Wales during this period by combining the results of two studies of areas, similar to that with which we are concerned, during the post-war era. The table shows a decline in the traditional manufacturing sector, which is partly compensated for by a growth in the chief 'modern' industries. It also shows, however, a decline in the share of manufacturing as a whole and the growth in importance of the service sector.

## West Glamorgan in the 1970s

West Glamorgan constitutes the local labour market area within which BSC Port Talbot is located and is also the travel-to-work area of its employees. It is thus the site of the market in which those made redundant had to sell their labour. West Glamorgan, rather than west Industrial South Wales, will constitute the reference point for tracing employment change during the 1970s. Table 2.2 shows the broad changes which took place in employment in West Glamorgan between 1971 and 1978. It is clear that the share of employment provided by traditional industries and by the manufacturing sector continued to decline and that the share of service industries increased. This continuation of trends already established for west Industrial South Wales in the 1950s and 1960s should not be allowed to obscure the reversal of others: the share of employment in the new industries (chemical, engineering and vehicles) fell and 'other manufacturing', which had increased its share from 6.5 to 9.5 per cent between 1961 and 1968 in west Industrial South Wales, actually fell in West Glamorgan by 0.5 per cent between 1971 and 1978. Most remarkable, however, was the decline in the share of the construction industry, which fell from 11.5 to 7.7 per cent.

There is in these figures cause for alarm. The decline of traditional industries and the failure of the new industries to replace the employment thus lost attests to the failure of post-war regional policy to achieve an expansion and diversification of the manufacturing base. As table 2.3 shows, only 'toys and plastics' and the chemicals industry showed net employment gains in the 1970s, while substantial net job losses occurred in construction, mechanical engineering and metal manufacturing; the net job losses in the other three categories, though small, together wiped out the net

TABLE 2.1 Percentage distribution of employees over industry type, 1951–1968

| SI classification | 'South West Wales' 1951 | | 'South West Wales' 1961 | | 'Swansea Region' 1968 |
|---|---|---|---|---|---|
| Extractive | 17.2 | | 13.5 | | 8.3 |
| Metal manufacture | 19.7 | | 19.1 | | } 22.1 |
| Metal (other) | 4.0 | | 4.4 | | |
| Traditional industry: total | 40.9 | | 37.0 | | 30.4 |
| Chemicals, engineering and vehicles | 8.2 | | 9.8 | | 12.3 |
| Other manufacturing | 7.7 | | 6.5 | | 9.5 |
| TOTAL MANUFACTURING AND EXTRACTIVE | 56.8 | | 53.3 | | 52.2 |
| AGRICULTURE | 1.0 | | 0.6 | | 0.6 |
| CONSTRUCTION | 8.9 | } 42.2 | 8.8 | } 46.1 | } 47.2 |
| SERVICES | 33.3 | | 37.3 | | |
| Total | 100.0 | | 100.0 | | 100.0 |

*Source*: Spence (1964) for 'South West Wales' 1951 and 1961 and Humphrys (1971a) for 'Swansea Region' 1968

TABLE 2.2 Percentage distribution of employees over industry type in West Glamorgan, 1971–1978

| SI classification | 1971 (no) | 1971 (%) | 1978 (no) | 1978 (%) | Change (%) |
|---|---|---|---|---|---|
| Extractive | 5,691 | 3.8 | 4,920 | 3.1 | −16.3 |
| Metal manufacture | 25,387 | 16.8 | 22,760 | 14.5 | −10.2 |
| Metal (other) | 7,270 | 4.9 | 6,231 | 4.0 | −14.4 |
| Traditional industry: total | 38,348 | 25.5 | 33,911 | 21.6 | −11.5 |
| Chemicals, engineering and vehicles | 13,418 | 8.9 | 11,730 | 7.5 | −12.4 |
| Other manufacturing | 13,551 | 9.0 | 13,339 | 8.5 | −1.6 |
| TOTAL MANUFACTURING AND EXTRACTIVE | 65,317 | 43.4 | 58,980 | 37.6 | −9.8 |
| AGRICULTURE | 949 | 0.6 | 877 | 0.6 | −7.6 |
| CONSTRUCTION | 17,190 | 11.5 | 12,296 | 7.7 | −28.0 |
| SERVICES | 66,932 | 44.5 | 84,665 | 54.1 | 26.4 |
| TOTAL | 150,388 | 100.0 | 156,818 | 100.0 | 4.3 |

*Source*: MSC ERII Returns

gains in toys and chemicals. It was the service sector's net contribution of nearly 18,000 extra jobs that resulted in the small overall increase in employment of 4.3 per cent shown in table 2.2.

Service sector gains were, however, chiefly in women's jobs as the right-hand column of table 2.3 shows. Nearly 16,000 of the 23,000 new jobs were taken by women. Male employment shows a net decline of 6,700 over the period, or 6.4 per cent. Female employment grew by 13,200, or nearly 29 per cent. The proportion of all employment formed by female employment increased from 30.5 per cent to nearly 38 per cent. The growth of female employment was slightly greater in West Glamorgan than west Industrial South Wales, probably due to the greater dominance of the county by Swansea, its administrative capital.

Male employment fell between 1971 and 1978 but industries experiencing the greatest percentage falls had provided only 16 per cent of all employment in 1971. Really major falls had yet to come in metal manufacturing, metal goods, chemicals, oil and coal, industries which constituted two-fifths of male employment in West Glamorgan throughout the 1970s.

## The Port Talbot labour market

The area most affected by the redundancies in the steel industry in 1980 was that based on Port Talbot, on the edge of which the BSC works is situated. The Port Talbot employment office area (EOA) or the Port Talbot travel-to-work area(TTWA) differ from other areas discussed so far in this chapter in that they are not sites of relatively self-contained local labour markets. In the 1970s, Port Talbot imported labour from outside its area to work in the steel and associated industries, but exported service sector workers who travelled to work in Neath and Swansea (Harris, 1982). The Port Talbot labour market is made up of two quite different areas: for the residents of Port Talbot, the area in which they sell their labour consists chiefly of the settlement of Port Talbot and its immediate environs. Port Talbot employers, in contrast, buy labour from the whole of West Glamorgan. The first section of this chapter has therefore been about that area from which labour was supplied to BSC: it is the labour market as seen from the standpoint of capital. The residents of that area do not share a common definition of their labour market area, each defining an area which is more narrow than BSC's area of supply, and is centred on the settlement in which each lives. A full study of West Glamorgan as a labour market would therefore require a series of related studies of its geographical sub-markets, a task outside the resources of the authors of this book. Since, however, we are concerned with the fate of redundant steelworkers in the labour market, the sub-market of Port Talbot - where the BSC works is situated and the majority of the redundant steelworkers live - is the sub-market most central to the understanding of their post-redundancy experiences and behaviour.

TABLE 2.3 Net job losses and job gains in West Glamorgan 1971–1978

| | *Job losses* (000s) | *Job losses* (%) | | *Job gains* (000s) | *Job gains* (%) | *Women only* (000s) |
|---|---|---|---|---|---|---|
| Construction | 4.9 | 28 | Manufacturing | | | |
| Manufacturing | | | Toys and plastics | 2.3 | 77 | 0.7 |
| Mechanical engineering | 2.6 | 54 | Chemicals | 1.0 | 52 | 0.1 |
| Metal manufacturing | 2.6 | 10 | Services | | | |
| Metal goods | 1.0 | 14 | National government | 7.8 | 328 | 5.7 |
| Remainder of manufacturing | 2.5 | 6 | Educational | 4.4 | 59 | 3.7 |
| | | | Professional and scientific (excluding education) | 3.5 | 41 | 2.5 |
| Services | | | | | | |
| Local government | 1.0 | 14 | Miscellaneous | 3.1 | 33 | 1.9 |
| Transport | 1.2 | 11 | Distributive, banking, etc. | 1.1 | 6 | 1.2 |
| Extractive | 0.7 | 13 | | | | |
| Total losses | 16.5 | | Total gains | 23.2 | | 15.8 |

*Source*: MSC ERII Returns

In terms of its employment structure in 1978, Port Talbot showed several distinct differences from West Glamorgan. As table 2.4 indicates, proportionately more of Port Talbot's *workers* (not residents) of both sexes were engaged in the manufacturing industry, fewer men were engaged in services in general, and fewer women were engaged in 'public administration' and 'other service industries' (the remainder of the service sector).

The structure of male employment has a distinctly old-fashioned look about it. Service employment had by 1978 not even reached the level recorded by Spence (1964) for 'South West Wales' in 1951 and manufacturing employment was 10 per cent above the 1951 figure for that area. Employment in Port Talbot was highly concentrated, the top ten categories of employer accounting for 80 per cent of all jobs, compared with only 56 per cent for West Glamorgan. Moreover, although Port Talbot provided only 20 per cent of all West Glamorgan's jobs, it furnished fully three-quarters of West Glamorgan's jobs in iron and steel.

During the 1970s the jobs in West Glamorgan's growing service sector were concentrated in Swansea, while employment in Port Talbot's central industry, metal manufacture, steadily declined. However, it did so more slowly than other forms of manufacture, so Port Talbot did not experience the same decline in manufacturing industry as that experienced by the county as a whole. In contrast, because in 1971 West Glamorgan's construction jobs were as heavily concentrated in Port Talbot as employment in iron and steel, Port Talbot took the brunt of the county's loss of construction jobs. As a result, the *proportion* of Port Talbot's jobs formed by manufacturing increased, in spite of their absolute decline.

TABLE 2.4 Employees working in Port Talbot EOA & West Glamorgan, June 1978 (percentages)

| *SI classification* | *Men* | | *Women* | |
|---|---|---|---|---|
| | *Port Talbot* | *West Glamorgan* | *Port Talbot* | *West Glamorgan* |
| Primary | 0.4 | 5.7 | 0.0 | 0.5 |
| Manufacturing | 69.7 | 45.9 | 31.0 | 19.1 |
| Construction | 12.3 | 10.5 | 1.4 | 0.9 |
| Services | | | | |
| Distributive and misc. | 4.9 | 11.9 | 31.1 | 28.9 |
| Other services incl. gas, etc. | 12.7 | 26.0 | 36.5 | 50.6 |
| Total | 100.0 | 100.0 | 100.0 | 100.0 |

*Source*: MSC ERII Returns

Port Talbot's occupational structure was old-fashioned not only in terms of its industry mix but also in terms of the proportion of jobs held by women. South Wales remained an area distinguished by the high proportion of jobs held by men during the 1970s, but Port Talbot's job structure was exceptional even for South Wales. In 1971 only 18 per cent of all jobs were held by women (West Glamorgan's figure was 30.5 per cent). By 1978 this figure had increased to only 23 per cent, compared to West Glamorgan's 38 per cent.

Changes in employment during the 1970s served therefore to accentuate the archaic characteristics of the sub-market's structure rather than modify them, thus increasing its difference from the labour market of which it formed part. The most important difference between Port Talbot and West Glamorgan is to be found, however, not in changes in its structure but in the level of employment during the 1970s. While employment in West Glamorgan increased over the period, in Port Talbot it fell: the number of employees in employment in Port Talbot in 1978 amounted to only 81 per cent of the 1971 total as a result of the loss of 7,500 jobs.

If we examine the incidence of these job losses by sex we find that in Port Talbot job loss among men (nearly 8,000) exceeded that of the county as a whole, while women's jobs increased by only 300. The greater proportion of jobs held by women was almost entirely the result of the decline in male employment and not of any significant increase in female employment. It was certainly not the result of 'feminization', in the sense of women taking over occupations previously held by men. The redundant steelworkers, predominantly men, were therefore offloaded onto a market which had already experienced a substantial loss of male employment. None the less, Port Talbot enjoyed some protection in the 1970s since its manufacturing employment declined more slowly than West Glamorgan's. The concentration of manufacturing which protected Port Talbot in the 1970s was later to become its Achilles' heel.

Between January 1976 and June 1980, 13,916 jobs were lost through redundancy alone from firms in the Port Talbot EOA, including 6,900 in metal manufacture. The 13,916 redundancies amounted to 40 per cent of *all* (not just manufacturing) employment at the beginning of 1976, and constituted 54 per cent of West Glamorgan's redundancies in that period. 60 per cent of these redundancies were in metal manufacture and 33 per cent in construction. This pattern was in marked contrast to that of neighbouring sub-markets, which experienced lower rates of redundancy in metal manufacture and construction but higher rates in heavy manufacturing and, in the Swansea sub-market, light manufacturing. Port Talbot suffered at the turn of the decade, partly because of its industrial mix but also because of a disproportionate contraction in construction employment.

By June 1980, when those made redundant by BSC were coming onto the market, employment was contracting sharply in other industries in areas to which those made redundant from BSC could have travelled to work. By 1981 the heavy loss of jobs in Port Talbot had abated, 'only' 2,309 redundancies occurring in Port Talbot that year, and the distribution had changed: the proportion contributed by 'iron and steel' had fallen to 34 per cent, but the contribution of other manufacturing industry had increased to 44 per cent. Increase in job loss rose less sharply in adjacent sub-markets, however, and redundancies continued after the worst was over in Port Talbot. Swansea and Neath lost 5,527 jobs through redundancy in 1981. It follows that after the period of mass steel redundancy in the summer of 1980 employment in neighbouring markets continued to decline, as did employment in other industries in the Port Talbot market. Those made redundant could not have improved their chances of obtaining employment in the year after the steel redundancies by switching either sub-market or industry.

Up to June 1980, 50 per cent of the non-steel redundancies were the result of closures. Thereafter the principal causes of redundancy were twofold: the completion or loss of contracts, and the knock-on effects of the scaling down of BSC's Port Talbot operation, that is redundancies at firms who supplied BSC. Job losses for the first reason constituted a significant proportion of all Port Talbot's redundancies at intervals throughout the period June 1980 to August 1982, but the BSC-related redundancies only contributed significantly in 1982.

Port Talbot is a local labour market dominated by one large concern, not only in terms of the proportion of jobs directly provided by BSC but also in terms of the business BSC creates for other employers. It is appropriate to speak therefore of BSC's *structural domination* of the market. In consequence, the scaling down of BSC's operations in 1980 had consequences for the level of activity in almost every other sector of economic activity and many of them would appear to have been distinctly lagged. As a result, the market's misery went on and on; the only sense in which things improved during the study period was that they got worse more slowly towards the end.

## The supply side of the Port Talbot market

Port Talbot lost jobs during both the 1970s and the 1980s on a scale which suggests that mass unemployment must have resulted. In fact unemployment rates, except for a short period after the BSC redundancies, were never significantly higher than those of the West Glamorgan labour market as a whole. Why? There are three reasons. First, the 1981 Census of Population shows a decline in the economically active population. The total population of Afan, within which district Port Talbot lies, fell by 8.4 per cent between 1971 and 1981, which might appear to be clear evidence of migration-response to job loss in the best 'on your bike' fashion. If, however, we examine the working population (defined as residents of over 15) we find that it actually *increased* by 0.73 per cent. This was largely due to increases in the numbers of older workers. If 'working age' is redefined to include those aged between 16 and 59, then we find only a tiny fall of 612 persons, or 1.8 per cent of the 1971 working population. Unemployment was not therefore significantly reduced by population loss and there is no evidence to suggest compensatory loss of population through net migration. There were, however, marked changes in the economic activity rates, that is in the proportion of residents in or available for work. Male rates fell from 82.5 per cent to only 69 per cent for those aged 16 and over, while economic activity among women rose from 35 to 51 per cent. The net result was a fall of 1500 persons (5.9 per cent) in the economically active population over the decade, the most substantial falls occurring among males over 50, the largest rises among women aged 21–9 and 40–9. If the 1971 rates had applied in 1981, the number of unemployed men would have increased by 2,400 and the number of employed women fallen by 850, a net increase of 1,550.

These changes are not enough to explain why Port Talbot's unemployment rate did not rise during the 1970s in proportion to its rate of job loss. The explanation is that the unemployment effects of Port Talbot's job loss were dispersed throughout the whole West Glamorgan market (which actually gained jobs during the 1970s) from which Port Talbot drew its labour. This would not have reduced the unemployment of Port Talbot's residents if their occupational distribution had corresponded to that of Port Talbot's jobs. It did not, however, falling somewhere between that of Port Talbot's job distribution and the occupational distribution of West Glamorgan as a whole (Fevre, 1984: 17–24). Port Talbot's *residents* had a wider variety of jobs than its industries could offer, and suffered less from the decline in construction and steel manufacturing than Port Talbot's *workers*. There is no evidence, therefore, of the operation of an economic 'guiding hand' which mysteriously adjusted supply downward to meet falls in demand during the 1970s.

When the combined effects of the national recession, the redundancies in steel and the continued decline of the construction industry hit Port Talbot at the end of the 1970s, unemployment in the Port Talbot market rose sharply. The numbers of both male and female unemployed in its employment office area were rising before the steel redundancies took place, and the travel-to-work area rates reached 17.1 per cent (18 per cent for men and 15.5 per cent for women) in October 1982, the last month before the change in the method of counting the unemployed. This was also the month in which the sample of those made redundant from BSC was interviewed for the last time for this study. The sharpest rise in the EOA figures occurred between June and December 1980, when 88 per cent of the steel redundancies occurred. This rise involved an increase of 2,000 in the number of male unemployed; the number of males in the EOA made redundant was approximately 2,800. The Port Talbot market would appear to have absorbed

28 per cent of the redundant, therefore. Similarly, the unemployment rate of the Port Talbot TTWA did not rise as far above West Glamorgan's level as the redundancies would have led one to expect. In December it stood at 13.5 per cent, only 0.7 of a percentage point above West Glamorgan. Since 75 per cent of the redundant steelworkers lived in this area, the number of registered unemployed who had previously worked in metal manufacturing should have stood at 4,350. In fact, it was 2,020 less. The TTWA seemed to have absorbed 46 per cent of the redundant. Moreover, by June 1981 the Port Talbot TTWA's unemployment rate fell below that of West Glamorgan, and by September 1982 was 0.7 of a percentage point *below* West Glamorgan's rate.

The relation between Port Talbot and West Glamorgan depends, of course, on what was going on in both places. The discussion of the redundancy figures above suggests that the rest of West Glamorgan suffered more badly from the recession after the impact of the redundancies had already manifested itself in the unemployment figures for Port Talbot. A large unemployment differential did not emerge as a result of the BSC redundancies partly because of the different *timing* of the impact of recession in Port Talbot and the rest of West Glamorgan. It is also the result of the apparent absorption of those made redundant by the Port Talbot market. We shall not explain this absorption at this point, since this whole book is concerned with 'what happened to the redundant', but we will return briefly to this issue at the end of the chapter.

## The composition of unemployment

The previous section has dealt briefly with unemployment levels and the impact of the BSC redundancies. However, redundancy and recession affect not only the level but the characteristics of the unemployed. In times of high employment the industrial and occupational structure of the unemployed population is as important a labour market characteristic as that of those in work. However, the impression given by a snapshot percentage distribution at any time point can be misleading, since it ignores the rate of change in the composition of the unemployed stock. This can be remedied if categories are distinguished in terms of an index of growth as well as in terms of their position in a distribution. As might be expected, the industry whose contribution to the unemployed stock had grown fastest between February 1980 and May 1982 was metal manufacturing. Its index of growth was 2.2 times that of all industries and was followed most closely by metal goods. The contributions of only two other major categories grew at above average rates: 'unclassified' and 'professional and scientific services'. Those contributing most to the unemployed stock were 'unclassified' (26 per cent), metal manufacturing (19 per cent) and construction (18 per cent). While there were differences in rates of growth, there was a marked similarity between the distributions of unemployment and of employment by industry. The character of the unemployed stock in May 1982 appears to be the result not only of decline in particular industries, but also of the general decline in the demand for labour. In this regard it is significant that service industries, although their contribution grew at below average rates, none the less had contributed 40 per cent to the unemployed stock in May 1982.

If we turn to the incidence of unemployment according to age and gender we find the unemployed to be over-represented among younger people (of both sexes) and older men. These well-known features of contemporary unemployment were not, however, altered by the steel redundancies. The elderly character of the redundant population (see chapter 3) did not create but merely accentuated a pre-existent feature of the market, while the proportional increase in the number of unemployed school leavers was greater in July 1980 (when the steel redundancies were at their height) than in any other month during the whole period between 1979 and 1982.

The combined effects of the recession in other industries and areas and the steel redundancies naturally resulted in increased durations of unemployment. The proportion of long durations in Port Talbot was below that of its neighbouring TTWAs in 1979 when employment in Port Talbot was increasing less fast than in adjacent markets. The year after Port Talbot's surge in unemployment levels the proportion of unemployed in Port Talbot with long durations overtook that of neighbouring areas, but was exceeded by its neighbours again in 1982, a year after their unemployment surge. The differences in duration would appear to be due entirely to the timing of increases in unemployment levels. There is no evidence that Port Talbot, as the centre of the steel redundancies, experienced a higher incidence of long-term employment as a result, at least in the two years after the redundancies.

There is no evidence, therefore, that the effect of the BSC redundancies was to create a pool of unemployed in Port Talbot highly untypical of the stock in neighbouring areas, and it should be emphasized that the situation under study is one of massive workforce reduction and not closure of a plant dominating a self-contained labour market. The analysis of data so far presented supports the hypothesis that, however dramatic the recession's arrival in Port Talbot, the drama of mass redundancy was merely a feature of that arrival and did not constitute or create a labour market situation atypical of the area in which it occurred.

## The response of the market

We have noted that the apparent absorption of the redundant is one of the main areas of enquiry of this book, as is the operation of the market which seems to have absorbed them. Absorption may be thought of as occurring in two stages. In the first stage redundants never reach the unemployment register because they either go 'out of the market' (that is, become economically inactive), retrain or obtain other work. Absorption at this first stage reduces the amount of work the market has to do in absorbing redundants at the second stage. This second stage involves getting them off the unemployment register. The labour market data make it abundantly clear that, for whatever reason, a significant proportion of redundants never reached the register. At the second stage an even more striking and mysterious form of absorption is apparent: the massive increase in flows on to the unemployment register produced by the redundancies were shortly followed by an almost equally massive flow off.

This is not what should have happened. Table 2.5 shows the relation between registered unemployment and job vacancies over the two year study period of the present work. Notified vacancies fell dramatically during the six month period during which redundant steelworkers were flowing on to the register. An increase in flows on, combined with a fall in vacancy notification which implies that flows off had fallen to a trickle, should have pushed up the unemployed stock and the whole market should have become stagnant. Instead, the market showed an unexpected dynamism: there were large flows both on and off the register (in spite of their being 52 unemployed for every notified redundancy), as figure 2.1 shows.

There is no way in which, from the available statistical data, explanations of these phenomena can be substantiated. It is, however, possible to produce a number of explanations on the basis of circumstantial evidence. First, some redundants could have gone 'out of the market' after some experience of being on the unemployed register. This is really a form of delayed 'stage one' absorption appearing as a flow off. Second, placement of redundants in jobs which would have been taken by recently unemployed

TABLE 2.5 Vacancies and unemployment in Port Talbot EOA (quarterly) 1980–1982

| | *1980* | | | | *1981* | | | | *1983* | |
|---|---|---|---|---|---|---|---|---|---|---|
| | *Feb.* | *May* | *Aug.* | *Nov.* | *Feb.* | *May* | *Aug.* | *Nov.* | *Feb.* | *May* |
| Unemployed | 2445 | 2665 | 3784 | 4889 | 4997 | 4921 | 5028 | 5215 | 5195 | 5184 |
| Unfilled vacancies | 196 | 182 | 167 | 94 | 137 | 143 | 179 | – | – | 139 |
| Number of unemployed for each vacancy | 12 5 | 14.6 | 22.7 | 52.0 | 36.5 | 34.4 | 28.1 | – | – | 37.3 |

*Source*: Employment Office and Careers Office. Employers sometimes notified vacancies to both but vacancies at Careers Office were few

workers who had not registered as unemployed would mean that the latter appeared for the first time in the figures as part of flows on without increasing flows off. Displacement of other workers (already on the register) directly or indirectly by steelworkers taking the jobs they otherwise would have occupied would have decreased flows off the register. Third, another form of displacement which could have contributed to the increase in flows off is the displacement of imported labour by local Afan people. Such a hypothesis presupposes a change in employers' recruiting practices: a movement from formal to informal means of recruitment motivated by the looseness of the market, and by the fact that redundant steelworkers, since they had their pay after redundancy made up to 90 per cent of their BSC wages, would be more willing to work for low wages (see chapter 3, p. 77).

A fourth explanation is that, coincident with the arrival of the steel redundancies and the more general recession, a change occurred in the character of labour demand. This explanation presupposes that job loss in the market during the period was in fact artificially high and reflected employers' desire to shed established labour and increase manpower flexibility, as well as to dispense absolutely with some of the labour shed. The replacement of permanent by fixed term employments would generate an immediate flow off and subsequently make the market more dynamic than is to be expected if we assume the character of labour demand to be that of the traditional post-war kind. This last hypothesis will be explored throughout the rest of this book.

## The 1980 climacteric

It was in the form of the 1980 BSC redundancies that the recession arrived in Port Talbot. In all, 5,800 workers were made redundant, yet in the Port Talbot TTWA, where 75 per cent of the redundants lived, the unemployed stock of ex-steelworkers never rose above 2,327 (in November 1980) or just over 50 per cent of the expected flow on, and by May 1982 had fallen to a mere 1,300. However, the level of unemployment did not fall as the ex-steelworkers moved off the register and it follows that they must have been replaced by workers classified under other heads. This does not necessarily imply that the steelworkers displaced other workers. If the steelworkers left the register for fixed-term employment in other industries, they would rejoin the register when their contracts ended, but under a different category.

In any case, there are explanations other than displacement for high unemployment levels: the reduction of manning levels to reduce unit costs across the whole range of manufacturing industry; the reduction of employment in line with a fall in demand, particularly in non-steel manufacturing and some private service sector firms; a fall in construction activity due to the

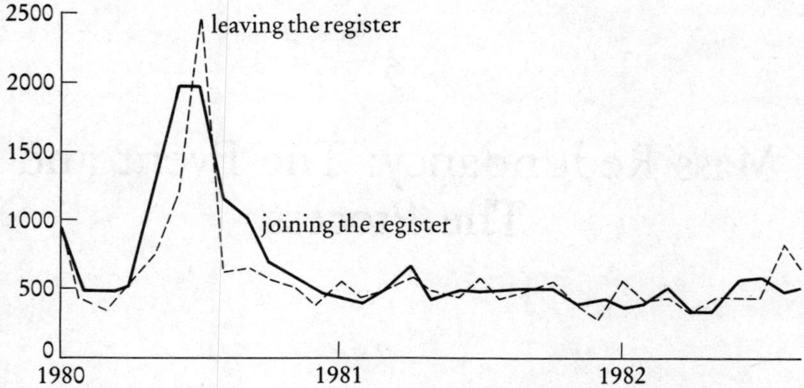


FIGURE 2.1 Monthly flows on and off the unemployment register among men in Port Talbot, 1980–1982 based on unofficial figures from Port Talbot Job Centre. (Statistics refer to Port Talbot EOA including Pyle, and Cymmer from July 1982.)

completion in 1981 of the Concast plant, the major technological innovation at BSC (see chapter 3); the knock-on effects of BSC lower operating levels manifested in 1982; the end of the domestic property boom of the 1970s and of a period of government investment in infrastructure; and, more recently, the end of expansion of government expenditure in the service sector.

If the market showed an unexpected dynamism, therefore, this was largely because a reduction in voluntary job-changing was counterbalanced by an increase in activity amongst workers who were compelled to change their jobs. It appears that more was changing in the Port Talbot labour market in the early 1980s than the number of jobs in BSC and the level of unemployment. The political and economic conditions characteristic of the period had transformed the way the market operated and the character of its demand. It is only human to assume that in the future the world is going to be like it was in the past. This chapter has shown that there is evidence which suggests that the market the redundant steelworkers entered was a changing one; one that was changing to a condition quite unlike anything which they had experienced before. We shall turn in the next chapter to the characteristics of those who found themselves adrift in the turbulent waters of this new type of market.

# 3

# Mass Redundancy: The Event and The Process

The previous chapter located the BSC redundancies of 1980 in the context of the sub-regional economy and the local labour market and examined its effects on the sub-market most affected. It is the purpose of this chapter to examine the redundancy process, that is the social process whereby certain people were selected for redundancy and the characteristics of the population of redundant workers which were its product. Before undertaking this task it is necessary, however, to locate the redundancies in the context of the steel industry in general and of the South Wales steel industry in particular.

## The plant and the industry

The Abbey works of the Steel Company of Wales at Port Talbot was completed in 1952 and formed part of the first, and most successful, phase of the post-war restructuring of the British iron and steel industry. It was designed to replace the old-fashioned production of steel strip for tinning by a large number of small plants in the western part of what is now West Glamorgan, and in the Llanelli area of Dyfed, by the new process of high speed continuous rolling of wide strip. The products of the new plant were to be processed by two new cold reduction mills sited in 'West Wales' to the north of Swansea and near Llanelli to absorb the redundant labour from obsolescent plant in those areas, in spite of the industry's view that 'the most economical arrangements . . . would have been for the two new . . . plants . . . to be located on sites adjoining the . . . new hot strip mill [at Port Talbot]' (Vaisey, 1974: 135–8).

A new company, the Steel Company of Wales was established to undertake the new developments. It took over the assets of the old works which were to be developed or superseded, owned variously by Richard Thomas and Baldwin; Guest, Keen and Baldwin; and Guest, Keen and Nettlefolds. Port Talbot was chosen as a site due to the availability of land, access to the sea and proximity to the proposed mills in 'West Wales'. This site is seaward of the settlement of Port Talbot through which the main railway line, trunk road and (today) the motorway run.

The Abbey Scheme at Port Talbot was part of a three works configuration comprising a new plant (the Abbey) and two existing plants, one at Port Talbot and one at the adjacent settlement of Margam. Iron for the steel furnaces was provided by two of the existing Margam furnaces, to which a third was added; coke was provided by the Margam coking plant whose capacity was increased. Steelmaking was initially retained in both the old works whose plant was modernized under the scheme. The scheme's major objective was, however, to develop on this new site, the Abbey, new steelmaking capacity, a slabbing mill, hot rolling mill, pickling and annealing lines and a cold reduction mill (Cartwright, 1952; Griffiths, 1952). The resultant three site configuration became the Margam and Abbey Works of the Steel Company of Wales at Port Talbot. Its main technological advance was the hot strip mill, but no such advance was made in either iron or steelmaking. Steelmaking involved massive investment in open hearth furnaces which were, as the plant's manager noted, 'of relatively conservative design and without many novel features' (Cartwright, 1952).

Iron-making capacity was increased in 1956 and 1959 to supply two new open hearth furnaces which were opened at the Abbey in 1957. In 1960 steelmaking at the Port Talbot works ceased and Margam's open hearth steelmaking capacity was replaced by four Bessemer convertors. Both these and the Abbey's original open hearth furnaces were closed in 1970 and steel was made thereafter by two large vessels producing Basic Oxygen Steel (BOS). The first changes had increased the capacity of the plant from 30,000 tons per week (1.5 million tons per annum) in 1952 to around 60,000 tons per week (3.1 million tons per annum) by 1960. The shift to BOS in 1969 provided a capacity of 3.25 million tons per annum with the possibility of expansion, by the addition of a third BOS vessel, to 6 million tons per annum (Heal, 1974).

In 1974, as a result of using higher grade foreign ores imported via the new harbour (see below), ironmaking was reorganized and the number of blast furnaces reduced. In the later 1970s the old sinter plant (which produces one of the basic ingredients for steelmaking) was phased out and a new sinter plant and a new bank of coke ovens was commissioned. The most significant innovation since the introduction of BOS steelmaking has, however, been the building of a continuous casting plant (Concast). This process bypasses the slabbing stage and reduces the amount of handling, with consequent reductions in cost and labour. The Concast plant was under construction before the redundancies were announced in 1980 and was not completed until 1982. It was therefore being built and generating demand for contract labour in the construction industry throughout the period of this study.

The first period of the plant's life was characterized by an increase in *capacity*. The second was characterized by major technological improvements in *steelmaking*. Both periods are remarkable for the absence of any improvements in *finishing*, that is, in the quality of the hot rolled strip whose production is the plant's *raison d'être*. A programme to refurbish the hot strip mill was, however, begun in 1984 to improve quality and adapt the mill for rolling the thicker slabs produced by the Concast process, which now operates alongside a conventional slabbing mill. The refurbished strip mill was opened by the Prince of Wales in the summer of 1986.

One further crucial development which must be mentioned is the completion in 1970 of a new tidal harbour on the seaward side of the site, together with a new processing and conveyor complex. This project was part of a scheme to provide both the Port Talbot and Llanwern plants of the Steel Company of Wales with direct access to harbours. The Port Talbot scheme was approved by the Docks and Harbour Board first, but the nationalization of the industry in 1967 stopped the development at Llanwern. As a result, since 1974, Llanwern has been supplied by imports from Port Talbot, giving the latter an advantage over its sister plant (Heal, 1974: 132–4).

The stages in the development of the Abbey Works closely paralleled the history of the British steel industry after the Second World War. There have been five industry plans, the chief concern of which has been to increase steel capacity. The first sought to increase capacity to 18 million tons nationally and the last to 27–30 million tons in 1970 (Vaisey, 1974: 162–3). The nationalized industry then produced its own 'Ten Year Strategy' which envisaged a further increase to between 36 and 38 million tons by 1980. This sequence of plans is characterized by underestimation of demand in the earlier plans and overestimation in the later. British steel production never rose above 30 million tons before the sharp fall in demand, triggered by world oil price increases, brought the boom of the early 1970s to an end. The British industry was not well placed to participate in that boom. For a variety of reasons the major investment which should have enabled the industry to take advantage of it was delayed and did not come on stream until the end of the 1970s when demand had slumped, while the proposed closures which the Ten Year Strategy had planned were postponed for political reasons, thus leaving BSC at the end of the 1970s with both a surplus of capacity and obsolescent plant (Cottrell, 1981; Aylen, 1984).

The problem of surplus capacity was greatest in what is now the Steel Strip Division of BSC and was a legacy of the period between the two nationalizations of the industry (in 1950 and 1967). In 1959 the Iron and Steel Board proposed a further strip mill in addition to the ones at Port Talbot, Ebbw Vale and Shotton. The industry regarded this expansion of capacity as unnecessary, but the plan went ahead and two sites were suggested: at Llanwern near Newport and at Ravenscraig in Scotland. Social arguments were put forward on behalf of both, and the Prime Minister at the time,

Harold Macmillan, decided on political grounds that both mills should be built. It cannot be doubted that, whether three was preferable to four, five was too many. Indeed, in 1964, Port Talbot's managing director had argued that major cost reductions could be achieved by concentrating operations at only two mills (Cartwright, 1964: 637–43). Ebbw Vale had been earmarked for closure by the Ten Year Strategy and steelmaking ceased there in 1978, which left four strip mills in operation.

## The redundancy event

In 1979 the British Steel Corporation produced a document called 'The Radical Review' in response to the outgoing Labour government's White Paper on the steel industry requiring BSC to bring capacity into line with demand. This paper was rejected in September by the new Secretary of State for Industry, Sir Keith Joseph, and 'The Radical Review' was replaced by a new BSC document, *A Return to Financial Viability*, which was adopted by BSC's Board on the 10 December 1979. It proposed a reduction in BSC's manpower by one-third, from 150,000 to 100,000, to cut back steel production to 15 million tonnes, and specified which closures and redundancies it required except those in South Wales (for discussion, see Upham, 1980).

South Wales was presented with three options:

1 the closure of either Llanwern or Port Talbot;
2 reduced production at both plants ('Slimline');
3 'the dogleg' steel to be made at Port Talbot and rolled at Llanwern.

The choice of the second option seems to have been settled upon as a result of informal negotiations between BSC management and local union officials at the two South Wales plants between the December Board meeting and the Christmas break. It was presented to the Board meeting on 17 January 1980 and then became part of BSC's strategy. A chronology of events is given below (p. 70).

The background to these events is complex, and there is space only to note two important features. The first is that all EEC steel-producing countries suffered during the late 1970s and by 1981 had cut back employment in their steel industries. Steel employment in the EEC fell by 17.8 per cent between 1979 and 1981. The British industry lost 43.6 per cent of its jobs during the same period. This was the result of the deliberate policy of the first Thatcher administration, which in BSC's own words 'deliberately created intense pressures on all BSC's operations' (BSC, 1981). In K. Morgan's words:

> The government's initial refusal to extend BSC's external financing limit, together with its imposition of an impossible breakeven target for 1980/1, represented the most stringent cash limits ever imposed on a nationalised industry in Britain [which] forced

BSC into a programme of entrenchment without parallel in the EEC [involving] a total reduction of 53,000 in the iron and steel labour force . . . concentrated into an eight month period. (pp. 181–2)

This was not, however, the way the steel cuts were presented in South Wales. Local press coverage of the announcement of the cuts emphasized falling demand and growing deficits as representing an economic necessity which steelworkers had to recognize if 'steelmaking was to be saved at Port Talbot.' Though neither of the other two options – 'the dogleg' and the closure of one of the two South Wales plants – seems to have been real, there was little doubt in anyone's mind that BSC was prepared to adopt them, if it failed to get worker agreement to 'Slimline'.

The reason for claiming that the closure of the Port Talbot works was not the Corporation's preferred option is their investment in the continuous casting plant at the Abbey. BSC's 1979 Corporate Plan proposed to expand production at Ravenscraig and Teesside at the expense of other plants. Morgan argues that this stemmed from BSC's investment in Ravenscraig in the form of a continuous casting plant (1983). The reason that Port Talbot was not similarly chosen as a site for expansion was because of the deficiencies of its 'finishing' end, that is, in its strip rolling and annealing operations. It was this weakness that made its closure or the adoption of the 'dogleg' option appear plausible.

Bryer, Brignall and Maunders (1982) argued convincingly that British Steel's problems in the 1970s arose from the concentration of the Ten Year Plan on increasing steelmaking capacity and the postponement of investment in finishing to the end of the period, an investment which never took place because the plan was abandoned before completion. As a result,

BSC did not have the kind of rolling and finishing facilities that its customers required and its continental competitors already had . . . the most urgent need for the enhancement of finishing facilities was at Port Talbot [where] 'the 80 inch hot strip [mill] was first designed in 1938 and had been rolling continuously since 1950'. (Second Select Committee, 1977–8: 147)

The result was the loss of home markets to foreign importers on top of falling global demand.

Someone, somewhere, however, seems to have decided to rectify this situation before 1979. Work had begun on replacing the coke ovens, on the new sinter plant and on the continuous casting plant in the previous year, and as the chronology below shows, a deliberate and well-thought out plan of modernizing the Port Talbot plant was being executed amidst the alarms and excursions of successive plans announcing redundancies and threats to close one of the South Wales plants.

| | |
|---|---|
| Aug. 16 1980 | expenditure of £12m was announced 'to improve quality' |
| Aug. 28 1980 | expenditure of £37m was announced on a new power plant |
| | expenditure of £1.4m was announced to improve metal handling |
| Nov. 14 1980 | expenditure of £60m was announced to improve finishing |
| Jan. 30 1981 | new coke ovens were lit |
| Mar. 8 1982 | purchase announced of 5 computers to improve production control |
| Aug. 19 1982 | Concast started production |
| Oct. 15 1982 | BSC estimated its investment over 4 years in Port Talbot at £400m |
| Dec. 17 1982 | BSC announced the provision of a new hot strip mill |
| Dec. 14 1983 | after long delays by the EEC work on the new mill started |
| June 1986 | new hot strip mill went into production |

The complex circumstances in which BSC's Corporate Plan was implemented in Port Talbot have a direct bearing on the subsequent behaviour of the steelworkers. Before the decision to build Concast was announced in 1978, morale seems to have been low among both management and workers, who knew that investment to modernize the finishing end was necessary and had been promised, yet was not forthcoming. Indeed, informants allege that significant numbers of management and workers left in the late 1970s, convinced that the plant had no future. Moreover, the plant had experienced continuous de-manning since it reached its peak of 18,352 workers in 1960, with notable falls in manning associated with the closure of the VLN (very low nitrogen) plant in 1969, the shutdown of open hearth steelmaking in 1971, and also in 1972 and 1975, when the sinter line and a blast furnace were decommissioned. In 1978 BSC implemented a Work Measurement Incentive Scheme (WMIS) which was designed to reduce manning among process grades. Partly because of this, total employment had fallen over the year from 13,139 to 12,155 by the end of 1978. A new scheme, Reduction in Fixed Costs, was applied to staff grades in 1979, and negotiations were under way with the trade unions over more flexible manning. None the less, at the time the redundancies were announced, actual manning had risen to 12,584.

It seems reasonable to suppose that in 1979 the future was seen by many workers to involve gentle reductions in manning levels combined with the progressive introduction of modern technology. The events of September 1979, following the election of the Conservative government, constituted a rude awakening. From then onward, BSC policy had at least three strands: massive manpower reductions to meet the government's cash limits;

investment to improve competitiveness and profitability; and highly flexible production levels to match fluctuating and uncertain demand. The events of 1979 and 1980 could be interpreted as the result of a temporary drop in demand, given that workers did not know of the coming recession, that demanning was represented as a market-determined economic necessity and not a political policy (for discussion, see Upham, 1980) and that BSC continued to invest in the plant. As one union official put it: 'There'd been redundancies before in 1972, and a lot of those got taken back on. Some of the younger ones thought it'd be the same this time.' The 'redundancy diary' below demonstrates that it wasn't.

| | |
|---|---|
| 1979 Sept. | Actual manning 12,584; crude steel output 2,314,528 tonnes |
| 1979 Dec. 12 | BSC announce **Corporate Plan**: 9–10,000 redundancies expected in Port Talbot and Llanwern |
| 1980 Jan. 2 | Steel strike begins |
| **Jan. 17** | **6,883 redundancies announced at Port Talbot; 4,500 at Llanwern, Port Talbot manning to fall to 5,701** |
| Feb. 9 | Tinplate redundancies in Port Talbot's associated plants estimated at 1,500 |
| Mar. 31 | Pay settlement of 15.5% recommended |
| Apr. 3 | BSC workers go back |
| Aug. 11 | Talks begin on Slimline implementation |
| Apr. 21 | BSC suggests 'hiving off' jobs to contractors |
| May 2 | BSC warns of possibility of further job cuts |
| May 16 | Management and unions agree redundancy plan<br>Redundancy flow starts |
| May 26 | BSC chairman-designate MacGregor says closure of Port Talbot not ruled out |
| June 20 | Last union signs the redundancy agreement at Port Talbot |
| July 7 | Tinplate workers to be put on short time |
| Aug. 20 | Loss of further 2,000 jobs in South Wales threatened by BSC |
| Sept. 18 | BSC Landore (Swansea) foundry to close with loss of 200 jobs |
| Oct. 2 | BSC to close Whitford Tinplate Works at Briton Ferry with loss of 30 jobs |
| Oct. 9 | BSC plans further reduction in capacity from 15m to 12m tonnes |
| Nov. 7 | Steelworkers set up action group to fight further cuts |
| Nov. 9 | BSC announces that 5,807 workers were made redundant at Port Talbot |

| | |
|---|---|
| Dec. 8 | BSC announces its '**Survival Plan**'. A further 2,500 jobs could be lost throughout Britain |
| Dec. 11 | Thatcher pelted with eggs at Cardiff |
| **Dec. 13** | **1,096 redundancies announced at Velindre; a further 796 at Port Talbot. Manning to fall to 5,560** |
| Dec. 24 | Workers asked to accept 6 month pay freeze |
| 1981 Jan. 20 | Velindre's redundancy agreement signed |
| *Jan. 23* | *Duport Steelworks in Llanelli close with loss of 1,100 jobs* |
| May 5 | Rumours that 2,500 more jobs to go in Port Talbot and Llanwern |
| *May 26* | *BP Baglan cuts 200 jobs* |
| July 17 | Tinplate works put on short time |
| *Oct.* | *British Aluminium closes, 560 jobs lost* |
| Nov. 3 | BSC's second **Survival Plan** involves a further 25,000 job loss |
| **Nov. 19** | **474 further jobs to go at Port Talbot. Manning to fall to 5,143** |
| 1982 May 20 | Over 1,000 jobs lost in South Wales coalfields in previous 12 months |
| June 7 | BSC to revise its survival plan in face of falling demand |
| June 10 | 400 jobs may be lost at Port Talbot |
| *June 17* | *BP cuts another 500 jobs* |
| Oct. 14 | Port Talbot goes on short time |
| Oct. 22 | 24 hour token strike against further closures |
| **Dec. 3** | **242 jobs to be lost at Port Talbot. Manning to fall to 4,907** |
| 1983 Jan. 26 | BSC chairman warns of plans to cut further 16,000 jobs nationwide |
| June 15 | Brynlliw Colliery Gorseinon to close; Blaengwrach Colliery to close |
| Sept. 22 | 200 more jobs to go at Port Talbot by Sept. 30 |
| Oct. 17 | Actual manning is now 4,848, representing a net loss of 7,567 jobs, 1979–83 |
| **Dec.** | **New agreement: 154 jobs to go. Manning to fall to 4,750; percentage loss 1979–85: 62%** |
| **1984** | **Actual manning 4,808. Crude steel output: 1,921,204 tonnes per annum. Output per man 400 tonnes per annum. (Output per man in 1978: 154 tonnes per annum.)** |

*Postscript*

| | |
|---|---|
| 1986 July | BSC announce profit for first time in decade |

The figures at the top and bottom of the diary referring to the beginning and end of the period covered are based on data kindly supplied by the personnel department at BSC Margam. A comparison of these figures taken in conjunction with the chronology on p. 69, demonstrates that the redundancies of 1980 were not the result of a fortuitous market turn down, nor even a result of the political pressures exerted on BSC *that year*, but part of a much longer term policy adopted by BSC. In the terms of this policy, investment and de-manning were not, as some BSC workers thought, alternatives. Rather, investment and de-manning marched together as twin means of reducing labour costs. They are twin means because they are both *related*, investment reducing the manpower required, and *separate*, since the policy also involved an attempt to employ fewer men to make a given quantity of steel with a given level of investment.

This policy has been highly successful. In 1984 Margam produced nearly the same amount of crude steel as in 1978 with only 38 per cent of the 1978 labour force. Policy implementation was enormously facilitated by the vicissitudes of the market for steel. Whereas an overt policy of what the unions would have termed 'job destruction' would have provoked worker resistance, successive reductions in manning were legitimated by quite genuine references to the falling market for steel, and the need to cut back manning to ensure 'survival'. A detailed study of the event chart from which the chronology on p. 69 and the redundancy diary are abstractions, makes it quite clear that Ian MacGregor (BSC chairman from summer 1981 onward) was a grand master of this art. Inspired leaks, horror statistics about losses, market falls and falling order books, and the continual reference to possible closure – 'none of the five main steel plants is safe' – were all skilfully timed to coincide with the emergence of worker resistance to new manning agreements. At the same time the BSC publicity machine ground out a whole series of items on production achievements, to which MacGregor would respond with statements of appreciation of the workers' efforts and assurances that BSC was becoming profitable and that their jobs would be safe – as long as they continued to co-operate. Mrs Thatcher has described MacGregor as 'Britain's most skilful politician'. We concur with that judgement.

In addition to redundancy events at Port Talbot the redundancy diary includes other major redundancies in west Industrial South Wales. There is no possibility of listing all redundancy announcements which appeared in the press, since these total 89 for the period 1980 to 1983 and involve 18,757 job losses or redundancies in all. The rate of loss was highest in 1980 and fell thereafter to half its 1980 level. The diary does not include mining or construction redundancies except in the cases of two colliery closures in 1983. Though the trend is downward over the period, peaks occurred in the fourth quarter of 1981, the second quarter of 1982 and the fourth quarter of 1983. These figures are not an accurate representation of redundancies or job losses in any specific labour sub-market. Our concern here, however, is with worker *perceptions* of the market. If some redundants thought they could 'get back in' to Port Talbot, they must soon have realized how mistaken they had been; and if they had read the local press and watched local news, they could have had little hope of getting a job anywhere else. One by one the major landmarks of the local economy – BSC tinplate, British Aluminum, Duport Steel, BP, Metal Box, Mettoys, Marx's – either shrank drastically or disappeared altogether.

These future events were, however, unknown when redundancy negotiations were in progress, effectively from November 1979 to May 1980. Informal negotiations continued during the steel strike which began on 2 January 1980. As one worker put it: 'While we were out there marching, they were inside talking.' 'They' were the union officials who formed the members of the Slimline Committee, and what they were talking about was how to implement the required cuts in manning levels in the various departments which made up BSC Margam. The full time union officers were busy conducting a strike over pay, which was surely what Sir Keith Joseph intended, since no body of workers, however 'moderate', could have been expected to accept the offer of a 2 per cent pay rise against a background of 16 per cent inflation. This left the way clear for management to use the local officials to implement the redundancies. Management informed the multi-union Slimline Committee which departments were to be closed and which jobs were to be cut; it was then left to each union to decide which workers, within given categories, were to go.

The unions' task was facilitated by generous redundancy terms which resulted in a large number of volunteers. However, the job loss pattern produced by the volunteers did not coincide with the pattern formed by the required redundancies. As a result, workers who were not made redundant but wished to be, applied for 'cross-matching' with another worker who was to be made redundant involuntarily.

It seems that age and 'last in, first out' were principles involved in the initial selection by unions of redundants. Volunteers who were surplus to particular redundancy requirements applied for cross-matching through their union official, who on occasion used the good offices of industrial relations officers to find a cross-match with an involuntary redundant in another part of the plant. (See the Redundancy Agreement, paragraph 4.5.)

The question of *who* was to be made redundant was, it seems, decided by a complex process of bargaining, initially between union plant officials and their members. Unions were able to persuade many workers in the categories management required to be reduced to accept the relatively generous redundancy terms on offer. Yet others who would otherwise have been required to go, but who wished to remain, were saved by offers of cross-matching from volunteers whose jobs were not scheduled to disappear. Just under 10 per cent of the Wave 3 sample had been involved in cross-matching and successful volunteers constituted what the unions called 'soft' redundancies. The residuum – those who did *not* want to take redundancy but had to in the end – was made up of 'hard' redundancies. Both unions and management estimated that the majority of the 1980s redundancies were 'soft'. 'Next time', said one official in 1980, 'it will be much more difficult.' The survey data confirms this judgement since 49 per cent of those interviewed on Wave 3 describe their redundancies as voluntary. The reasons for this fact are not far to seek. Half of BSC Port Talbot's labour force in 1979 was over 45, and as many as one-third were over 50 and had had more than 15 years' service (BSC, Port Talbot, personnel department). Age provided the motivation and service-related redundancy payments the opportunity for 'early retirement' from, at least, the steel industry.

Formal negotiations could not, however, begin until the strike over pay ended on 3 April 1980. The outcome of these negotiations was a draft redundancy agreement as required by the Employment Protection Consolidation Act of 1978.

## The Redundancy Agreement and its effects

The Preamble to the Memorandum of Agreement made on 15 May 1980 begins with these words:

> WHEREAS . . . the Board . . . in the light of the sharp and pronounced falling-off of demand for Steel Products in the UK and its other markets . . . instructed the Welsh Division to . . . reduce costs and modify capacity . . .

The 'General principles' (paragraph 1.2) include the phrase, 'Having regard to . . . the overriding need to become and remain internationally competitive given the alternative of closure . . . ', while paragraph 1.4 contains the following sentence:

> In these circumstances, the plant configuration, work patterns and manning levels will need to be *flexible* in order to provide for *rapid expansion* when and if market factors permit. (*stress added*)

The Preamble is of crucial importance in understanding the reasons for the unions' co-operation and the attitude of the redundant workers. Demanning, it claims, was required because of market forces which necessitated a low volume of production and a reduction in labour costs. The 'General Principles' embody the threat of closure, present throughout all stages of the negotiations, and assert the need for flexibility of manning, but this is cleverly tied to future *increases* in production, not to further *reductions* in authorized manning. The meaning attributed to the redundancies was, therefore, that of a reduction in manning to 'save steelmaking at Port Talbot' until the market *picked up*.

This was not, however, all that the workers were required to accept. The terms of the redundancy agreement are summarized below.

| The unions agreed to: | The unions received: |
|---|---|
| reductions in manpower | quarterly lump sum *bonus* payments in addition to the National Pay Settlement of 11% for the **employed** |
| **revised working practices** | special *ex gratia* payments for the **redundant** |
| a new operating system | |
| **the restricted use of contractors** | |

In terms of the meaning the redundancy had been given these seem perfectly reasonable terms. In fact, as subsequent events showed, they established precedents for further redundancy agreements. The restrictions on the use of contractors to do work which would otherwise have been done by BSC employees were subsequently eased; the renegotiation of revised working practices became normal and the precedent of bonus payments was used by management to move away from national agreements on pay to a system of plant productivity bargaining. What appeared to be a gain in 1980 was, from the union standpoint, to become a distinct liability and by the spring of 1983 some members of the chief union, the Iron and Steel Trades Confederation (ISTC), were pressing for a return to national agreements as opposed to local productivity bargaining.

It is in the context of these later events that the redundancy terms should be considered. What is a reasonable or even generous payment when understood as a 'disturbance allowance' to cover periods of retraining and job search lasting for perhaps a year before eventual re-employment, seemed quite different three years later, when BSC employment was still shrinking, even though output had risen to pre-redundancy levels and the labour market was still loose with unemployment to vacancy ratios remaining high.

The Redundancy Agreement states that each person made redundant shall receive, in addition to his or her entitlement under the Employment Protection Act and the BSC Supplement to it, 'an additional ex-gratia payment' equivalent to between 20 and 45 weeks of pay proportionate to length of service (Redundancy Agreement, appendix 9). The existence of this *ex gratia* payment meant that those with under two years' service not entitled to redundancy money under the Employment Protection Act none the less received redundancy payments of equivalent to 20 weeks' wages. The net effect of these provisions was to produce a population of redundants, 76 per cent of whom received over £1000, 59 per cent over £5000, and 34 per cent over £10,000. 25 per cent received £5–10,000, 27 per cent £10–15,000 and 6.3 per cent over £15,000.

There are two points to be made about this distribution. First, most workers received a very substantial 'cushion'. There was no immediate financial incentive to get on their bikes: destitution did not stare them in the face the day they left the works. The absence of a need to obtain a job at any cost, or to move away from the area, was a direct result of the government's providing BSC with funds to buy off worker opposition to demanning. All the government had left to encourage worker mobility was moral exhortation – which Mrs Thatcher duly supplied in her speech in Cardiff in July 1980. The second point is that the distribution is distinctly odd in shape, having two peaks, one in the £3–5,000 range and one in the £10–12,000 range. This is immediately explicable in terms of the length of service of the redundant.

The length-of-service distribution demonstrates even more clearly the existence of two distinct sub-populations of redundants: one with a mode and median of 6 years' service and an upper limit of 15 years; the other with a range from 16 to 48 years' service and a median of 26 years. These two statistical sub-populations correspond to the 'hard' and 'soft' redundancies respectively. The former were forced on to the market by the exigencies of the new BSC manning schedules (set forth in an appendix to the redundancy agreement) and the latter drawn out of employment by the attraction of large lump sum payments deriving from their many years of service.

There were, however, other inducements, *directly* associated with *age*, not merely length of service. In the first place, those over 54 were entitled to draw a small works pension of between £20 and £30 immediately on redundancy. Secondly, they could increase this by paying in their redundancy money to the pension fund. Thirdly, those over 54 were entitled to have their increase 'made up' to 90 per cent of their previous BSC wages for two years after the redundancy point. Though this enhancement would cease, it would of course be partially replaced, at the end of the redundants' official working lives at 65, by the statutory old age pension. It was therefore possible at the age of 63 to withdraw fairly comfortably from the market, and the nearer you were in age to 63 the easier it was to withdraw. There was for these reasons a strong incentive, built into the financial provisions for redundancy, for workers over 54 to retire, an incentive which increased with age (Bytheway, 1985).

Table 3.1 shows the proportion of each age group made redundant. This distribution also has two peaks or modes: in the 20–9 age group corresponding to the 6 years service peak in the first length of service distribution and 55 plus corresponding to the second length of service distribution's mode of 26 years. The Abbey Works at Margam had been in operation for 28 years at the redundancy date. Longer-service workers would have come from the smaller Port Talbot and Margam works amalgamated by the Abbey development. The most notable feature of table 3.1 is of course the leap in percentage at the age of 55 in response to the special conditions of severance offered to workers of that age. The other feature is the relatively high proportion of redundancies in the 20–9 and 30–9 age groups, which may be interpreted as a result of the application of the last in first out (LIFO) principle by the unions in the case of hard redundancies. On Wave 3 of the interviews conducted for this study, 13.5 per cent claimed to have been made redundant on this principle; that is, 26 per cent of the non-voluntary redundancies.

Workers under 55 were also entitled to make-up pay, which, like the enhancement of statutory redundancy provision, was financed out of EEC funds under 'The Iron and Steel Employees Re-adaptation Benefits Scheme'. Paragraph 3(i) of that scheme entitles redundant iron and steel workers under 55 to have their pay made up to 90 per cent of their previous earnings for 78 weeks. This benefit is only available to those *in work*, and therefore make-up is an inducement to take any job that is offered, not only to preserve unemployment benefit entitlement but also to avoid the diminution in income which the substitution of unemployment benefit for BSC pay would involve. The two-peaked (bimodal) age distribution of redundants reflects the operation of these regulations as well as the redundancy process itself and represents two populations of redundant workers: those over 55 motivated, in Bytheway's words, 'to re-adapt *out* of the market', and those under 55 motivated to stay *in work* if at all possible. The motivation provided by make-up pay to obtain work quickly moderates the effect of high redundancy payments – it encourages redundants not to recline too long on the cushion of redundancy pay. It would, however, be more correct to say that these cushions and incentives would have so operated in a market where the redundant had any choice in the matter. But we have seen that, given the market conditions in the post-redundancy period, there was no way in which, however strongly motivated, the redundant workers could all have found work. We have also seen, however, in chapter 2, that the market appeared to have 'absorbed' the redundancies,

TABLE 3.1 Numbers of steelworkers made redundant as a percentage of each age-group

| *Age* | *% redundant* |
|---|---|
| <20 | 13.6 |
| 20–9 | 43.0 |
| 30–9 | 38.5 |
| 40–9 | 29.0 |
| 50–4 | 29.3 |
| 55–9 | 86.0 |
| >60 | 100.0 |
| Total | 45.0 |

partly as a result of many workers never reaching the register and partly as the result of their flow on being counter-balanced by significant flows off.

The above account of the redundancy event and redundancy process enables us to go some way towards a resolution of the absorption problem. It is clear that a significant number of redundants never reached the register because they withdrew from the market. There are two ways that someone may go out of the market: They may retire or they may become sick. Approximately 9 months after being made redundant, 8 per cent of respondents said they had not looked for work because they had retired. However, 41 per cent were in receipt of a BSC works pension. This indicates the ambiguous and shifting nature of the category 'retired', for the figures indicate that only one-fifth of those drawing a pension considered themselves to be out of the market in the sense of not looking for work. In addition to the 8 per cent retired, a staggering 27 per cent were receiving either industrial injury or sickness benefit, of whom over a third were looking for work, only 16 per cent of the sample claiming not to be because of ill health. We may conclude therefore that, 9 months after redundancy, over one-fifth of those made redundant genuinely withdrew from the market by defining themselves as sick or retired, but many more could have withdrawn by so defining themselves in the face of failure to find employment.

In addition to being diminished by the numbers of those who never arrived, the flow on to the market was further reduced by those who took up retraining places. The first status after redundancy was retraining for 4 per cent of those interviewed in Wave 3 of the interviewing. These men therefore did not go directly on to the employment register, but constituted elements of flows on and flows off the register at later dates.

There is, however, another sense in which a redundant worker may 'go out of market.' He or she may move away from the local labour market area in search of new employment. Financial assistance was made available to workers who were offered and had obtained new work 'beyond daily travelling distance'. These provisions did not amount to an incentive to move: they merely defrayed part of the costs of moving, and they did nothing to diminish the largest disincentive of all, the difference in house prices between South Wales and the more prosperous parts of the country. Were these provisions, combined with job loss, sufficient to motivate workers to move?

There is no answer to this question. As Reynolds pointed out many years ago (1951), it is vital to make a distinction between actual movement and propensity to move. 'Opportunity must be added to willingness before any actual movement will occur' (pp. 240–8). However, *perceived* opportunity itself affects propensity: 'If workers become convinced that unemployment is general, however, that "things are just as bad there as they are here", their resistance to movement may be reinforced' (p. 241). In the present case, the meaning given to the redundancy, the age distribution and health of the sample and the local and national news coverage of the developing national and world recession after the redundancy period, were all likely to have created a perception of opportunity which would have decreased rather than augmented any propensity to move.

As regards actual movement, out of the original Wave 1 sample of 1,020 (contacted 9 months after the peak of the redundancies), 17 had moved out of the UK, 9 had moved out of South Wales to England, 10 had moved within South Wales and 38 had simply 'gone away'. None of these last respondents was successfully traced or interviewed. Of those who were interviewed, 28 had moved within the area of West Glamorgan and 10 outside that area. It is possible to estimate from these figures the total amount of movement and this is done in table 3.2 which, by distributing the 'gone aways' in the same way as the rest of the sample, arrives at a figure of 10.9 per cent of gross movement, but at a figure of only 5.3 per cent for those moving outside the local labour market of West Glamorgan. Movement is therefore unlikely to have accounted for more than 310 of the 5,807 redundants not appearing on the unemployment registers of West Glamorgan. This may be compared with an estimated 930 off the market through sickness, 465 who had retired and 238 who had retrained immediately. Failing to come on to the register through leaving the market in one sense or another seems to account for the absorption of 1,943 (33.3 per cent) of those made redundant, and only 5.6 of those 33.3 percentage points are the result of movement.

We have seen that the operation of the make-up pay ought to have motivated those remaining in the market to behave as 'snatchers' rather than 'stickers' (Mackay, 1972a). A snatcher takes the first job that comes along rather than waiting for a more attractive offer. On the other hand, the generous lump sum redundancy payments should have motivated workers to stick out for an attractive offer since they could draw on their lump sum to supplement their unemployment benefit. It may be argued, however, that the longer the depressed state of the market lasted the more willing they would have become to 'snatch', since the more convinced they must have become of the market's looseness, and the nearer they would have been to the exhaustion of unemployment benefit. Savings of over £1,999 were **not** disregarded by DHSS for Supplementary Benefit purposes and workers were therefore forced to live on their savings alone after exhausting unemployment benefit, until they fell below £2,000.

We shall leave the discussion of the workers' labour market behaviour and the character of flows on and off the register to subsequent chapters. Our primary concern here is the effects of the redundancy agreement and in particular the way it produced an absence of flows onto the register. Someone who 'organized' themselves a job before being made redundant is neither a sticker or a snatcher, nor is their behaviour to be understood as a consequence of the redundancy terms offered by BSC. However, to

TABLE 3.2 Movement among the redundant 9 months after redundancy

| | *Not interviewed; location but not new address known* | *Interviewed at new address* | *Total with known location* | | *Not interviewed; no known location; no longer at old address* | *All movers* | |
|---|---|---|---|---|---|---|---|
| | | *No* | *No* | *%* | *No* | *No* | *% of drawn sample* |
| West Glamorgan | 9.65[a] | 28 | 37.65[a] | 51.0 | 19.4[a] | 57.05[a] | 5.6[a] |
| Elsewhere in S. Wales | 0.35[a] | 1 | 1.35[a] | 1.8 | 0.7[a] | 2.05[a] | 0.2[a] |
| Elsewhere in UK | 9 | 7 | 16.00 | 21.5 | 8.2[a] | 24.20[a] | 2.3[a] |
| Abroad | 17 | 2 | 19.00 | 25.7 | 9.7[a] | 28.70[a] | 2.8[a] |
| Total | 36 | 38 | 74 | 100.0 | 38.0 | 112.00 | 10.9 |

[a] These figures estimated.
Wave 1 drawn sample: Base 1020

complete the discussion of the category of redundants who did not 'flow on', it is necessary to note that 11.5 per cent of the Wave 3 sample went straight into work following redundancy. This is equivalent to another 670 of those being made redundant and brings the total of those 'absorbed' by virtue of their not 'flowing on' to 2,613, or 45 per cent.

### The characteristics of the redundant

Of Port Talbot's workforce on 3 March 1979, 46 per cent were made redundant between May and December 1980. The official figure of 5,807 does not accurately reflect job loss during the period since jobs can also disappear where natural wastage exceeds recruitment and labour is of course being recruited to replace losses even when redundancies are taking place. None the less, the distribution of redundancies between different operational departments in the plant does provide some indication of which operations were most severely affected by the de-manning.

The first point to make is that various types of service department were cut back the hardest. Of catering employees, 74 per cent left, and 65 per cent of those engaged in transport activities. In addition, all those who worked in the quarry which produces limestone for the furnaces were made redundant, and the quarry operation closed. These were the only departments with losses massively above the plant average. Other 'above average' departments were hot sheet finishing, where 59 per cent were made redundant, and the coke ovens (54 per cent). Engineering services (52 per cent) is a category which hides relatively high redundancy rates of 66 and 62 per cent in mobile plant engineering and general engineering services respectively. Redundancy rates in the core process departments – iron- and steelmaking and the hot mill – approximated to the average. Departments least affected were technical services where only 37 per cent were made redundant, energy engineering (36 per cent), the slabbing mill (33 per cent) and management services (27 per cent) (raw data supplied by BSC).

Despite these differences it would appear that the 46 per cent redundancy rate was chiefly the result of reducing steel output: crude steel production in 1980 fell by 50 per cent after allowing for the effects of the steel strike. Certain core functions which are not directly related to output were reduced by less than the average, while those departments (catering, transport and certain types of engineering services) which *were* highly output-related and whose functions could be outsourced (that is performed for BSC by other firms) were reduced by more than average.

The mention of so many different activities may surprise some readers who have assumed thus far that steelworkers are men in safety helmets tending massive furnaces, pouring molten metal in a shower of incadescent sparks, since this is the part of the process always shown on television whenever the world 'steel' is mentioned (unless of course the reference is to the political rather than the manufacturing process). In fact, a steelworks is not only not like a factory, it is not even like a foundry. It is the size of a small village and consists of an assemblage of what in other industries would be large freestanding 'plants'. Vast quantities of material have to be transferred from one 'plant' to another; a bewildering range of technical expertise is required; a great deal of waste is generated which has to be cleared up and the entire array of increasingly complex plant has to be maintained. As a result, a wide array of occupations is involved which, if the plants which make up the 'works' were independent, would result in the distribution of employees over a number of different categories of the industrial classification instead of their all belonging to one: that of metal manufacture. Table 3.3 gives some idea of the complexity of the occupational and industrial structure of a steel plant by listing the Abbey's departments under six headings. The bottom line shows the distribution of redundants between these headings (source: Wave 1 sample). It is apparent that half the redundants were engaged in activities which the public would think of as metal manufacture. Another way of classifying occupations is provided by the CODOT system used by the MSC. Under this classification only 40 per cent of the redundants had been in metal processing occupations, and 21 per cent in transport; professional and managerial, catering and clerical contributed 7 per cent each and 'other' 18 per cent.

If we turn to the distribution of redundants across the hierarchy of occupations we find that there too there is as much diversity as in the general population. Of the redundants, one-twenty-fifth were classified as management, a fifth as staff and three-quarters as works. A quarter were in supervisory positions. If we apply the hierarchical classification devised by Goldthorpe and Hope (1974) to the occupations of the redundant steelworkers, we find that 23 per cent were in managerial, professional, non-manual or technical occupations (which is roughly equivalent to the proportion in staff and managerial BSC grades), 24 per cent had transferable skills, 19 per cent non-transferable skills and 34 per cent were in semi-skilled, unskilled or service occupations. Generally the distribution between grades was similar in the different types of BSC Departments (see table 3.3) with the exception of staff in indirect services who constituted over twice the sample average. The size of the plant and the heterogeneity of its occupational structure could have provided the Abbey works with a larger internal labour market: members of its workforce could have pursued varied and extensive careers by moving between different grades and departments within the works. In other words occupational mobility was in theory possible without recourse to the open market. Was BSC Port Talbot an internal labour market?

It is difficult to answer this question. The criterion of recruitment only through entry points at certain levels in the works' structure is not relevant

TABLE 3.3 The occupational and industrial structure of BSC Margam

| | | | | Services | | | |
|---|---|---|---|---|---|---|---|
| | *Ironmaking* | *Steelmaking* | *Finishing* | *Primary* | *Secondary* | *Tertiary* | |
| Departments | Blast furnaces<br>Coke ovens | Cold mills<br>Hot mills<br>BOS plant<br>Melting shop | Hot sheet finishing<br>Galvanizing<br>Hot strip mill | Control engineering<br>Slab yard<br>Ore terminal<br>Sinter plant<br>Power plant<br>Heating and ventilation<br>Technical services<br>Water and compressed air<br>Stores | Maintenance<br>Permanent way<br>Administration etc.<br>Computing<br>Building<br>Engineering | Vehicle and locomotive repair<br>Catering<br>Transport<br>Janitors<br>Services<br>Quarries | |
| % of those made redundant who previously worked in each category | 19.3 | 25.0 | 5.7 | 20.7 | 14.5 | 14.8 | Total 100 |

since in recent times the works was de-manning, not recruiting, and vacancies must have been filled *ad hoc* when a suitable person could not be found within the existing workforce. However, it is possible to test the hypothesis that the redundant workers had moved around within BSC. Of those made redundant, 44 per cent had moved between what they considered to be different departments during their time at the works. Comparing BSC departments at the redundancy point with previous departments in which they served reveals no clear pattern of movement. There was a tendency for job transfer to be restricted to cognate departments, particularly from the cold mill to hot mill, which field data suggests was considered by most workers as a 'step up'. There was little difference in mobility between types of department but it has been highest among those who at the point of redundancy were working in steelmaking and finishing. It would seem that in the service departments movement into process departments was unlikely among non-manual workers, while for manual workers movement into process work represented occupational advancement.

Understanding mobility patterns is complicated by the fact that, while the age of redundants and the length of their employment in service departments did not differ significantly from each other or the sample average, there was variation within process departments. Those who had worked in steelmaking were over-represented among those over 50, those in ironmaking among those under 45, and those in the finishing sections among 'prime' age employees aged 30–49. It is of course from the process departments that most workers with steel-specific skills were made redundant.

The redundant population, then, by virtue of its length of service and the character of the works within which it was employed, had extensive experience of an internal labour market but little experience of the external market. We shall consider workers' experience of the latter in the next chapter, which concerns those active in the market after redundancy. Taking the redundant population as a whole, however, it is possible to investigate the relation between internal labour market mobility and the initial labour market outcome of the redundancies measured by their 'current labour market status' nine months later.

Throughout this work, 'current labour market status' (or 'current status') will refer to the following range of statuses: (1) employed full-time; (2) employed part-time; (3) self-employed; (4) unemployed; (5) retraining; (6) retired; (7) sick. This range can be collapsed so that the basic categories become in work (statuses 1, 2, 3); unemployed; retraining; withdrawn (statuses 6 and 7). The term withdrawn will also refer to those not looking for work at any given point in time; it will also be used to refer to those whose labour market histories, collected during the interview held two-and-a-half years after redundancy (Wave 3), show that they had been withdrawn throughout the study period.

No relationship was found between workers' experience of internal labour market mobility and their labour market status 9 months after redundancy. That is to say that such mobility appears neither to facilitate nor hinder redundant workers' search for work, nor affect their decision whether to withdraw. What needs to be considered is the character and recency of their external market experience, not their experience of the internal market.

The previous section had demonstrated that, because of the terms of the redundancy agreement, the redundant workers were relatively privileged. As one letter-writer to the *South Wales Evening Post* put it:

> What the 2,000,000 in Britain who have lost their work do not share with the redundant steelmen is £8,000 redundancy payments; no caravans are set up by building societies to advise them . . . there is no special arrangement . . . to have their benefit made up in the next two years . . . If these 'brothers' are special . . . [they] owe it to the other thousands . . . to disclose why members of the cheque club are going to be well placed in the queue for the trickle of newly created jobs . . . (7 December 1979)

The hostility to the redundant steelworkers felt by other sections of the working class in West Glamorgan reflected that felt by those who had failed to obtain employment in the Abbey works towards those who worked there. This hostility to what was seen as an isolated area of privilege is aptly captured by the local name for the work, 'Treasure Island'. Were the steelworkers privileged in employment, as well as in redundancy? By their own testimony, when interviewed on Wave 1, they were: 81 per cent were satisfied with their pay, 76 per cent found their jobs interesting, 94 per cent thought working conditions friendly, and 80 per cent were content with their hours of work, 75 per cent thought their travel-to-work time reasonable. Least satisfaction was expressed with working conditions and union–management relations (65 per cent satisfied) and with the chances of promotion (45 per cent) and fringe benefits (only 35 per cent). By and large the redundants were better pleased with their employment than they were with their unions: only 54 per cent were satisfied with union support of workers' interests in general, though 68 per cent thought that the unions did a good job in supporting individual workers.

Privilege in employment and in redundancy is not the same as privilege in the labour market. Privilege there entails the possession of certain skills and experience for which demand is high and supply low, and having personal characteristics which are valued by employers. We shall return to the issue of 'personal characteristics', but here it is merely necessary to point out that the majority of redundants were not of what employers considered to be 'prime age': in the words of many of Bytheway's respondents, 'their age was against them' (1985). We noted in chapter 1 that there is almost universal agreement among students of redundancy that the prime determinants of labour market success are age and skill. Whereas skill, in itself, is of great importance in occupational stratification, what matters in the market, as opposed to employment, is *negotiable* skill, or, as some theorists prefer to term it, 'human capital'. The estimation of skill is, however, a matter of considerable difficulty once the worker is out of employment. Most skill measures refer to the skill required by the job rather than possessed by the worker. In this study, we have constructed a worker-based skill measure by combining educational qualifications with type of training required by the worker's previous job at BSC. Only 23 per cent of those made redundant had any educational qualification. A further 23 per cent had served an apprenticeship; 11 per cent had some other marketable qualification, but over 40 per cent of the sample had only on-the-job training at BSC or at a similar job elsewhere. Combining these two dimensions, it becomes apparent that 59 per cent of the sample had neither educational qualifications nor negotiable skills.

In terms of the labour market therefore the redundants were not 'privileged'. As a population they were older, less skilled and less experienced in selling their labour as a result of their long service with BSC. Their market prospects were not good. In human terms it is difficult to over-emphasize the shock of redundancy. It would sound odd to any one who has been round the Abbey works to hear it termed a 'Garden of Eden'. But BSC's corporate plan expelled the workers from an Eden of employment, and moreover placed an angel in the shape of Ian MacGregor at the gates, whose sword of 'financial viability' was thenceforth to prevent their return - at least as BSC employees.

# 4

# All Sorts and Conditions of Men

### Withdrawal from the market

In chapter 3 the occupational variety of the workers made redundant has been emphasized. There was, however, one respect in which they were not heterogeneous: 94 per cent were male. This study is therefore a study of male redundancy, and, except where otherwise stated, we have eliminated the 47 women respondents from our analysis since they constitute a distinct sub-category which is not large enough for analysis by itself. This is not, however, to say that we ignore the effects of redundancies on women. We shall consider those effects by examining the households of sub-samples of redundant workers in chapters 6, 7 and 8. In doing so we are not assuming that women are significant social actors only in the private sphere. We consider women in the context of the household merely because, in a sample of male redundants, it is through their membership of the redundant workers' households that women were affected by the redundancies.

It was also noted in chapter 3 that the age distribution of those made redundant, combined with the provisions of the redundancy agreement, resulted in many redundants withdrawing from the market. Because of the ambiguous nature of the 'retired' status and the fact that 'sickness' does not necessarily preclude future work, the only certain means of identifying those who have withdrawn from the market is to examine their post-redundancy labour market histories. However, at this stage we are concerned with the response to redundancy in the year following it. At that point, when the first wave of interviews was conducted, respondents were defined as withdrawn if they claimed that they had not looked for work since being made redundant for reasons other than that they already had a job, were self-employed or retraining. Forty one point seven per cent had 'not looked', 4.6 per cent because they had another job, 2.2 per cent because they were self-employed and 3.5 per cent because they were retraining. On *this* definition 31.4 per cent were therefore withdrawn from the market at the time of first interview.

What disposes a redundant worker to leave the market, that is, to stop actively searching for a paid job? The most obvious answer to this question is that such workers believe that employment is just not available. Only 7 per cent of those who had not looked for work gave this as their reason, however. In fact, the only other substantial categories of response to the question as to why those who had withdrawn were not looking for work was that the respondent was retired (26 per cent) or sick (51 per cent); indeed, over 70 per cent of those receiving sickness or injury benefit appear to have withdrawn. It is only necessary to explain why the remaining 23 per cent withdrew. In addition to the 7 percentage points contributed by what have been termed 'discouraged workers' (Mackay et al., 1980: 72), 8 percentage points are contributed by those who cite their age or the benefit make-up available to older workers. There is probably no substantive difference between these workers and those who describe themselves as retired. Miscellaneous reasons account for the remaining 8 per cent, the largest group being 'other' at 4.5 per cent.

In a sense, we need go no further to explain why the workers considered here withdrew from the market. To halt the analysis at this point would, however, be to take our respondents at their own word and a brief discussion must therefore be given of the characteristics of 'the withdrawn' in comparison with the sample as a whole. The first question to address is whether there were any major differences between those who withdrew and the rest of the sample, in terms of the characteristics derived from their work at BSC. There are no major differences in the proportions of those in different types of department who withdrew, nor in terms of their occupational classification. There is, however, a difference by BSC grade: more managers (44 per cent) left the market than in the sample as a whole (31 per cent), while fewer of those in staff grades withdrew from economic activity (24 per cent). This difference is explicable in terms of age distribution: the managers were over- and the staff under-represented in the oldest age groups. When experience of the pre-redundancy external labour market is considered we find that the highest rate of withdrawal (45 per cent) is to be found among those who had only experienced one short (under five months) spell of unemployment prior to joining BSC. Those with no previous experience of unemployment had the same withdrawal rate as the sample as a whole, while those having experienced more unemployment (in terms of length of spell or number of spells, or both) had rather lower withdrawal rates.

These figures must be interpreted with caution. The older the worker now is, the less likely he is to have experienced unemployment and the more likely to withdraw. The fact that those with no unemployment experience had only average withdrawal rates suggests that age rather than lack of unemployment experience is the chief factor promoting withdrawal. Little unemployment experience also implies lack of experience of the market, and lack of market experience is likely to inhibit immediate withdrawal: as we shall see in chapter 9, some men only withdrew after experience of the market Unfortunately, even in a relatively large sample (n = 707), given the concentration of respondents among those with no recent experience of the market/unemployment, these issues cannot be pursued further here.

The second question concerns whether those who went out of market differed in any significant way from the sample as a whole. The answer is clear and fairly obvious: they were older. Of those who withdrew 86 per cent were over 49, compared with only 59 per cent in the sample as a whole. Because of this, 56 per cent had lived at their present address for more than 19 years, compared with 38 per cent of the sample; more had long periods of service with BSC, they tended to be at a later stage of the family cycle, and more of them spoke Welsh. While there was no difference in the proportion drawing unemployment benefit, the proportions drawing sickness benefit (56 per cent) and BSC pension (81 per cent) were more than double those in the sample as a whole. Because their length of service was longer their redundancy payments were larger, and more of them had income from savings. Because of their age, slightly fewer than the sample average had worked at BSC all their lives.

We have already noted that the chief characteristics of the population of redundant workers were its elderly character and the high incidence of ill health, and this examination of the characteristics of those who withdrew implies that in such a population these are the chief factors associated with withdrawal. It is therefore of some importance that we examine the incidence of withdrawal by age: see table 4.1.

There are three points to note about this table. The first is the substantial proportions of those who went out of market at relatively early ages (35–49). The second is the converse of the first: it would be quite wrong to suppose that a majority of older workers went out of market: only 45 per cent of

TABLE 4.1 Labour market withdrawal by age, nine months after redundancy (percentages)

| *Age group* | *Withdrawn workers* | *Withdrawn due to ill health* | *Base* |
|---|---|---|---|
| 18–20 | 12.5 | 12.5 | 8 |
| 21–34 | 1.0 | 1.0 | 152 |
| 35–44 | 9.1 | 7.8 | 77 |
| 45–9 | 9.8 | 8.8 | 51 |
| 50–4 | 13.0 | 13.0 | 115 |
| 55–65 | 63.0 | 28.3 | 304 |
| Total | 31.5 | 16.1 | 707 |

those over 44 withdrew. The third involves a modification of the second: the terms of the redundancy agreement quite clearly succeeded in encouraging those of 54 and over to 'readapt' out of the market.

The percentages of withdrawals attributed by the respondents to ill health account for the vast majority of withdrawals at younger ages. It is of course possible that this ill health was a product of redundancy rather than simply a cause of withdrawal. It should, however, be remembered that the ill health referred to is cited by a respondent as a reason for not having looked for work during the previous twelve months, not a measure of ill health at the time of interview. Moreover, the respondent was not forced at once to admit that he had not looked for work and then asked to explain this. Respondents chose to claim the less socially acceptable of two answers to the question, 'Have you looked for work since being made redundant?', and when asked 'Why not?' cited ill health as a reason. The assumption must be that, whether or not they were too ill to work by any objective measure, these respondents believed this to be the case, and had therefore not looked for work. The proportion of those out of market who were receiving sickness benefit (56 per cent) at the time of the interview is greater than the proportion claiming to have withdrawn by reason of sickness (51 per cent); this does not suggest that respondents' beliefs that they were ill were illusory, whatever reservations one may have about using sickness benefit receipt as an indicator of the level of ill health.

The picture presented by the table is, therefore, of increasing withdrawal with age. This withdrawal is chiefly as a result of ill health, except in the 55 to 65 age group. In this group 63 per cent withdrew, but those withdrawing because of ill health (28.3 per cent) form under half. Only 19.5 per cent claimed to have retired in this age group, however, the remaining 15 per cent attributing their withdrawal to a variety of other reasons, notably the lack of jobs. Withdrawal in the oldest age group is therefore a result partly of the financial pull of special provisions, but is also the result of two push factors: an increased incidence of ill health and the difficulty of obtaining work by older workers in a loose labour market. It is curiously enough in the over 55 age group that the 'discouraged worker', who gives up job search in despair of ever finding employment, is to be found.

It is not the case, therefore, that those remaining in the market are the original population minus the aged and infirm. While most of the latter seem to have gone out of market, older workers have only been thinned, not eliminated, by withdrawal. It must be asked what social attributes distinguished those older workers who withdrew from others who continued the fight. Unfortunately our findings here are inconclusive as we were unable to establish any pattern of characteristics not associated with age which distinguished withdrawers from non-withdrawers. One negative finding does, however, warrant mention. In view of some variation in unemployment rates, unemployment–vacancy ratios, industrial structure and, probably, methods of job recruitment in the different settlements which make up west Industrial South Wales, respondents were coded by settlement and settlement type. No differences were found between those who went out of the market and those who remained in terms of these variables. The inference must be that structural differences in market demand have little effect on the decision to *withdraw*. This is not of course to deny that an increase in general demand for labour would have an effect on withdrawal rates. Our finding refers only to conditions where the aggregate level of demand is low relative to supply.

The rest of this chapter (and indeed the rest of our study and this book) is concerned with those steelworkers who, although redundant, remained in the market. In this chapter they are defined as those who claimed at the time of the first wave of interviewing, nine months after the redundancies commenced, to have looked for work since being made redundant or had not looked for work only because they had jobs, were retraining or were self-employed. Those who went out of market will henceforth not be considered until we return briefly to them in chapter 9. Those aged over 54 have been the subject of a special study by W. R. Bytheway (1985, 1986a, 1986b).

## Those who remained active in the market

Because such a substantial proportion withdrew, chapter 3 did not attempt a detailed description of the characteristics of those who were made redundant. This task is attempted here using data for those who remained active in the market nine months after the redundancies commenced. Outcomes at this point will be termed 'initial outcomes'. The characterization of a population, though a fundamental sociological task, is one fraught with difficulty since the properties according to which any population *can* be characterized are not delimited. The descriptions of populations contained in sociological enquiries are therefore structured either by categories specified by a more or less theoretically informed research tradition ('the standard variables'); by the categories used by population members themselves in characterizing each other; by characteristics which the investigator intuitively thinks important, or some combination of these alternatives. It is rare for descriptive strategies to be articulated, but we shall attempt to make clear our principles of selection.

The previous chapter has described the population of redundants in terms of attributes derived from our respondents' employment at BSC. However, a worker is not defined merely by his or her location in and experience of the labour *process*. He or she is defined also by his/her position in and experience of the labour *market*.

The most important attribute of the redundants' *labour market experience* was their lack of it. Just over a tenth had worked only at BSC: they had, that is, *no* experience of selling their labour on the market. Over a quarter had had only one job before their employment at BSC: over a third therefore had little labour market experience of any kind. While their internal was less extensive than their external labour market experience – only 45 per cent had moved within BSC – it was none the less substantial and, by definition, more recent than their external experience. Only 12 per cent had ever been self-employed. Only 25 per cent had ever experienced unemployment, and only 12 per cent a long spell.

Nearly two-thirds had acquired their job at BSC by direct means, the majority by direct application, though a minority had been recruited by BSC. The proportion recruited by formal means (advertisement, employment exchange) was only half that recruited by informal means. The data on job acquisition at BSC reflect the state of the market at the period of recruitment: they attest to the effectiveness of direct application and the presence of labour-seeking behaviour by firms. It should be noted that, even in the relatively tight market conditions of the past, nearly a fifth of the workers acquired their jobs by informal means and that formal means of acquisition were used by only 11 per cent of the sample (for further discussion, see chapter 5 below). It may be said, therefore, that the redundants had little experience of the external labour market or of unemployment, and what experience they did have was obtained in a market in which firms were seeking workers rather than workers jobs: an epoch of *employment* exchanges rather than *labour* exchanges.

It should therefore be noted that, in terms of their competence in job search and acquisition, redundants' previous experience was such that we can say that even those redundants who remained in the market were negatively privileged, and this negative privilege must be balanced against the advantages given by the redundancy agreement. They were better equipped to wait, to retrain and more cushioned against the economic effects of 'trading down' – taking less well paid jobs – than other job seekers, but they were inexperienced or lacked recent experience of job search in relation to other workers. Of course *all* those on the market, that is, looking for work, in the early 1980s lacked experience of job seeking in a very loose and falling market, and all had to cope with making decisions under conditions which were unstable and with background expectations which turned out to be inappropriate.

## *Labour market attributes*

In attempting to characterize the redundant population in terms of its labour market attributes we have drawn heavily on the research tradition of the redundancy studies reviewed in chapter 1. Previous research has been concerned with *labour market outcomes* defined in terms of the employment status of the redundant at the time of interview and sought to explain differences in outcome in terms of both the attributes and behavioural responses of individuals. The most basic attributes are gender and age, but, as we have noted, gender differences cannot be used to explain outcomes in the present sample, since 94 per cent of those made redundant were male.

Although the redundant workers included a high proportion of older men, they were by no means all old; neither did all of those in the older categories withdraw. As a result, though those remaining in the market were younger, as many as two-fifths were over 49, a tenth were under 25 and the remainder were prime age (25–49) workers. Altnough represented in all age groups, even those still in the market were disadvantaged in terms of age: a large minority were 'over the hill' in terms of their desirability as employees.

If we turn to the difficult matter of assessing workers' skills, using the Goldthorpe-Hope classification we find that in terms of their BSC jobs the redundants were not particularly disadvantaged, only 38 per cent being unskilled or semi-skilled. However, if we split the skilled category into two sub-groups and distinguish those with transferable and non-transferable skills, the proportion of workers who lacked a *negotiable skill* rises to 56 per cent.

An alternative way of estimating skill is to examine educational qualifications and the training required by BSC. A fifth had neither qualifications nor did jobs for which BSC required training. If, however, we add together those who had no qualifications and only on-the-job training at BSC, the proportion of the sample with no negotiable skills rises to 59 per cent. Both measures therefore suggest that around 60 per cent of the redundant population who remained in the market lacked a negotiable skill. Their long service, the characteristics of the steel industry and the operation of BSC Margam as an internal labour market resulted in a redundant population which was relatively disadvantaged in the market in terms of *negotiable* skill, as well as by its age.

While it is widely accepted that age and skill are each determinants of labour market outcomes, it is less often recognized that these two variables interact. Of those remaining in market and aged 21–4, 46 per cent had no qualifications; this proportion for those aged 50–4 was 88 per cent, with a gradient between those points. Of those aged 21–24, 36 per cent had a marketable skill, compared with only 20 per cent aged 50–4, with a gradient between the points. There are not two separate disadvantaged sub-populations of the redundant – the old and the unskilled. An elderly population is disadvantaged twice over: those of an advanced age are also likely to lack skill.

### *Labour market entry and search commencement*

Every redundancy event of whatever size has an effect on the market in which the redundant firm is located. Even when the market is initially tight, the flow on produced by the redundancies can produce at least a temporary excess of supply over demand. It is not surprising that redundancy studies have showed that the timing of the commencement of job search is an important determinant of labour market outcome. If you can get on to the market while labour is still scarce, your chances of obtaining comparable employment are greater than if you do not arrive until the supply of labour is already in excess of demand. Although, as we have seen, the BSC workers did not enter a tight market, they did enter a falling market. Hence the same rule must apply: 'the race is to the swift'.

Two factors determine the point of market entry: the date when the worker concerned is made redundant and the point at which he or she starts the search for a job. Nearly 60 per cent of those who stayed in the market were made redundant at the same time, July and August 1980. This massive flow on cannot have improved the chances of getting a job swiftly. Moreover, the time of year coincided with the period of 'shut downs' and 'stop weeks' in manufacturing industry; summer is not a season during which firms are 'taking on'. It is, however, a season in which firms are contracted to move into plants for maintenance work and there is a possibility that the timing of the redundancies encouraged those workers who were affected to begin what turned out to be careers as contract labourers.

The timing of the redundancies was unfortunate in another sense. More workers were made redundant after the summer onflow (27 per cent) than before it (15 per cent). The relatively disadvantaged were therefore more numerous than the relatively advantaged. Moreover, those who remained in the market came on to it slightly later than those who withdrew; this appears from field data to be because BSC retrained prime workers beyond their original redundancy date to ease the shift to new production methods and levels. In other words, because of the pressures BSC was under the redundancies were not well managed: they were not timed to maximize the chances of the market absorbing the redundants with minimum friction.

An examination of the distribution of those made redundant in different months in 1980 over various types of labour market outcome approximately nine months later shows that of those made redundant in the last three months of the year, 82 per cent had been continuously unemployed since redundancy compared with a rate of only 47 per cent for the sample as a whole. Those made redundant in the months before July had lower rates of continuous unemployment but higher rates of both employment and a mixture of employment and unemployment than the sample mean. Though the concentration of redundancies in July and August means that the sample numbers involved in early and late redundancies are small, the available evidence supports the view that redundancy date has some effect on outcome in the way described above. An unexpected finding was the relative lack of variation by redundancy date in the proportion who were in employment when first interviewed, though what variation there is again supports the hypothesis that those made redundant earlier fared better. The hypothesis that contracting work and therefore broken employment histories is associated with the August redundancies receives only limited support from the evidence, which suggests rather that those made redundant in the last four months were less likely to have experienced broken employment or to have been in employment at first interview. Overall, however, the available evidence does support, if only weakly, the hypothesis that redundancy date affects initial labour market outcome.

If we turn to the other dimension of market entry, the point at which job search began, we find that only 22.6 per cent started their search for work before they were actually served redundancy notices, and over two-fifths did not start until after they had left. These figures must be interpreted, however, in the light of the history of the redundancy event. Only six weeks elapsed between the end of the steel strike and the signing of the redundancy agreement. The 'cross-matching' procedure, however valuable in minimizing 'hard' redundancies, induced uncertainty about whether or not any given person with a redundancy notice would in fact be made redundant. While these considerations suggest that the substantial proportion not looking for work until after redundancy cannot be attributed to workers' complacency about their prospects in the market, they do not account for the low proportion of those attempting to improve their prospects by 'jumping the gun', that is, seeking work before receiving notification of redundancy. This may be explained in terms of possible attrition of the workforce in the pre-crisis period by the departure of those with negotiable skills who were anxious about the future of the plant.

At the time of the redundancies there was a media 'moral panic' about the behaviour of redundant workers who were alleged to be uninterested in working, but taking expensive holidays and generally living it up on their redundancy money. Our concern here is solely with market entry. Did those who did not look for work until after leaving BSC delay in their search for work because of the redundancy cushion? Over a half started the search for work immediately, and rather under a fifth delayed for between a week and a month. This proportion is in fact surprisingly low, since the majority of redundancies took place in the holiday season and it would not be unreasonable to spend some of the redundancy money on a holiday, especially as money earmarked for the annual holiday was likely to have been spent during the three months' strike which preceded the redundancies. In fact, only 16 per cent of workers claimed to have spent any of their redundancy money in this way.

A significant proportion did, however, substantially delay their search for work for more than a month (26 per cent of all those 'in market' and 28 per cent of those who delayed search until after their redundancy). This was, to say the least, unwise of them. It is, however, understandable. There was confusion after the redundancies as well as before them. The labour market histories (discussed in chapter 9) include statuses such as 'retired' or 'sick' early in the histories of those who remained in the market, and it should be remembered that whether or not 'unemployment' is a contributory factor in ill health, redundancy, especially when compounded with personal and collective uncertainty and a national strike, is a highly stressful experience clearly not beneficial to the health of a relatively elderly workforce. Without rejecting the use of causal language in the explanation of aggregate outcomes, it has to be remembered that they are the result of human action and interaction and of the negotiation of meanings of events, circumstances and identities. It is consequently not unreasonable to suppose that in the period immediately after redundancy a certain amount of juggling went on among workers over whether to adopt the identity of sick or retired before they rejected those identities and began the search for work. However unwise postponing the search may have been in the utilitarian sense, it is intelligible in terms of the categorical liminality of many members of the workforce. A quarter, even of those who remained in the market, were in receipt of a BSC pension.

What factors affect the point at which job search begins? Among those who remained in the market, workers receiving BSC pensions started to look later than those who were not, and this on the whole supports the hypothesis that the market liminality derived from age, reinforced by the categorical liminality involved in receiving a pension (pensioner = retired), generates a period of identity negotiation. Pension receipt apart, it would appear that, among those who did not look for work until after being made redundant, the timing of job search was unrelated to previous labour market experience or level of skill. It seems therefore to have been determined by personal factors. In any case, since only a quarter of those concerned waited longer than a month to look for work, the numbers are too small to show any clear relationship with other variables.

Of more importance is whether search began before, during or after redundancy. Internal labour market experience showed no relationship with the timing of job search, but some types of pre-redundancy labour market experience did. Previous experience of unemployment was not, however, one of them. We had expected either that previous unemployment would encourage early search, or that previous unemployment and late job search would go together as the result of a more generalized attitude to the market. In the event, neither experience of unemployment before joining BSC, nor its length, showed any relation to the timing of job search. It should be remembered, however, that much labour market experience was, as we have noted, somewhat remote. More recent experience might well have been related to search timing.

We also expected that there would be some relation between search timing and methods used to obtain the original BSC job, the only proxy we have for pre-redundancy search behaviour. This, however, was not the case; the only connection between the two was that those recruited directly by BSC were more likely to have looked before they left.

Those recruited directly by BSC are more likely to have had no previous work experience. Work experience, defined as the number of pre-BSC jobs held, showed no relationship to when job search began, but more of those whose only job had been the one they lost on redundancy looked early than did the rest of those remaining in the market. Lack of labour market experience, if not its type, would appear to affect positively the timing of search commencement and compensate somewhat for lack of market experience. At least those with no market experience *knew* that they did not know; those with irrelevant experience were not forced to acknowledge its irrelevance until they started job search.

Length of BSC service also showed a relationship to search commencement. If length of service is divided into short and long, we find that only a third of those with short durations waited until they left, compared with half of those with longer durations. The short duration workers of course included more who had only worked for BSC, and those with longer durations more of the sick and the pensioned and older age groups. Nearly two-thirds of those over 49 did not look for work until after they left, compared with a third of those under 50.

Search commencement does relate to skill in terms of qualifications: nearly half of those without qualifications did not start looking for work until after redundancy, compared with a third of those qualified. However, we have noted that older workers are less qualified and less skilled. Since there were good reasons for older workers to postpone job search, there is no reason to attribute the observed difference to lack of qualifications. No differences were found among those with different skill levels alone.

Age-related factors therefore appear to be more significant than prior market experience, or the cluster of variables associated with qualification and skill, in determining the timing of job search. This is chiefly due to older workers' knowledge of the way in which age affects job opportunity on the market, together with the effect, and these workers' knowledge, of institutional measures which are age-related. In so far as age leads to late search, which leads to poor labour market outcomes, then advanced age may affect outcomes by delaying entry as well as reducing the chance of job acquisition once the worker is on the market.

## *Labour market attitudes*

We have been concerned so far with labour market experience and attributes and the initial response to redundancy. Redundant workers can also be characterized in terms of their attitudes. Four attitude questions asked during the first wave of interviewing concerned what may be loosely termed 'labour market attitudes'. Two-thirds of the sample disagreed with the statement that 'all things being equal, I would prefer a job which gave me a high level of pay over one which gave me security', only just over a quarter agreed, only a twentieth strongly. This tells us something about the meaning of redundancy to those directly affected: for the majority it meant loss of job security rather than loss of high earnings. It also highlights the character of the privilege which 'Treasure Island' (as we have noted BSC was called) bestowed on its employees. While what hit the headlines in its days of prosperity were the high wages steelworkers could earn, what they really valued and others envied was the relief from having continually to *come on to the market*.

Only two-fifths of the sample *dis*agreed with the statement that they had felt degraded by unemployment. One of the ways in which unemployment may be degrading is that it involves having to ask for work as opposed to fighting for wages/rights. To fight (however unsuccessfully) is never humiliating but to ask (or beg) for work is. Fear of degradation through unemployment appears to be stronger than the desire to earn more. This interpretation fits well with the history of the west Industrial South Wales labour market and the moderate character of the chief steel employees' union, the ISTC, and the willingness of workers to accept redundancy to 'save' jobs for others. It suggests that redundant steelworkers would be unlikely to stick out for jobs with comparable wages rather than 'trade down' to avoid unemployment, even if the redundancy provisions (through make-up) had not encouraged such an attitude. Those interviewed were also asked to respond to the statement, 'it is important to maintain a high standard of living'. This is not a statement likely to provoke a large amount of disagreement, so it is important to record that over 40 per cent failed to agree with it, and this is further evidence of willingness to trade down to obtain employment.

If many of our respondents did not emphasize the importance of maintaining a high standard of living, many were naïvely optimistic about the ability to do so, only 37 per cent failing to agree with the statement that 'people with any drive or initiative will always be able to maintain their standard of living'. 'Drive', however, does not appear to have included moving out of the *local* market since nearly two-thirds failed to agree with the cautious statement, '*if you can find job opportunities elsewhere* you ought to be prepared to move away from the area to take them'. This reluctance to move by those remaining in the market to jobs elsewhere (for discussion of the amount of geographical mobility in the sample see chapter 3) can be explained chiefly by reference to the elderly character of the redundant population.

We may therefore conclude this section on labour market characteristics and attitudes by noting that those who remained in the market were elderly, relatively unskilled, with little recent labour market experience; they arrived on the market in a way which did not facilitate successful job search, few of them engaged in early search, and a significant proportion hesitated for some weeks before committing themselves to trying to obtain work. They were, on the whole, unwilling to move to acquire work (let alone to search for it), were more concerned with security than high pay but believed that their standard of living could be maintained by people with drive and initiative.

It may seem odd, in the light of the conditions at the time, that redundant workers could believe drive and initiative would see them through. It was apparently not other people's drive and initiative they were thinking of, since 66 per cent of the sample felt that 'whatever happens to the economy I reckon I'll get by' and claimed 'I'm optimistic about my own future'; less than a third acknowledged feelings of despair ('things will never get better for me'). These optimistic views are all the more remarkable since over 80 per cent, far from failing to recognize 'the state of the country', agreed that 'it makes me anxious and pessimistic'. Before the reader assimilates this discrepancy to the familiar 'it can't happen to me' syndrome, which is the target of attack by those selling insurance or seeking to improve road safety, he or she should recall that these are respondents who were, at the point of survey, either in work, retraining or looking for work. There is nothing in the life situation of those in the first two categories which would make for personal pessimism. In the case of the third, however, maintaining an optimistic attitude is a necessary condition of continuing the search. To believe that you won't get by, that things will never get better, would logically necessitate the abandonment of the search as fruitless. Unsuccessful search over a long period (even without the benefits of newspapers and broadcasts) must make one 'anxious and pessimistic' about 'the state of the country'. This displacement of the anxiety over personal troubles on to public issues functions to maintain both individual morale and, paradoxically, the belief that personal success is the result of individual moral attitudes. Present failure has a collective cause, but future success will be a personal triumph.

## Location in social structure

Characterizing a population involves attributing its members to the social categories constitutive of their society. By virtue of belonging to those categories and that society, each individual becomes embedded in a network of relationships between particular persons. Such networks, whether or not viewed from the standpoint of a given subject, are necessarily composed of relations between persons who are not distributed geographically in a random fashion but clustered in space. Each person develops, therefore, what may be termed a field of social relationships which increases with time, and if that person and the other persons in the field remain in the same geographical area, the fields of the area's inhabitants are likely to overlap. The population of a settlement with a relatively stable population is therefore likely to constitute an interconnected social network composed of the overlapping social fields of its members. However, all persons will not stand in relationship to all other persons, any more than members of one social category will all be members of any other. Network and category set are the two most primitive aspects of social structure whereby population members are both connected *and* separated from each other. The existence of a locally based network does not thereby constitute its members as a community, since they need not constitute either a group or a social category, nor have anything else in common other than residence; but the fact that their relationships with each other are structured enables us to speak of members of a population of a settlement as occupying different locations in the structure of that settlement, locations that is in local social structure.

The settlements composing west Industrial South Wales are both distinct and interconnected. They are not interconnected through a central place: people move up and down the valleys and back and forth between the different settlements on the coast which constitute what Humphrys has termed 'Swansea Bay City' (Humphrys, 1971c). The redundant population was drawn from the whole of this area and we have noted that those remaining in market were distributed in the same way as the redundant population as a whole, over half coming from Port Talbot and adjoining settlements. Of the redundant, 85 per cent were born in West or Mid Glamorgan and only 12 per cent outside Wales. Because of the elderly character of those remaining in the market it is reasonable to assume that these redundants were deeply embedded in the networks associated with the settlements where they lived, and hence involved in extensive local networks. Half had been living in their present house for more than 10 years and a third for more than 18. Two-thirds of those married had been married for more than 13 years and a third for more than 27 years; only one eighth were single. The majority were in the later stages of the family cycle: nearly two-fifths had adult children living away from home and less than half had children living in the household. Kin contact rates were extremely high: over 70 per cent of respondents with each category of parents outside the household had seen them within the week; the figures for children outside the household were above 60 per cent. The least seen category of kin were siblings where weekly contact rates were only in the 30 per cent range.

It is a mistake to suppose that being embedded in the social network, which can be inferred from long residence and high rates of kin contact, entails high levels of communal participation. Involvement in private and home-centred activities featured more regularly than attendance at clubs and associations. The two most popular activities outside the home were going to pubs and places of worship, over 50 per cent claiming to visit pubs often or fairly often, compared with only 10 per cent who made a similar claim in respect of attendance at churches or chapels. Only 7 per cent denied any religious affiliation, however, and because of popular misapprehension about religious allegiance in Wales it is worth recording that 52 per cent claimed allegiance to the Anglican church, 12 per cent to the Roman Catholic church, 15 per cent to English-speaking and 10 per cent to Welsh-speaking denominations. In spite of low levels of attendance at worship, denominational allegiance remains an important type of social classification in South Wales, which suggests it has implications for social action and no sociologist can assume that its implications do not extend to the various forms of economic action of which labour market behaviour is one. We shall return to this issue in chapter 10.

Further insights into network embeddedness and locality attachment emerge from the data on geographical mobility, attitudes and behaviour. Of those in market, 57 per cent owned or were buying their own home, which is a major impediment to mobility. The Conservative dream of a property-owning democracy would be a major disincentive to mobility; there is usually a large discrepancy between house prices in the high-unemployment areas in which workers reside and the low-unemployment areas to which they are expected to move. House purchase is therefore a sign of commitment to an area of residence defined by parity of price for property of similar type. As we saw in chapter 3, only a tiny proportion of all redundants had moved since redundancy: in the case of those remaining in the market, less than 2 per cent had moved out of the west Industrial South Wales labour market area. A further 13 per cent were thinking about moving, but only 5 per cent had definite plans. The most frequent reason for moving was 'to find work', but that only accounted for 4.4 percentage points, the remainder being accounted for by reasons unconnected with employment. Only 5.5 per cent of those considering moving were thinking of moving out of the local labour market area.

The majority intended to stay and only 10.4 per cent of those mentioned factors which did not involve the house, the locality or the disruption of social ties moving would involve. Of those remaining in the market, 61 per cent said they had no intention of *ever* moving but 22 per cent declared themselves willing to consider moving in the future for a variety of employment reasons. In view of the findings so far presented it is not surprising that when asked to agree or disagree with the statement, 'moving away from my family and friends would be a very great hardship', 80 per cent agreed.

We are not suggesting that the people of South Wales, the labour market area under study or those made redundant are more embedded in local social networks than is the case in other areas. We have argued that people's social fields are generally local, that attachment to locality is likely to increase with age, and that in consequence those made redundant showed strong locality attachment arising from long residence and involvement in local social relations. Such relations constitute both a constraint on, and a resource for, social action and a person's location in such a network must be considered potentially important in determining his or her actions and their outcomes.

## Theoretical issues

So far in this chapter a number of different terms have been used to clarify our analysis and exposition. We have spoken of employment attributes (discussed in chapter 3), pre-redundancy labour market experience (of both the external and internal labour markets), labour market attributes and attitudes (including the initial response to redundancy). The assumption is, of course, that reference to these factors explains labour market behaviour and that labour market characteristics and behaviour together with labour market conditions (discussed in chapter 2) determine labour market outcomes (whether individual or collective). Labour market outcome can be defined as the *current status* (employed / retraining / unemployed) at a given point, or it can be defined in terms of the *labour market experience* of workers, that is, the variety of statuses they have occupied since redundancy; such sequences may also be termed 'labour market careers'. The terms 'labour market experience', 'outcome' and 'career' therefore overlap. Another term has, however, been introduced: 'labour market position'. In contrast to the other terms, it is analytic and not descriptive and refers to the chances that a given worker in the market has of different types of employment, different types of labour market experience or different types of career in the market. It is important to distinguish 'labour market position' from 'labour market location'. The latter term refers to the location of a worker in the social structure of the population of the set of settlements which constitute the local labour market. 'Social structure' is used in the sense defined at the beginning of the previous section. A person's labour market location is therefore defined in terms of his or her membership of the different social categories used by members of the local population which define their social identity; but it also refers to his or her location in the network of social relations between population members which bind and separate them.

This chapter has also therefore paid some attention to those characteristics of workers remaining in the market which specify their location in the structural sense. Central to the approach of this *book* is the assumption that social identity, personal network type and location in the population network are always potential determinants of both labour market behaviour and outcomes. It is not, however, an assumption upon which the *study* was predicated, but emerged out of an attempt to understand the data we were collecting. The difficulty attaching to a redundancy study in a loose or falling market is that, to put it briefly, it is not the case that those who are advantaged in terms of the classic standard variables all quickly get good jobs, and the disadvantaged get them later, or worse ones, or none at all, but that not even *all* the advantaged workers get a job of *any* kind. The question this study is concerned with is the same as that often put by unemployed men and their wives: 'why is it, when some people get jobs, that others don't?' The categories conventionally used by both sociological observers and market members no longer seem to work as predictors of individual outcomes, and their power to predict aggregate outcomes is weakened in loose market conditions. We are now in a position to put the matter precisely. Labour market position (the chances of a particular outcome occurring) is determined not only by age, skill, timing of job search commencement, redundancy date and so forth; it is also determined by a worker's labour market location within local social structure which defines his or her social identity.

## Initial outcomes

What determines labour market outcome will be discussed in chapters 9 and 10, and R. M. Lee's investigation of job search and job acquisition form the subject of the next chapter. We conclude this chapter by presenting briefly the outcome of the search for work by those remaining in the market *nine months to a year after the redundancy period.*

There are two quite different methods of determining which workers were still in the market. This chapter had used data generated by asking respondents whether they had looked for work, and if not, why not, in order to define two sub-populations: the withdrawn (31 per cent) discussed in the first section of this chapter, and the in market (69 per cent) who constituted the sub-population discussed in subsequent sections. The alternative method is to use the current statuses 'retired' and 'sick' (which together account for 24.6 per cent of the sample) to distinguish those out of the market from those remaining within it. This latter method has been rejected, because it only provides information about those currently out of the market and inflates the number of 'unemployed' (those who had failed to obtain work) by including among them those who had never sought it. Table 4.2 sets out the initial labour market outcome for the whole sample (including withdrawers and the small number of women) in the left hand column. The remaining columns refer only to those men classified as in market according to whether they had 'looked for work' or not. Of those who had looked for work, 10 eventually reclassified themselves as 'retired' and may be thought of as having withdrawn; withdrawal is therefore one possible outcome even among those who are not classified as 'withdrawn' on 'looked for work' criteria. Two nominal measures of outcome are used: current *status* at interview, and a constructed one, 'labour market experience', which combines the first measure with an element of unemployed respondents' labour market histories. This is a very limited proxy, at this point after redundancy, for the full classification of outcomes in terms of workers' labour market histories which are discussed in chapters 9 and 10. The current status and experience measures are presented in Table 4.2.

TABLE 4.2 Labour market outcomes 9 months after the redundancies

| | *Current status: whole sample* | | *Current status: those still in market* | | | *Labour market experience: those still in market* | |
|---|---|---|---|---|---|---|---|
| | *(n)* | (%) | *(n)* | (%) | | *(n)* | (%) |
| Employed full-time | 150 | 20.1 | 144 | 29.8 | Employed | 157 | 32.5 |
| Employed part-time | 21 | 2.8 | 13 | 2.6 | | | |
| Self-employed | 45 | 6.0 | 44 | 9.1 | Self-employed | 44 | 9.1 |
| Retraining | 57 | 7.6 | 55 | 11.5 | Retraining | 55 | 11.5 |
| Retired | 65 | 8.7 | 10 | 2.1 | Withdrawn | 10 | 2.1 |
| Unemployed | 283 | 37.7 | 216 | 44.8 | Unemployed continuously | 180 | 37.3 |
| Sick | 119 | 15.9 | - | - | Unemployed with occasional jobs | 36 | 7.4 |
| Housewife | 9 | 1.2 | - | - | | | |
| Not classified | 4 | - | 3 | 0.1 | Not classified | 3 | 0.1 |
| Total | 753 | 100 | 485 | 100 | Totals | 485 | 100 |

*Source*: The data were collected in the first wave of interviewing. The redundancies took place between April and December 1980 with a peak in July and August; interviewing took place during April, May and June 1981. Women are included in this table.

The facts revealed by the 'experience' variable are that nearly 45 per cent of the redundants still in the market were unemployed a year after the redundancies commenced. The majority (83 per cent) of those classified as unemployed had been continuously unemployed since being made redundant. Those employed (full- or part-time or self-employed) constitute a slightly smaller proportion of the sample than the unemployed, and are only slightly more numerous than the continously unemployed. The balance is made up by those who were undergoing retraining or had withdrawn when interviewed.

This result was described by one local newspaper, after we discussed our findings with the steelworkers themselves at a Workers' Educational Association seminar in Port Talbot, as 'the grim fate of the redundant steelworkers'. It is not surprising, given the character of the market and the timing of the recession in relation to the redundancies, that the unemployment rate of the economically active redundant should have been double that for males in the local labour market. Considering the market disadvantage of the redundant population, it is surprising that it is not higher. It must be recalled, however, that BSC Margam did not *close*; and that neither the manufacturing sector of the Port Talbot market, nor that of even more diverse west Industrial South Wales, though structurally dominated by the steel industry, was exclusively composed of it. Nearly a third of those in the market were employed a year later. Wales was not 'closed': we are not dealing with an area of economic devastation where the market has ceased to operate, but one where it is extremely loose. The question which must be dealt with is how do workers behave in these market conditions and what determines how successful the outcomes of their actions are? This study is an attempt to widen our understanding of the behaviour and fortunes of those who came on the market in 1980, by focusing on the relation between their market behaviour and demand-side factors, and locating workers' actions in the context of their wider social circumstances at both individual and collective levels.

# *Part II*

# Effects and Responses

# 5

# Looking for Work

In the previous chapter we posed the question: what determines who is employed and who is unemployed when the supply of qualified labour exceeds demand? The inverse of this problem – where does the extra labour come from when demand exceeds supply? – is not difficult to solve. At the lower levels those designated 'unemployable' are suddenly discovered to be 'employable' after all, while at specialized skill levels 'shortages' occur.

Clearly, in the case of very loose labour markets the behaviour of the work seeker can act as a determinant of job acquisition. This chapter is therefore concerned with a description of the *job search* behaviour, its determinants and its consequences in terms of getting jobs. Here we shall be concerned with those redundant workers who, when interviewed in the first wave of interviewing, said they had looked for work. Those looking for work may be described as 'job seekers' and job acquisition is simply one possible outcome of job search at a given point.*

The chapter is also concerned with a different sub-population: not those among the redundant who were 'on the market' and who sought work, but those seekers who actually obtained it. (Women respondents have been included in this analysis.) We are concerned with two closely related but analytically distinct questions which have not always been clearly distinguished in the literature: what were the methods of job search and what were the means of job acquisition? That is, how did those made redundant seek work and how did they get it?

### Search methods: formal and informal

A substantial part of the job search literature has been concerned with the usefulness of different kinds of information sources about jobs to those in

* The sub-population considered here is not all those who remained in the market, since a proportion of these went straight into training or self-employment. It is therefore smaller than the sub-population described in chapter 4.

need of work; distinctions are commonly made between *formal* channels of information (advertisements, employment agencies and the like), *informal* channels (friends, relatives and acquaintances), and the use of a direct personal approach made to a prospective employer.

To classify methods of job search by distinguishing those which are formal, those which are informal and those which are direct, is to compress into a single rather crude typology a range of complex processes which go on within the labour market (Reid, 1972). To take a particular instance: all three approaches may well co-exist within a single job acquisition episode. For example: an individual hears about a job from a friend, makes a direct approach to the firm concerned but is then told to make a formal application which leads to a job. Again, an individual might routinely, while on the market, rely on a given method or combination of methods but in fact may secure a specific job through some other unanticipated means.

In the present context, however, the distinction between formal, informal and direct methods of job acquisition is useful since it reflects the ways in which the labour market is socially structured and socially organized. These are, on the one hand, the presence or absence of agencies, circumstances or relations which form mediating structures between the job and the person obtaining it, and, on the other, the extent to which mediating structures, where they exist, are formally organized.

Although the distinction between these three methods of finding employment (formal, informal and direct) is common to both labour economics and sociology, the underlying assumptions of the two disciplines stand in contrast to one another. The labour economics approach has a conception of labour market activity which is individualistic and strategic. A key assumption is that those active in the labour market act most rationally when they engage in 'job search', that is, where they purposively explore the opportunities presented on the demand side of the labour market. Thus, for example, labour economists have attempted, within a tradition initiated by Stigler (1961, 1962), to model in a fairly abstract way the costs and returns attendant on attempts to acquire information about jobs (for a review of this approach see Lippman and McCall, 1976). Much of the writing in this area takes its basic assumptions from neo-classical economics. Where the post-redundancy situation has been studied, the literature has relied heavily on survey methodology to the exclusion of other, less atomistic, strategies for data collection. As was noted in chapter 1, it has also often been underpinned by an explicit policy orientation aimed at discovering ways in which the labour market may be made more efficient in terms of manpower allocation and utilization.

By contrast, sociologists have tended to be interested in the context of job acquisition and have attempted to understand it in a structural way, focusing on the ways in which job information is socially organized, channelled and mediated. Looked at in more detail, two distinct but complementary approaches can be identified within the sociological literature dealing with how people find jobs. One of these – predominantly American in origin – concerns how job information is disseminated through social networks. Thus, Granovetter (1974, 1981) has criticized the notion of search underlying the labour economics approach by pointing out that studies of job search show that there is a substantial degree of reliance for job information on sources which can be categorized as informal. For labour economists, the theoretical significance of this pattern is that it reveals an 'imperfect' knowledge of the labour market. However, as Granovetter points out (1974 and 1981), the equation of the informal with the imperfect is misguided. Job information gained informally is often richer in the quality of its information than that obtained by more formal means.

Granovetter further points out that a detailed investigation of the role of informal relations in bringing together persons and jobs makes it unclear how far those who find fresh employment engage in a purposive and active exploration of the labour market. In the first place, jobs may be offered to those not on the market. In Granovetter's sample of professional, managerial and technical workers, about one-third were not actively 'on the market' at the time the job offer was made. Second, job information is often passed on in chance encounters, or within some kind of pre-existing relationship. As Granovetter says (1981, pp. 23–4):

> job information is deeply imbedded [*sic*] in . . . social structural processes, in a way that makes it difficult to assert that workers act *as if* they were conducting a rational search . . . By this I mean that information, unlike most other commodities, may often be acquired as the by-product of other activities. A prototype of such a situation is learning about a new job at a party or in a tavern. It strains credulity to assert that the cost of having attended such occasions ought to be called a cost of job search and that one could expect workers to equate, either consciously or unconsciously, the marginal costs and benefits of such 'search'.

Granovetter's demonstration of how much those in the labour market rely on informal sources of job information raises fundamentally sociological questions about the ways in which knowledge is socially distributed, channelled and constrained within a social structure.

More specifically, Granovetter has attributed an important role in the dissemination of informal job information to what he calls the '*strength of weak ties*'. According to Granovetter, the strength of a relational tie between two individuals can be thought of as the 'combination of time, the emotional intensity, the intimacy (mutual confiding) and the reciprocal services which characterise the tie' (Granovetter, 1973: 1361). Weak ties have a greater potential utility to an individual in the provision of job information, Granovetter argues, because those weakly tied to an individual tend to move in different social circles and therefore have access to information not likely to circulate in the individual's own network. Using frequency of contact as a measure of the strength of the tie, Granovetter found support for this contention among a sample of male professional, managerial and technical workers in Newton, Massachusetts. In this sample, job information was considerably more likely to come from those weakly tied to the searcher in the sense of their meeting relatively infrequently.

In contrast to the network approach, the work of British sociologists has focused rather more heavily on the demand side of the labour market by investigating employers' recruitment practices. Much of the literature has its origins in work on gender and racial discrimination and has therefore tended to focus on the useful distinction which Jenkins et al. (1983) and Jenkins (1986) have made between 'suitability' and 'acceptability'. This approach is concerned with the relative importance of 'functionally specific criteria which relate to job performance and competence' (Jenkins, 1986, p. 10), that is, those personal attributes which in labour economics have traditionally been thought of as 'human capital' variables, as opposed to 'functionally non-specific criteria, which relate to "manageability" and the predictable control of the workforce and the organization' (1986). Acceptability is judged on the basis of social attributes and personal knowledge, on the basis of location in the market as a social structure rather than as the site of the exchange of commodities.

The recruitment process in these studies is seen to involve three aspects, each of which is assumed to become more marked as finding jobs becomes more difficult. First, recruitment, although ostensibly an *economic* transaction involving the buying and selling of labour, takes place within the context of an unequal *power* relation between employer and potential employee. Second, recruitment practices are assumed to be shaped by the interest of the employer in controlling the workforce, or as Jewson and Mason (1986, p. 57) put it, recruitment can be conceived of 'as the interface between the labour market and the labour process'. Third, the recruitment process is judged to assist in the reproduction of patterns of social disadvantage, as acceptability criteria often tend, directly or indirectly, to produce discriminatory outcomes.

Both the approaches outlined here tend to pay rather more attention to the role of informal methods of job acquisition than they do to formal methods. Where they differ, however, is in the emphasis they place on the character of informal relations. Those writers who focus on the recruitment of labour and on its relationship to control in the workplace tend to stress the 'moral' aspects of informal relationships, such as trust and obligation. Granovetter, on the other hand, while not discounting the importance of such factors, is rather more concerned with what might be called the 'technical' character of social networks; the relative 'efficiency', in other words, of differing kinds of network ties in disseminating job information.

**Modes of job search and acquisition**

At the time of their first interview (Wave 1), 22.9 per cent of the sample of workers made redundant from BSC and 32.5 per cent of those who said they had 'looked for work' had found their way back into full- or part-time employment. Table 5.1 compares workers' methods of post-redundancy job acquisition with those they had used to obtain their job at BSC. The very marked differences between the two columns strongly suggest that workers respond to different labour market conditions by adopting different search strategies. However, part of this difference is due to the different behaviour of employers; expanding firms in a tight market seek to recruit labour directly. This difference (12 per cent) does not, however, account for the major differences shown by the table which are that, after redundancy, direct application declines and other methods of acquisition, both formal and informal increase markedly. There is no sign of a shift from formal methods in the pre-redundancy era to the use of informal methods in an era of recession. Rather, *both* methods appear to have been more favoured after redundancy than before it, at the expense of direct application.

For comparison, table 5.2 shows figures taken from the *General Household Survey* (OPCS, 1984: Table 6.50) for a national sample of individuals who had changed jobs in the previous 12 months, together with data for BSC redundants showing how those who were unemployed when interviewed on Wave 1 had heard of the last job for which they had applied. Overall, differences between ex BSC workers who had found employment and the national figures are not great. However, those who were in employment at the time of the Wave 1 interviews were slightly more likely to use formal methods and slightly less likely to use informal methods than the GHS respondents. They also made somewhat less use of direct application, but were twice as likely to have received an offer of employment direct from an employer.

TABLE 5.1 Methods of BSC and post-redundancy job acquisition (percentages)

| *Method* | *Pre-redundancy (how obtained BSC job: whole sample)* | *Post-redundancy (re-employed BSC workers)* |
|---|---|---|
| Formal | 11 | 45 |
| Informal | 20 | 30 |
| From employer | 20 | 8 |
| Direct application | 44 | 13 |
| Other | 5 | 4 |
| Base | 754 | 171 |

*Source*: Wave 1 Survey Data

TABLE 5.2 Modes of job acquisition (percentages) in comparison with data from the General Household Survey 1980

| *Method* | *Re-employed BSC workers* | *GHS 1980* | *Unemployed BSC workers: last job applied for* |
|---|---|---|---|
| Formal | 45 | 41 | 56 |
| Informal | 30 | 37 | 32 |
| From employer | 8 | 3 | - |
| Direct application | 13 | 15 | 10 |
| Other | 4 | 4 | 2 |
| Base | 171 | | 163 |

*Source*: Wave 1 Survey Data

Of the unemployed, a similar proportion to those who were re-employed had heard of the last job for which they had applied from an informal source, but a rather greater number – over half – had gained information through a formal channel of one kind or another.

Turning now to look at those in the Wave 1 sample who had found work, there appears to be a fairly marked relationship between the kinds of occupations and industries entered by respondents and the use of particular job acquisition methods. To take occupation first, the association between the occupational level of the job currently held by the respondent and the method by which it was obtained is shown in Table 5.3. Formal methods were used by some 59 per cent of those who entered non-manual employment following redundancy. Among *manual* workers the proportion using formal methods was rather less substantial, markedly so in the case of skilled manual workers, only 25 per cent of whom had used formal means to find a new job, but less so for those in the other manual group where those

TABLE 5.3 Job acquisition method by occupational level of job currently held (percentages)

| | *OCCUPATIONAL LEVEL* | | |
|---|---|---|---|
| *Mode of job acquisition* | *Non-manual* | *Skilled manual* | *Other manual* |
| Formal | 59.0 | 25.8 | 44.5 |
| Informal | 20.5 | 29.0 | 35.9 |
| Direct from employer | 2.3 | 16.1 | 6.5 |
| Direct to employer | 9.1 | 25.8 | 9.8 |
| Other | 9.1 | 3.2 | 3.3 |
| Base | 42 | 30 | 91 |

*Source*: Wave 1 Survey Data

using formal methods totalled 44.5 per cent. The likelihood of using informal methods increases as skill declines from only 20 per cent among non-manual workers to 36 per cent for those in the 'other manual' category.

The most noticeable difference between the three groups, however, is to be seen, as the table shows, in the 'direct' category. Among non-manual workers direct application to an employer amounted to 9.1 per cent, while in 2.3 per cent of cases an offer of employment had come direct from an employer. In the 'other manual' group a similar proportion (9.8 per cent) had applied to an employer while a slightly larger number (6.5 per cent) had been offered a job. In the skilled manual category, however, a 25.8 per cent of those finding jobs had used direct application and in 16.1 per cent of cases the job had been offered by an employer.

The jobs found by respondents in the sample were also classified by industry group. Five groups were distinguished on the basis of the Standard Industrial classification. These were primary, manufacturing excluding vehicles, manufacturing, construction and services. Vehicle manufacturing was singled out for special treatment since, as was apparent both from the survey and field data, the second phase of recruitment associated with the expansion of the Ford Motor Company plant at Bridgend had coincided with the beginning of the redundancy period and Ford had employed a number of ex-BSC employees. Ford used formal methods of recruitment (MSC, 1982). How those who were re-employed found their jobs in various industries is shown in table 5.4.

TABLE 5.4 Job acquisition method by industry group of current job (percentages)

| | *Industry group* | | | | |
|---|---|---|---|---|---|
| *Mode of job acquisition* | *1* | *2* | *3* | *4* | *5* |
| Formal | 33.3 | 47.3 | 50.0 | 25.3 | 47.0 |
| Informal | 44.4 | 33.3 | 37.1 | 20.7 | 28.2 |
| Direct from employer | – | 9.7 | – | 25.3 | 5.8 |
| Direct to employer | 22.2 | 9.7 | 7.8 | 25.3 | 12.5 |
| Other | – | – | 5.2 | 3.4 | 6.5 |
| Base | 5 | 36 | 23 | 17 | 84 |

Key
1 = Primary
2 = Manufacturing excluding vehicles
3 = Vehicles
4 = Construction
5 = Services

*Source*: Wave 1 Survey Data

The number of those in the sample who subsequently found employment which was located in the primary sector (column 1) is small (n = 5). In the manufacturing sector excluding vehicles (column 2) 47.3 per cent used formal methods, 33.3 per cent used informal methods and less than 10 per cent each type of direct method. Though 37.1 per cent of those who found a job in vehicle manufacture had heard of the job from someone known to them and 7.8 per cent made a direct application, 50 per cent of those finding employment in this industry got their job by formal means – a reflection, perhaps, of Ford's recruitment methods.

Formal methods were most common, too, in service industries (column 5), having been used by 47 per cent of those finding work in this sector. Informal methods were used by 28.2 per cent of service employees; 12.5 per cent obtained work through direct application and a further 5.8 per cent had been directly offered a job by an employer. The greatest diversity of methods used for finding work is apparent in construction (column 4). Here formal application, direct application and offers of work amounted to 25.3 per cent in each case, with a slightly lower proportion (20.7 per cent) using informal methods.

These patterns relating to occupation and industry become more interesting if they are compared, for example, with the distribution of modes of job acquisition by age. There appears, in fact, to be some relationship between weak labour market position in terms of age and the use of formal methods, since close to half of under 25-year-olds and of those aged between 50 and 64 had found their present job by formal means. Apart from this, however, the patterns found in the present sample with respect to the age of the respondent are not entirely clear-cut. Over 33 per cent of those in the 25–34 age group had used informal methods, compared with slightly less for each of the other age groups. Direct application was favoured slightly more by those over 35, being used by over 14 per cent of those aged between 35 and 64, in comparison with only 10 per cent of those aged 34 and under. Age differences in the proportions of those offered work by an employer were not great.

The relatively weak influence of age compared with either the occupational level of the job found or its industry suggests that the use of particular modes of job acquisition is rather more a product of how the demand for labour is structured through the recruitment process, than of factors such as demographic characteristics. There are, however, changes in the proportion using different methods to obtain jobs as the volume of labour coming onto the market alters.

Changes in the competitive environment facing a redundant worker at any given time are difficult to determine on the basis of survey analysis. One crude measure refers to the time when job search began, on the assumption that the later one starts the search for work, the greater the likelihood that others will be similarly engaged. Wave 1 respondents were asked when they had started to look for work. Had they been looking for a new job before the redundancies were announced, or had job search begun (1) after the announcement was made, but before the workers knew they were to be made redundant; (2) after they had been selected for redundancy; or (3) after leaving BSC? Those who had found employment, but who had already been looking for a job when the redundancies were announced, most often acquired jobs through formal methods or through direct application. This is not entirely surprising, of course, since it is reasonable to assume that those on the labour market while still at BSC and before the redundancies were announced were actively searching for new jobs, and both formal methods of job acquisition and direct application are search-related methods.

The proportion of respondents who found jobs using formal methods rises the later search was begun, from 38.9 per cent among those who started looking for work after the fact of the redundancies became known, through those who started looking after they had been told of *their own* redundancy (42.4 per cent), to 49 per cent among those who looked for work after they left. At the same time, there is a slight but perceptible decline in the proportion using informal methods the longer after the announcement of the redundancies the search was started. In all, 38.9 per cent of those who had obtained jobs and who looked for work after the redundancies were announced used informal methods, compared with 33 per cent of those who looked after being told, and 28.8 per cent of those whose job search commenced after their dismissal. A similar though slightly more marked pattern is seen for those making direct application. Here the proportions are 19.8, 15.2 and 8.9 per cent respectively. The proportions of those being offered work by an employer rises, however, the further the start of job search is from the announcement of redundancies.

The increased use of formal methods by those successful in finding work the later job search was started is in some ways a little surprising, since we have seen in chapter 2 that the number of registered unemployed per unfilled vacancy in Port Talbot rose very sharply in the period immediately following the redundancies. In other words, for those making use of at least the job centre, competition for jobs was very fierce indeed.

One possible explanation for the trend might be based on an - often unstated - assumption found in job search studies based within the labour economics tradition. This tradition posits an association between job search and social learning, that is, the abandonment of less efficient methods in favour of those more likely to produce a job. This association would explain the observed trend combined with the assumption that the informal is usually a less efficient means of job search than the formal.

If this explanation were correct, it might be supposed that workers would rely more heavily on formal methods of job acquisition where they had greater or more recent experience of the labour market, for example, by having been unemployed at some time prior to working for BSC, or by having had a relatively short tenure at the steelworks. In fact, those in the sample who had had experience of unemployment before working for BSC were actually rather *more* likely to use informal methods and less likely to use formal methods than those who had not previously been unemployed. What this pattern reflects primarily, however, is the greater tendency of manual workers (who are more likely to have experienced unemployment) to use informal methods. Controlling for occupational level, there appears to be no relationship between prior unemployment and the use of particular methods of finding work.

The amount of time the respondent had worked continuously for BSC measures the period since he was last exposed to the labour market. Length of service was divided into 0 to 14 years, and 15 years and over. To control for the effect of age, both categories of length of service were further divided by age into those under 50 and those aged 50 and over. Among those aged under 50, recent exposure to the labour market made little difference to the way in which jobs had been found; there were only marginal differences in the use of different modes of job acquisition whatever the respondent's length of service. Among the over-50s, those who had had long service, and therefore relatively little recent experience of the labour market, were more likely to use formal methods. Older short-service workers also made substantial use of direct application, but there was relatively little difference according to length of service in the proportions using informal methods.

It may be that the higher proportion finding jobs through formal means among those who looked later simply reflects special efforts made by the local job centre on behalf of ex-steelworkers. Fevre has suggested, on the basis of official figures, that ex-BSC employees may have been relatively fortunate in finding jobs and that, indeed, unemployment may have been displaced on to those who were not redundant steelworkers (1984). A further possibility is that as the volume of workers coming on to the labour market rose, those who sought work later rather than earlier had fewer interpersonal resources to draw on in the search for work than those who began to look for work earlier. In part, this might explain the findings on recent labour market experience seen above, if it is assumed that the contacts of older long-service workers were concentrated within BSC leaving them badly placed to find work by these means outside it.

A relevant piece of evidence on this point concerns how hopeful the respondent was of finding another job at the point of redundancy. Having been 'hopeful' of finding fresh employment when made redundant made virtually no difference to the proportions using formal methods in acquiring a job: among those who had found employment, hopefuls used these methods in 47 per cent of cases, non-hopefuls in 47.5 per cent. However, there was a fairly clear tendency for more of those who had expected to find fresh employment to have obtained a job by informal methods, than those who had not. Specifically, 33 per cent of hopefuls used informal methods, as opposed to only 20 per cent of those who professed themselves to have been pessimistic at the time of redundancy about finding another job. There was a slight tendency for the *non-hopefuls* to use direct application to a greater extent than the hopefuls (17.5 per cent to 12.9 per cent). At the same time, *non-hopefuls* in work were substantially more likely to have obtained a job as the result of an offer from an employer (12.5 per cent to 3.5 per cent). Non-hopefuls, fewer of whom had found work by informal methods, were most dependent on direct methods of job acquisition.

One possible explanation for the relationship between being hopeful and the use of informal methods is not that hopefulness of itself leads redundant workers to use these means, but that those who were better placed in terms of informal contacts could view their situation in a rather better light than those without. It may also be that among the less optimistic there were those who, devoid of informal network resources, felt themselves impelled to engage in a direct search for work.

It should be emphasized that throughout the sample much use was made of the formal means of acquiring employment: job centres, newspaper advertisements, employment agencies and so on. Yet, the substantial proportions of redundant workers who used informal means to obtain and look for jobs, the variations in method of job acquisition by occupation, industry and labour market optimism, and the extent to which jobs were obtained by direct methods, all suggest that a simple equation of the formal with the efficient search for job opportunities is far from adequate. So what are the features characteristic of the social relationships that actually produced jobs and how useful were informal relations in terms of finding work?

## Informal relations and job acquisition

Those interviewed on Wave 1 who had found a job by informal means were asked about the nature of their relationship to the person who told them about the job; about frequency of contact with that person, how the contact knew about the job, and whether or not he or she had 'put in a good word' for the respondent. The same questions were also asked of those not currently in employment with reference to the job for which they had most recently applied and which they had heard about through informal channels. It is therefore possible to draw some conclusions about the relation between the use of informal sources of job information and success in job search, something which is, curiously enough, missing from most studies of job seeking.

Looking at those in the Wave 1 sample who had obtained their current job though informal means, and excluding those cases in which the job had been offered to the respondent by an employer, some distinctive patterns emerge, as table 5.5 shows. Overall, those supplying job information were

TABLE 5.5 Job seekers and their contacts, excluding direct approach by employer (percentages)

| | *Employed: Current job* | *Unemployed: Last job applied for* |
|---|---|---|
| How contact known | | |
| Relative, friend | 52.5 | 55.9 |
| Acquaintance | 47.5 | 44.1 |
| Location of intermediary | | |
| Employed in firm | 81.9 | 69.7 |
| Other | 18.1 | 30.3 |
| Influence | | |
| Good word put in | 77.6 | 38.3 |
| No good word *or* don't know | 22.4 | 61.7 |
| Frequency of contact | | |
| Very frequent | 39.4 | 42.8 |
| Fairly frequent | 33.1 | 45.2 |
| Infrequent | 27.5 | 12.0 |
| Base | 51 | 50 |

*Source*: Wave 1 Survey Data

only slightly more likely to be friends or relatives than acquaintances, whether the job was eventually secured or not. Where a job had been obtained there was a rather greater tendency for the contact to have been employed in the firm than where it had not. A large proportion of those who had found employment through someone who worked at their eventual place of employment said that their contact had put in a good word for them. Such attempts by contacts to exert influence on a job seeker's behalf were, however, much less frequent in cases where a job had not been obtained. The proportion of contacts seen frequently was similar in both instances and (at around 40 per cent) not insubstantial in either case. However, 27 per cent of those who got jobs reported that they had seen their contact infrequently in contrast with those cases where the respondent remained unemployed: only 12 per cent saw their contact infrequently.

This last pattern is consistent with Granovetter's assertion that a competitive edge is given to job seekers whose weak ties to others give them access to more selective information. However, if one compares the different elements of the relationship between the job seeker and those who informed him about the job, it seems clear that what strongly distinguishes those who became re-employed from those who did not is the extent to which positive influence is exerted. Whatever the nature of the tie and the position of the intermediary, those who remained unemployed were much less likely to have had a good word expressed on their behalf. In the case of those who did find employment, all those intermediaries who worked in the firm and were strongly tied to the job seeker exerted influence, as did two-thirds of those in the same position who were weakly tied, and three-quarters of strongly tied intermediaries outside the place of employment.

This of course raises the question of the social conditions under which influence was exerted. Where a job originates with an informal contact, it is likely that the nature of the relationship between the contact and job seeker produces an active tendency for the former to wish to exert influence on the latter's behalf. As Harris (1983) puts it:

> When jobs are scarce, information about vacancies is a scarce resource the provision of which can be used to discharge a moral obligation incurred in a social-exchange process, or be a means of discharge of social duties such as constitute the relationships between members of solidary groups (chiefly domestic and work groups) and ascriptive ties (locality and kinship). When there is competition for resources, people look after 'their own' as socially defined, and channel resources to those to whom they feel morally bound thus giving them a competitive advantage over those to whom resources have not been channelled. The importance of the moral element is therefore correlative to the importance of the competitiveness of social life and not its opposite.

At the same time, as Jenkins et al. point out, in times of recession employers are likely to develop a positive preference for informal recruitment methods which, in turn, are likely to encourage the development of links between the locality and the firm, based on networks of strong ties. In a context where managers are trying to minimize costs, informal recruitment methods are cheap and administratively convenient. More importantly, such methods aid attempts to increase control over the labour process by providing 'a privileged source of information, operating as a pre-interview screen against the "trouble-maker" or the "layabout"' (Jenkins et al., 1983, Bresnen et al., 1985).

Strong ties between those in employment and those recommended for recruitment are crucial in this context, for two reasons. In the first place, it might be assumed that employers are likely to look for recruits who have characteristics similar to those in the existing workforce who are judged to be satisfactory. Such individuals are most likely to be available through strong ties. Second, in exerting influence on behalf of someone else, the reputation of the intermediary is potentially put at risk. Such risk, presumably, is most likely to be minimized where a relation of trust exists between the intermediary and the potential recruit. Again, such relationships are most likely to be found where strong ties exist. Or, putting this another way, in Port Talbot at least, the 'moral' character of informal relations outweighs their technical importance as channels of information.

## Informal relations and job outcomes

Existing studies (Daniel, 1974; Granovetter, 1974) tend to suggest that those who find their jobs through informal means are likely to be more satisfied with them. In the case of the redundant steelworkers from BSC Port Talbot this appears *not* to have been the case. Those respondents who had jobs were asked to indicate their level of satisfaction with a number of features of their present job. In general, relatively high levels of satisfaction were recorded. However, on every single item the proportion of those who said they were very satisfied with their new job was greater where the job had been obtained by formal means. Differences were striking in relation to the questions on relations between management and workers, the ability of trade unions to advance members' interests or to support individuals, working conditions, hours of work, promotion chances and the fringe benefits. These findings using subjective measures are paralleled in interesting ways by objective measures. Two-thirds of those who had used a formal method to find their present job were in a trade union, as opposed to just over half of those who had used an informal method.

If workers who have re-training are excluded, there is a strong suggestion in the survey data that those in the sample who found full-time work after redundancy tended to be downwardly occupationally mobile. Some 43 per cent of routine non-manual and technical workers reported themselves to be in semi-skilled post-redundancy jobs at first interview. A similar figure is found for workers with transferable skills (that is, skills not specific to the steel industry) moving into semi-skilled or non-transferable skilled jobs. Among those who had been employed as semi-skilled operatives at BSC, the downward pattern is not quite so marked, for 17 per cent had moved upwards as against 25 per cent who had moved into unskilled work. Some of this upward movement, however, is apparently due to formerly skilled workers, who had taken semi-skilled but highly paid jobs in the steelworks, moving back into the trades they had been in before working for BSC (a similar pattern among 'affluent workers' in the car industry in Luton is described by Goldthorpe et al. (1969)).

One important factor linking informal modes of job acquisition to inferior job outcomes is likely to be the operation of what might be termed the 'ancillary employment structure'. The ancillary employment structure comprises those short-term jobs which arise as a result of a firm employing workers on a fixed term basis or through contractors. Such a structure appears not to be a novel feature of the labour market within which the Port Talbot steelworks is located; BSC and the other large firms in the area have always made use of contractors to provide certain services. In addition some process jobs, for example, in canning, have a seasonal character for which short-term labour is required. It is not known precisely how extensive the role of contracting firms is in the local labour market. However, as we have seen in chapter 4 and as Fevre's work (1987) indicates, an impetus to the demand for contract labour has been given by the internal restructuring of BSC's Port Talbot plant which required the greater use of contractors on site.

Access to contract employment is likely to be heavily dependent on informal social relations as a vehicle for obtaining labour. This is so, first, because there is relatively little incentive for a contract employer to advertise formally for a position which may only last a short time and which would require an expenditure of resources to screen a large number of applicants. Second, contracting firms require labour for fixed periods: they continually come onto the market to recruit such labour. They therefore need to know who is currently available. Field data indicate that many contractors operate with 'lists', which suggests the association of contracting with a direct approach by an employer. This was certainly likely to have been the case just after the redundancies since in the redundancy agreement BSC undertook to 'use its good offices' to encourage the contractors it employed to recruit the workers it was making redundant; knowledge of the steel industry and the works must have been a factor in employers' estimates of a worker's 'suitability' for working on a BSC contract. However, lists go out of date and working with them is not incompatible with a contract worker 'putting in a good word' – even if this only amounts to providing information about availability.

Third, there appears to be a degree of continuity between legitimate contract work and the use of the 'hobble', a term used in South Wales to refer to various kinds of ancillary and usually informal economic activity or income, but used in the present context to denote a job, income from which is not declared to the income tax or social security authorities. We know that redundant steelworkers were formally employed by contractors, for example, while they remained eligible for 'make up' payments (see chapter 3). Such payments, which supplement the redundant's wages in new employment for a finite period after redundancy, allow the contractor to pay a low basic wage, and, presumably, to obtain contracts on the basis of low wage costs. With the ending of the period of eligibility for make up payments, the worker *may* remain in employment with the contractor, but this time 'off the cards' (Lee et al., 1983) still at a low wage, but without tax deductions or the docking of social security payments. This is more likely to occur the greater the distance of the worker from the firm who has put the work out, contractors themselves using sub-contractors and sub-contractors sub-sub-contractors, and so on; field data suggest that this sequence is one of increasing informality and eventual illegality.

The need to obtain labour readily and the potentially questionable nature of some types of contract labour render trust and reputation extremely important factors in the operation of the ancillary employment structure. It seems to encourage the employer to offer work to a suitable and 'worthy' candidate about whom the former has information, as to both his or her suitability and acceptability, such information concerning social category membership, relational social attributes and personal characteristics.

### Conclusion

Although access to contract employment through contact with former workmates does ensure that some redundants are able to find work in an unpromising labour market, one consequence of the burgeoning of the ancillary employment structure has been the marginalization of workers formally located in a well-protected internal labour market. Such workers may in some cases find themselves back in employment doing work similar to their old job and even in their former place of work, but under conditions of employment rather different from those they had previously enjoyed. Once again, this is most notable in relation to job stability. An association of informal job acquisition methods with contract employment would explain the lower rates of satisfaction and union membership among those who used informal means of job acquisition.

Of course, it is not being suggested that a short-term contracting job with inferior conditions will form the inevitable fate of redundant workers or even of those who use informal methods of search. Nevertheless, as Sengenberger (1981), assessing the labour market consequences of the recession in Germany, has pointed out, a dominant employer strategy in times when labour markets are slack involves the attempt to encourage increased interchangeability between internal and external labour markets.

It is unclear how far overt strategies of this kind have been used by employers in Britain as the recession has deepened. Certainly a recent Institution of Manpower Studies (IMS) study of temporary work found that 7.6 per cent of the workers in its sample were temporary and that the proportion had increased since 1980. The rationale of 'flexibility' (which we have noted was embodied in the BSC redundancy agreement) had, according to the study, emerged particularly strongly in the manufacturing sector (Meager, 1985, 1986). This study was not, however, specifically concerned with contracting. The *Financial Times* (13 June 1986) forecast that as much as half of a projected 8 per cent drop in employment in production and agriculture would be caused by the adoption of flexible strategies. In so far as temporary workers are recruited informally, it may be that there is a shift taking place in local markets, as a result of the recession, towards what might be described as employment relationships which are 'substantively closed', rather than being 'formally closed' in the Weberian sense (1915 [1978]:43). That is, access to employment is coming increasingly to be based on the restricted availability of knowledge about possible opportunities rather than governed by rules which specify who is eligible.

It is not, however, being suggested that all employment is now distributed as a result of information passed along informal channels or as a result of the influence exerted by intermediaries strongly bonded to the applicant. Nor do we wish to claim on the basis of our data that all contracting work is necessarily obtained in this way. What we do wish to suggest is that in loose markets, in general, job information is scarce resource and, for some categories of workers, can act as an important determinant of job acquisition and that, given the appropriate social conditions, information is likely to be directed along networks of informal relationships.

The importance of moral influence by intermediaries must be understood in terms of the employer's, not the employee's, need of information. In a loose market the employer can choose what sort of qualified workers he or she wants, that is, those who are 'acceptable' in terms of their social and personal character. That information cannot be ascertained by formal means but it can be provided by intermediaries. A loose market is a buyer's market, one in which the buyer has greater power and choice than the seller. The looser the market, the greater the importance of recruitment strategies by labour buyers relative to the labour market behaviour of the sellers of labour power. In such markets it follows not only that those labour market attributes which constitute human capital will be much less reliable predictors of success in finding employment, but also that the labour market behaviour of workers, particularly their method of job search, will also be a weaker predictor of success in obtaining employment. Respondents who said, 'then I had a bit of luck' in their inability to fathom the cause of their success, ignore the fact that while they were out there searching, those on the other side of the market - even a loose one - continue looking for 'acceptable' labour.

The existence of an operating labour market necessarily involves the existence of relationships between the parties between whom power in the market is unequally distributed. It is the action of the more powerful party that will be most effective in affecting outcomes. This inequality in market power (as opposed to workplace authority) is not, however, fixed: it varies with market conditions, as the terms 'buyers market' and 'sellers market' imply. In a loose market for labour, the power of buyers is immeasurably enhanced and takes the form of their greater ability to choose. Hence it is employers' recruitment strategies rather than workers' job search strategies that require study.

In order to make the choices which their enhanced power opens to them, employers require information. Information about human capital is available through formal recruitment procedures. The greater the choice between persons equivalently qualified in formal terms, the greater will be the resort to informal procedures which can deliver information about social and personal characteristics. However, the market power of the employer will vary according to the tightness of the market for different types of worker. MSC's Bridgend study (MSC, 1982) reported skill shortage even in 1980 in the Port Talbot travel-to-work area. Hence we would expect to find increasing resort by employers to informal means of recruitment the lower the occupational/skill level. And that is precisely what table 5.3 shows.

A labour market is a process as well as a set of relationships and needs therefore to be understood as a series of inter-related flows. Even after redundancy and in recession, as chapter 2 demonstrated, the unemployed flow off the register as well as on, and they do so as a result of employers' search for labour as well as workers' search for jobs. Data on job search and acquisition methods must be understood therefore as the result of a dynamic relation between the actions of employers and wage labourers and not as the result of choices made in isolation by either party. In this relation, as in all others, 'it takes two sides.' However, in a labour market the need of both sides for information means that the relation at the level of personal interaction is frequently mediated by third parties. The character of an employer's or employee's social field will determine whether or not such mediation is available. Hence the relative location in social structure of buyers and sellers to one another must constitute an important determinant of search outcomes, whichever party is doing the searching.

# 6

# The Household in the Labour Market

When this research began, one of our main objectives was to distinguish between workers who were successful and those who were unsuccessful in the labour market – the employed and the unemployed – and then to identify differences between the two groups which might help to explain their post-redundancy experiences in the search for employment. It very quickly became clear, from a detailed study of the households of a representative sub-sample of 40 married men under 55, that our research intentions were ill-conceived. In some senses our preconceptions and proposed system of classification were inappropriate to the situation we wished to study. One case study will show why.

Mr Parker is 36 years old. He was made redundant by BSC in September 1980, and claimed unemployment benefit for 3 weeks before beginning an 8 month course in engineering. During this course he received a retraining allowance equivalent to his previous salary, and signed on as unemployed when it ended. He was immediately offered 4 weeks' work as a steel erector, with a small firm of contractors working for BSC. As his job drew to a close an old workmate, who had set up his own firm and was also under contract to BSC, telephoned to offer him work back on the job from which he had been made redundant. This work lasted another 4 weeks. Mr Parker then applied through the local paper for a job as a sales representative for a clothing firm, which paid commission only. He tried this for three weeks, then moved to a different job, selling aluminium windows, again advertised in the local paper, which he again abandoned after a few weeks. In each of these jobs Mr Parker received make-up pay which brought his salary up to 90 per cent of his BSC earnings.

This chapter draws substantially on detailed research findings, published elsewhere. See Morris (1983, 1984a, 1985b) and Harris and Morris (1986).

For the 2 months which followed, Mr Parker was again unemployed and claiming benefit. He then began a second course of retraining as a welder, throughout which he received a generous retraining allowance, and which was followed by 6 weeks with a firm, where a friend from the local rugby club was a manager and used his influence on Mr Parker's behalf. After this he remained unemployed for 2 months, at the end of which the workmate who had previously provided work back on his old job contacted him again, offering more work. Mr Parker accepted, but for one week only. By this time, in fact, he had been taken on by a hotel chain as a trainee manager, and was to commence his introductory training the following week.

This 'official' job history was made yet more complicated by short spells of paid work which were not declared when Mr Parker signed on as unemployed. He had taken one day's employment loading a lorry for a contractor in the steelworks; 8 days' work over Christmas (while officially on a training course) for the friend who had employed him on his old job; and occasional work for a cousin who ran his own building firm.

Not all cases are so extreme, or indeed so fortunate, as that of Mr Parker. In fact there is considerable variety not only within the employment experience of one individual worker, but also between the experiences of different workers. For example, some men had not worked since redundancy, while others found a new job soon after and have remained there since. More common was some mixture of the different statuses as in Mr Parker's case so that over a period of roughly 18 months after being made redundant men had known different combinations of employment, unemployment, self-employment and retraining. A brief discussion of certain aspects of special provisions for redundant workers may help to explain why.

## Retraining and make-up pay

The EEC Iron and Steel Employees Readaptation Benefits Scheme offered retraining on an income equivalent to BSC salary for a maximum period of a year. Workers took up such opportunities for a number of different reasons. Some hoped to gain a marketable skill, others were attracted by the money and yet others, unaware that the market would fall further, judged it advisable to delay entry onto the labour market at a time when it was flooded by redundant workers.

The provision of make-up pay (see chapter 3, p. 77) is rather more complicated in its operation and its effects. Where a redundant steelworker was able to find new employment, then EEC benefits were used to make up low wages to 90 per cent of previous earnings for a maximum of 18 months after redundancy (2 years in the case of men over 55 and women over 50). Hence, during the period covered by these provisions an ex-steelworker could be offered an almost nominal wage and left to claim his make-up pay. The arrangement is not without disadvantages for the worker, however, as 'Mr Lloyd's case shows. For the 3 months immediately following redundancy Mr Lloyd claimed unemployment benefit, but then found work with a firm of industrial cleaners on contract to BSC. Mr Lloyd explained:

> The boys were talking in the pub, so I turned up and was lucky. The work was terrible, mind, £50 a week, but I'd have done anything, and the rest of the boys were the same. We'd take turns to go on the sick – we've got a doctor down here who'll give you a paper any time. It wouldn't have been so bad if the make-up had come through. I spent a fortune on phone calls to Sheffield [central office dealing with claims].

When the contract ended Mr Lloyd found work after a few weeks, again through the boys in the pub, driving an overhead crane for a firm of contractors working at Port Talbot harbour, work he had previously done for BSC:

> It was the same thing though. Seven shifts for £36 a week, and if you complained it was just, 'Well, you've got your make-up'. I only lasted two weeks, and I've been out of work since. A lot of the boys couldn't afford to work 'cos they hadn't the bus fare.

One man explained that he had found work through his father, at a very low wage, with a firm of industrial cleaners: 'They're looking for make-up men. Mind you, for every job down there, there's another ten hobbling' [working off the cards].

## Short term employment

An inspection of post-redundancy job histories makes clear the importance of short-term employment with contracting firms. The use of contractors by large-scale enterprises is by no means new, but as chapter 5 notes, there has been some evidence of recent growth in the use of such firms in the UK, as well as an associated growth in the employment of temporary workers. Large and long-established contracting firms are likely to operate with a unionized workforce and be party to national agreements on levels of pay and conditions of employment. For this reason they are unlikely to benefit directly from the make-up provision. Advantages could, however, accrue to firms without such commitments, which tend to be smaller and more recently established. We should note, however, that the local branches of large-scale, long-established contracting firms may well sub-contract work to smaller, less reputable organizations (see Fevre, 1985).

It would appear that large firms have responded to the recession by increasing the use of contractors. As we have seen from earlier chapters, BSC is a prime example. The redundancies from the Port Talbot plant were the result not only of cutbacks in production but also of a restructuring of the labour process which involved a reduction in the number of permanent jobs and the creation of what Lee (see chapter 5) has termed an ancillary employment structure. Such reorganization on the part of the largest local source of employment seems likely to lead to shifts in the opportunity structure, and one notable feature of post-redundancy work histories is a recurrent reference to short-term contract work, some of which is actually back in BSC.

## The steel redundancies and the informal sector of the economy

While the reaction of BSC and presumably other large-scale enterprises to the recession has involved an increase in the use of contractors, such firms themselves will respond to the recession by offering their services more cheaply to gain a competitive edge and pass on the costs to the workforce. They do this by taking advantage, wherever possible, of the make-up provision, and also by employing labour 'off the cards'. It seems likely that this kind of arrangement has been increasingly used as an alternative means of keeping labour costs low when the period covered by make-up pay ends. In other words, this strategy represents another way a firm could take on labour at extremely low wages, offering cash payment to a worker claiming unemployment and/or supplementary benefit. By combining his wage with such benefit, a man would conceivably arrive at a viable income level.

Many of the men I spoke to had had a few *days or weeks* of such work, but for a man to have accepted full-time employment over a longer period of time, while also claiming benefit, was rare. As 'Mr James' explained:

> That's not what it's like mostly. What suits a firm, especially on a contract, is to avoid taking someone onto their books just for a week's work. The main thing is to let people know you're out of work, and if you have enough contacts something always turns up. Word gets round and the jobs come in. The other day, now, one of the boys asked me was I working, and I knew he was going to offer me a hobble.

Of course, work off the cards for a contractor is by no means the only kind of 'hobble' to be found in Port Talbot. Interview data reveal a range of different types of activity, all covered by the use of this term, for example: Odd jobs for friends, relatives and acquaintances; occasional work for an employer (driving, panel-beating, construction, and so on); full-time employment at low pay undeclared to the DHSS (such as builder's labourer); private building and central-heating conversions on a scale which approaches that of a small business. Any of these types of work could have been, and often were, taken on while the person concerned was still employed by BSC, and equally, a number of men who found new employment continued to take on odd jobs in their spare time, as did others who were in receipt of benefit – a topic we return to in chapter 7.

Since a large proportion of men used their redundancy payment to finance substantial alterations to their homes, there is likely to have been an increase in the informal demand for both labour and goods. This demand eventually abated as redundancy money was exhausted, however, while 'off the cards' *employment* seems likely to have increased with the termination of make-up money.

The workings of the informal market for labour, however, merit further attention, since they represent part of a general system of informal recruitment. In practice, this means that opportunities are made available and services offered on the basis of belonging to a social collectivity which serves both to distribute information and to confer upon its members a 'moral identity'. The worker is thus put in touch with an employer or client, while the employer is assisted in the search for appropriate labour, and any subsequent transaction is grounded in the social and moral ties which brought them together.

## The importance of moral identity

Precisely what is meant by the term 'moral identity' is perhaps best illustrated by example. Mr Smith, like many men in South Wales, has a lively interest in racing pigeons, and his social life has for many years revolved around the local pigeon club, the more so since his redundancy, which began with a period of two years' unemployment. It is through this club and his general familiarity with people in his neighbourhood that Mr Smith has been able to pick up casual employment 'off the cards', work which may, however, be unpredictable, and in many ways undesirable.

> A lot of boys from the club work as painters, plasterers or brickies, and they'll call on me if there's a job they can't handle . . . it might go a month or so without anything, then there'll be a knock on the door . . . We're all mates from way back, at school together, racing pigeons together, drinking in the same pub . . . They'd pass a job to me before it would go to an outsider.

The notion of the 'outsider' not only implies the preferential channelling of opportunities; it also suggests a social world which is divided into the known and the unknown, those to be trusted and those not to be trusted. Given the illicit nature of undeclared employment, the need for mutual trust between employer and employee, and the guarantee of a degree of secrecy, an outsider to a local network can be something of a threat. Mr Smith, on the other hand, is the employer's ideal choice:

> They know I'll always do it quietly. I don't shoot my mouth off bragging in the pubs, and I only take work through people I know I can trust, tidy boys. You could cut their hands off and they wouldn't tell . . . and if one of the boys wants a hand you go along on Friday and there'll be a couple of pints behind the bar. Or if it's painting the side of a house, an afternoon's work, say, there could be £10 in it for you.

For Mr Smith, the work provides much-needed additional income, but he also clearly derives some satisfaction from his ability to track down such opportunities, which he attributes to his qualities as a worker. These qualities are, of course, critically important to whoever takes him on, for they are not engaging in a formal market transaction. While payment is expected this will usually be at rates lower than the formal market value of the labour. The employer or client has to be assured that the worker will be available when required, will actually appear, and will perform the task adequately. This will be guaranteed partly by the hope of future work and also by the nature of the ties which brought them together. In the case of Mr Smith, the contacts were direct and the mutual obligations personal. It may equally be the case that some third party, a member of the same social network and bound by the same social conventions, will bring worker and employer or client together, vouching for the reliability of each by placing their reputations on the line.

## Informal recruitment

The same processes which operate in the allocation of informal work opportunities will provide access to certain kinds of formal employment – hence the argument: 'I have to go out drinking, or I'll never get a job.' Some examples will illustrate the process of informal recruitment, and give some idea of the kind of employment which results.

*Example 1: 'Mr Evans'* At the time of his redundancy, Mr Evans heard talk among the men he worked with about a firm in Port Talbot which was taking on workers. He turned up to enquire and was given work in his trade, painting and signwriting, although there was no guarantee that this would be a permanent position. The job lasted 3 months and was followed by 7 months' unemployment. One day an old workmate called at his home unexpectedly to say that he was starting his own firm, had a contract with the steelworks, and could offer Mr Evans a job. The wage was £50 a week, made up to 90 per cent of Mr Evans's BSC salary. The job ended the day his make-up entitlement ran out – though Mr Evans could not be sure that there was any connection.

*Example 2: 'Mr James'* After being unemployed for 5 months, Mr James took on work with a contractor at British Petroleum. He had been introduced to the job by a friend from the local rugby club who was already working there. Both men worked for a short spell off the cards but were eventually taken on to the official workforce for a period of 12 months. 'To tell the truth I was glad when it ended . . . dirty work, cleaning up spilt oil; emergency work, so there was always pressure to do long hours and you couldn't really refuse . . . All the jobs BP men wouldn't do went out to contract.'

*Example 3: 'Mr Smart'* In contrast to the above cases, Mr Smart, after 4 months being unemployed, found a job he has been in ever since:

> You'd hear talk around the club of who had heard of work, and I knew William Press was taking on because there was work on the new blast furnace. Being so near the works you always hear, but I knew it wouldn't be secure and I thought I'd rather hang on for something better, not to miss my chance like. Fords' were advertising in the paper at the time so I applied and got in there. I've been with them ever since.

Informal acquisition of employment is minimally dependent upon information about where work is available (as with Mr Evans's first job), while the most certain access is through a personal acquaintance who can offer employment (Mr Evans's second job). Almost equally helpful, however, is a well-placed friend, someone who can influence an employer and speak on behalf of a prospective employee. This usually happens when the friend is already working for a firm when a vacancy arises. An example is Mr James's recruitment to the job at BP.

This system is of considerable advantage to the employer who, in the absence of direct personal contact with the potential recruit, can rely on the reputation of the referee to guarantee that the quality of work and reliability of the worker will be acceptable. As Mr Jones explained:

> Obviously, you look after your own, don't you? My mate pulled me in there and maybe I'll do the same for him some time. Only if he'll do the job, mind. You're not going to have someone in who'll let you down 'cos it comes back on you, see. Take my mate now. My work is his reputation if you like. He's guaranteeing it. The whole set up would break apart if I let him down.

## Differential labour market locations

It is time now to rephrase the original research question, for we must try to understand the fate of workers after redundancy not in terms of a status division between employed and unemployed, but in terms of a work *history* and the different types of opportunities, both formal and informal, which go to make it up. This finding challenges the adequacy of any *over simple* version of the polarization thesis (Pahl, 1984) which suggests a society increasingly divided into working and workless households. Households where workers move constantly between employment and unemployment cannot be classified in these terms.

It remains to consider the ways in which different individuals gain access to employment opportunities, and how that access relates to their location in a world of social contacts which, at least potentially, link the household with the labour market. We must therefore, as the previous chapter has argued, consider opportunities for employment in the context of both the varying types of social contact of individual workers and the varying recruitment strategies of employers.

In chapter 5 it was noted that there are good reasons for expecting different types of recruitment to correspond to different sorts of employment. For example, a small-scale enterprise working to a contract and offering short-term employment, often for low pay and under poor conditions, is likely to use informal channels to advertise and recruit. This system of recruitment allows employers to minimize costs, avoid troublemakers, and identify workers with an appropriate skill, while also fostering loyalty and co-operation by involving the existing workforce in selection. Where the work involved is not recorded by the employer and not declared by the worker, that is, 'off the cards', there are additional reasons for the emphasis on informality, loyalty and privileged access to information.

As we have seen, the networks involved in acquiring employment are usually based on some form of local institution, such as a pub, sports or social club which serves as a focus for social interaction. Men whose social activity does not have this institutional, collective dimension, and does not involve them in a highly developed network of acquaintances, are much less likely to fall into short-term employment with a contractor, and tend either to acquire more secure employment through formal channels or to remain unemployed in the long term. A secure job is only usually achieved, however, after a relatively long spell without employment.

In other words, the character of a particular worker's social world will influence both the means of access to employment and also the nature of the employment that results. Informal channels may increase the likelihood of finding work but also seem to increase the probability that the work will be short-term and held under poor terms and conditions of employment, this is an additional reason, from the point of view of the employer, to exploit these informal means.

## Role reversal

Under the variable circumstances which I have described it is not surprising that responses to redundancy at the household level cannot be clearly and easily identified. Role reversal will only be seen as an option where a man's unemployment is *expected* to be long-term, and where the woman has at least a reasonable hope of getting full-time employment. Given the chequered employment pattern experienced by many of the men, the informal procedures for recruiting both men and women, and increasing demand for part-time female labour, the consequences of any set of employment decisions for the household can be both complex and unpredictable. Under these circumstances the central research questions to be addressed are (Morris, 1983; cf. R. E. Pahl, 1984: 150):

How is work outside the household distributed among its members?

How is work inside the household distributed among its members?
What is the relationship between these two divisions of labour?

When we look at changes in the structure of the national economy we find major shifts in employment from manufacturing to services, and from male to female workers. It therefore seems reasonable to assume that since men have been losing employment and women – especially married women – have been gaining, then within the household women could be taking over from men as principle earners. This turned out to be another mistaken assumption, for what goes on inside individual homes cannot be inferred in any simple manner from aggregate statistics.

There are other sources available which suggest that male joblessness is not commonly dealt with by a reversal of roles within the home. Figures from the *General Household Survey* (OPCS, 1984: Table 6C) show that the wife of an unemployed man is less than half as likely as the wife of a working man to be in paid employment. This is one aspect of the 'polarization' thesis which our research findings confirm, and there are a number of factors which contribute to an explanation:

1 There was a fall in employment opportunities for women as a result of recession.
2 The rise in employment for married women throughout the 1970s was predominantly in part-time work which could not replace husbands' lost full-time occupations.
3 Recent increases in employment opportunities for women have also been part-time.
4 It is popularly believed, usually correctly, that a woman, even in full-time employment, could not earn as much as the household could claim in state benefits.
5 At the time of our research the better part of a wife's earnings (all but £4) was deducted from supplementary benefit.[1]
6 Contemporary gender roles emphasize a woman's domestic obligations, especially in the rearing of young children.

It was quite common to discover that in homes which had for some time depended on two incomes, both husband and wife lost their jobs in fairly quick succession, and we should remember the particular vulnerability of part-time (and therefore often female) workers in times of cut-backs and lay-offs (Meager, 1986). It was also the case in some homes that once the household came to be dependent on supplementary benefit the woman felt it no longer worth her while continuing in paid employment. Other women felt they should nevertheless keep their jobs, on the assumption that their husbands would eventually find work and that they themselves were by no means sure of finding another job should they leave their present one.

## Household strategies

How does any given household arrive at a 'strategy'? Let us take the example of Mr and Mrs Lewis. The couple were unconvinced of the viability of a role swap, although Mrs Lewis was no stranger to paid work:

'I don't see it really. For a start he'd be hopeless, and it's not fair on them [the two children] is it? And, anyway, I can't get the money, you know.'

Mrs Lewis has a history of part-time employment, having worked as a cleaner in the local club, and on different occasions in two of the shops in the town: 'I've always done part-time, with these [children] still little. I want to be here when they get in [from school], and there's the dinner to get for him. He likes it as soon as he's through the door, you know what they're like.' She worked in the mornings as a cleaner when her husband was made redundant, but once he became dependent on supplementary benefit she gave up the job:

Well, you know, it was like working for nothing. But wouldn't you know, not long after, he rolls home full of himself; one of the lads at the club says they're taking on where he works, they need a driver. It might be just for a month or two but never mind. He turns up on the Monday and he's in.

After two months Mrs Lewis was offered a temporary job at a nearby shop, as a part-time assistant:

It was the lass a few doors down told me they needed someone over Christmas, but I think she had it in mind to leave after, being pregnant like. Anyway, once the few weeks were done they asked me to stay. It just suited, only the middle of the day and I was home soon after three o'clock. Now Evan was still driving, so we were set up. I stayed on, but about 6 weeks later he came home with a face as long as your arm and I knew. The job was finished. But they might need him again; they'd be in touch. Well, I'd already lost one nice little job, so I stayed put. Chances were he'd be working again. He didn't like it, mind, not with him being out of work himself, you know.

This is not a *typical* example, but it is a case which illustrates the fortuitous and haphazard way in which a 'strategy' and a work history are worked out. It is an account of experience shaped by the opportunities available, calculations about future prospects, and ideas about gender roles. A major constraining factor is the presence of young children. In the few homes with women continuing in full-time work in the face of their husband's unemployment there were no pre-school children, and indeed national figures show that a woman is increasingly likely to take paid employment as the youngest child gets older (Joshi, 1984).

Couples who had some experience of the woman as sole earner emphasized that the arrangement was unsatisfactory to both of them, and certainly only a temporary expedient. Given the variable nature of many men's work histories after redundancy, this often proved to be the case. Nevertheless, the force of the dominant gender ideology should not be underestimated. Its character was eloquently expressed by some of the few people who had made attempts to change their domestic roles: 'A housewife means just that. She's supposed to stay at home . . . while I was out of work I felt I wasn't playing a part in things, ashamed that I wasn't keeping my family.' Or as one rare woman breadwinner put it: 'If there was any way that I thought giving up my own job would help him get one I'd do it like a shot. It's hard on any man to be out of work.'

## The maintenance of gender ideology

The history of the local Welsh economy has encouraged a rigid division of labour between the sexes, with men traditionally employed in heavy industry and supported by the domestic services of wives and mothers. In Wales, the participation of women in paid employment has always been low by national standards (see chapter 2), but ideas about what it is to be a man or to be a woman, which have grown up around these traditional divisions of labour, have powers of endurance that go beyond the economic logic from which they arose.

Their persistence is, ironically, to be understood in part as a reaction against change in the economic underpinnings of gender identity. There is a strong feeling on the part of both men and women that it is the man's place to be the main earner and as a result any other arrangement is experienced as stressful for one or both partners. The availability of opportunities for short-term employment and/or retraining make it difficult for many couples to rethink their situation.

It seems reasonable that under threat people should cling to the familiar, and attempt to deal with change by stating all the more firmly the principles upon which they have organized their lives in the past. The challenges posed by male job loss may be seen in this context as a temporary disruption of the familiar order which is soon to be re-established. Clearly, such a view cannot persist indefinitely, but as long as there are a significant number of jobs available, albeit temporarily, and as long as the unemployed man knows of others who have recently found work, then faith in a resumption of the old order will seem justified and he will continue to be motivated to seek work. (See the discussion of the attitudinal data in chapter 4.)

## The role of social networks

I remarked earlier in this chapter on the role of informal social contacts in providing access to employment. A tendency for small-scale contractors to recruit workers through such channels has meant that the workers involved are likely to be those with highly developed social networks. These networks also perform the rather different function of sustaining and reinforcing traditional ideas about gender identity and appropriate gender behaviour. The men involved in such a social world, which commonly revolves around the pubs and social clubs in South Wales - shown by the survey data to be the most popular non-domestic activities - are thus in a strong position for gleaning information about short-term employment, both formal and informal, and are also likely to find constant reinforcement of their gender identity. This will discourage any radical reorientation of their domestic lives.

We have so far said little about the position of women in this complex of local social contacts. As in the case for men, informal channels of information and support can play a significant role in access to opportunities for employment, but just as the traditional source of male identity has been paid employment, the traditional basis for female identity has been the domestic sphere, child care and domestic labour. Apart from the need to explain why these gender divisions persist in the absence of male employment (the focus of the following chapter) we need to ask more generally why women's association with domesticity has not been shaken by their increased participation in paid work, which grew steadily throughout the 1960s and 1970s.

## Women's networks and the labour market

It is apparent from our research that the labour market participation of married women cannot be understood simply by reference to a rational decision-making model which examines the labour power available to the household and weighs the relative labour market strengths of household members. Although the notion of a household strategy is used by some authors in the discussion of contrasting divisions of labour in different households (for example, Pahl, 1984) the rational-calculative connotations of the term take little account of the location of particular households within a local social network, a network whose influence is brought to bear both on beliefs about appropriate gender behaviour, and also on access to opportunities for employment.

Given a well-established pattern of female responsibility for domestic and child care tasks, a woman's paid work must either take account of her domestic obligations, or those obligations must accommodate her paid employment. Broadly speaking, there are three possibilities:

1 Hours in paid employment must leave the woman free at the appropriate times for the fulfilment of domestic and child care obligations.

2 An arrangement may be made with female friends or relatives whereby they assume some of the domestic labour, either for financial reward or on a reciprocal basis.
3 A husband may assume a share of the activities previously defined as the responsibility of his wife.

It is in deciding which of these possibilities is viable, and which easiest to realize, that the social network comes into play. This is not to suggest that there is no room for the notion of choice in our understanding of entry into paid employment by women; rather, decisions about work can only be fully understood in terms of constraints and possibilities which derive from the woman's location in a web of social contacts.

Entering paid work was found to be largely the result of exploiting informally acquired knowledge of suitable work opportunities, 'suitable' being defined as opportunities which did not interfere too severely with traditional patterns of domestic organization. Wives' participation was structured by their position in the traditional nuclear family-household, and the ability of their social contacts to provide, minimally, information about the availability of suitable employment. Just as informal access to employment allows women with heavy domestic obligations who are seeking paid work to identify jobs which accommodate those obligations, so informal recruitment operates to the advantage of employers by encouraging the creation of low cost, low security, part-time work for women.

We have only to understand the way these labour market conditions interact with social security regulations to appreciate the complex of influences whose effects support a traditional sexual division of labour. It is only if a woman's wage substantially exceeds the household's benefit claim that her assumption of employment *in place of her husband* is a logical outcome. This is unlikely to arise where women are offered only part-time work, yet their domestic responsibilities have traditionally been such that this is often the work they seek out.

While a woman with an extensive network of contacts is more likely to be presented with opportunities for employment, she is also likely to be married to a man with his own extensive social pattern. He will consequently be likely to have access at least to temporary opportunities for employment, while his resistance to any challenge to the established gender order will be strengthened by peer group pressure. In sum, loss of employment for a man might seem to encourage the renegotiation of gender roles in the sphere of paid employment, but there are strong social and labour market constraints which militate against it. Where a man finds secure employment after redundancy the idea of renegotiation does not arise, despite the fact that these men may be married to women whose part-time employment makes a significant and often much-needed contribution to household funds. For men who are less fortunate in finding work, any serious challenge to their notional bread-winner role may held at bay as long as job opportunities for *some* men continue to arise – and it is in the nature of temporary work that they will. Correspondingly, while women's domestic obligations *and* their labour market opportunities lead them into part-time jobs, there is every reason for both partners to remain in conformity with traditional gender roles.

## Conclusion

The field data presented in this chapter make clear the complexity of the redundant workers' social situations, and highlight the limitations of the social survey as a method of enquiry. It is clear that labour market histories collected through structured interviews represent an ordered abstraction from a complex reality. Respondents are engaged in multiple forms of economic activity which make it difficult to attribute a definite status at any given point. The fact that these statuses were often of relatively short duration means that being in and out of employment at a given moment is not a valid indicator of any sort of final outcome, for both may be part of an enduring pattern of fixed term employment punctuated by periods of unemployment.

The data also support the contention that, in loose labour markets, job acquisition is the result of a complex process shaped by labour search strategies on behalf of employers, the character of demand, the mutual relation of buyers and sellers to one another through their location in a common social milieu, the importance of intermediaries, as well as attributes such as age and skill which can be more easily measured by survey techniques.

This chapter has, however, widened the focus of enquiry into labour market experience to include household dynamics in an explanation of the way the economic activities of spouses are interrelated. Households as well as individuals are located in the labour market in the social structural sense, and individuals' labour market behaviour and futures will be influenced by their household circumstances. In our consideration of the household we have dealt here with what Homans termed many years ago the external organization of the group. The next chapter will examine its internal organization.

### Note

1 The White Paper on Social Security Reform (1986) proposes a minor change in this ruling.

# 7

# Domestic Circumstances

The previous chapter offered an explanation for the continuation of the traditional *domestic division of labour*, that distribution of roles in which the man has prime responsibility for providing the income to support the household whilst the woman has prime responsibility for domestic tasks. In this chapter the division of *domestic labour* is discussed, that is the way in which responsibility for and performance of household tasks is distributed among household members.

It has already been argued that a number of factors limit the probability of a woman taking over from her husband as the main earner in the household. Nevertheless, because of the chequered nature of the employment experience of many men after redundancy, we found a number of cases in which the woman *temporarily* continued in employment for a period during which her husband was seeking work. Below we consider the circumstances of one such household, a case which has been selected because it demonstrates a relatively high degree of male involvement in the domestic sphere.

Mr and Mrs Barton have 3 children, aged 6, 8 and 10, and live on a large council estate. After his redundancy, Mr Barton was continuously unemployed for 10 months. His wife had taken on an evening job as a factory cleaner about a year prior to her husband's redundancy. Despite the fact that her husband's benefit was reduced because she was working, Mrs Barton decided to keep the job, on the assumption that he would eventually find work (as he did). Later, the couple jointly decided that Mrs Barton should take on an additional part-time job as a home help. Mr Barton had originally suggested that his wife seek full-time work, thinking she might have a better chance than he had of finding a job. Mrs Barton was not enthusiastic: 'Well, I wasn't very keen on the idea of him doing the

This chapter draws substantially on data from a number of articles published elsewhere. See Morris (1984b, 1985a, 1985b).

housework because he wouldn't do it properly anyway, and I'd still have the lot to do after work.'

During the period in which Mrs Barton held two jobs and Mr Barton remained unemployed, Mrs Barton worked in the morning until 2 p.m. and in the evening from 5 until 8 p.m. The children had their midday meal at school and Mrs Barton would prepare their tea before going to work at 4.45, leaving the dishes for her husband. She would then return from work to cook an evening meal for herself and Mr Barton.

Although in theory Mr Barton took on the task of keeping the house clean, Mrs Barton was far from satisfied with the arrangement:

> He doesn't like housework anyway. I suppose he thinks it's not manly. He'd dust and tidy downstairs but he won't do upstairs because no one sees it, and he won't clean the front windows in case the neighbours see him. I don't mind housework myself as long as I've got time to do it, but I get irritable at the weekend when there's a backlog of things to do and he won't help. He just tells me to leave it. He doesn't understand that it's got to be done sometime. A full-time job would have been just impossible, but I think we'd have driven each other mad if one of us hadn't been out of the house for a bit in the day.

The couple shopped together while Mr Barton was out of work, a change from the previous pattern, because Mr Barton was available to drive his wife to the cheaper shops: 'I'd try to get him to come round the shelves with me and I was glad of the chance to show him the prices. I try to tell him now they've gone up but it doesn't sink in.' Nevertheless, Mrs Barton had total responsibility for budgeting and planning for the household's weekly needs.

The point about this particular case is that although the couple perceived the arrangement as a 'role swap' (albeit one expected to be temporary), in effect the woman continued to run the house, with minimal assistance from her husband. From his point of view, however, he had made a significant shift in the extent to which he participated in domestic labour within the home, in response to his wife's employment. He was also going against a well-established cultural tradition in the area. His comments may be taken as fairly typical, and were echoed by other men in similar situations: 'I'd spend sleepless nights. I'd get up and come downstairs at three in the morning, worrying that I'm the man and it's my job to see that everything's right between these four walls. If it's not, then it's my fault.'

Mr Barton, however, was more flexible in his behaviour than most. One woman, who had held a full-time job pre-dating her husband's redundancy by about a year, spoke of his 6 months out of work and whether he could use the time at his disposal to relieve her of the burden of domestic work:

> It wouldn't work. He wouldn't stand it and there'd be more quarrels than it's worth. I'd rather do the work myself . . . His mother used to throw it up at his family that she worked, you see, and he'd never let it happen here. Anyway I couldn't stand the strain. He'd be out with the horses most days (his friend runs a stables) and I'd get

home at tea-time to find nothing done. He wouldn't do a thing. 'What do you think I am?' he'd say, 'some old housewife?'. It killed him some days seeing me getting up for work, though. I'd like to have dropped the job just to show him, but we just couldn't do without the money.

## Male unemployment and domestic labour

Our basic reference in this discussion will be what we have termed the 'traditional' pattern of domestic responsibilities (Morris, 1983). It was clear from the data collected that there are culturally established spheres of responsibility which guide the division of domestic labour within each home, although some men will offer assistance in the 'woman's sphere' more readily than others.

It is possible to distinguish degrees of difference between households in the allocation of domestic responsibilities, and I have elsewhere used the terms traditional, traditional-rigid, and traditional-flexible (Morris, 1983) to denote such difference. Complete 'renegotiation' of domestic roles was rare.

Male participation in tasks culturally defined as women's work was usually in the nature of 'occasional help'. By this I mean reasonably frequent assistance which, though not in any way regularized, is not so rare as to be insignificant. The areas in which this kind of help is most commonly offered are preparation of food, transport for shopping, help with the dishes, minding and playing with children (for short periods). In contrast to these areas of activity we find that the woman is always solely responsible for washing and ironing clothes, bathing children, cleaning the house and planning the weekly shopping.

It is clear that a number of men have reacted to unemployment by slightly increasing their contribution to domestic labour but without significantly departing from the traditionally established pattern. In other words, while there may be an increase in general tidying about the house, help with the dishes, and possibly with food preparation, this in no way represents a major assumption of *responsibility* for domestic tasks by the man, and is in almost all cases viewed as a temporary arrangement. Mr and Mrs Barton provide a good example. On the other hand, in certain cases where the wife lost her own job at the same time as her husband's redundancy, there has actually been a contraction of the man's contribution to domestic labour because the wife was then considered to be fully available to carry out such labour herself.

It is possible, however, to see an increase in male participation in domestic tasks, again within the traditional framework outlined, in cases where the woman is not gainfully employed, and usually as a response to the man's boredom. This pattern is likely to be short-lived for two reasons: the woman usually finds 'interference' disruptive of her own routine, and judges the standard of work performed by her husband to be low; men soon tire of domestic work, often in response to irritation on the part of their wives, and anyway seem reluctant to make a commitment to regularly performing particular tasks. As one man put it: 'It got me down in the end. I'd have a go and then she'd come and do it all again anyway.'

An illustrative case study may be helpful here. Mr and Mrs Jones (aged respecitvely 27 and 25) have an 18 month-old child. Since his redundancy, Mr Jones has experienced 3 months' unemployment, followed by one year's retraining and a further year of unbroken unemployment. Mrs Jones took a shop assistant's job towards the end of her husband's retraining course, lasting a month into this second period of unemployment. She left the job because her earnings were deducted from her husband's benefit claim. During the 3 months she spent in paid employment, Mrs Jones continued to have full responsibility for running the home, while her mother-in-law looked after the child. During Mr Jones's time of unemployment and while Mrs Jones was employed, he was to have responsibility for the child, but in fact went with her up to his parents' home.

Although Mr Jones has difficulty filling the day, he takes minimal responsibility for domestic labour within the home. Rather, he gets out of bed as late as possible, reads, gardens, watches TV and spends occasional afternoons watching his father's video. He did some work on the house during his earlier spell of unemployment:

> Then you start slowing down. I'm often not up till 11 because there's nothing to do. At night you can sit up late watching TV and reading. You lose your energy, can't be bothered with anything. The wife thinks I could do more. At first I did, but you lose interest in everything. I'd rather go out and dig the garden – anything to get out of the house. She's always on the go and gets on at me to help, but if I try I do it wrong, or she does it again anyway, and gets annoyed at my interfering.

Mrs Jones gave much the same account:

> I like to do the housework myself really, because I need something to do, and don't want to be bored. If he does something I just do it again, but I still get cross to see him sitting about doing nothing and getting in the way . . . it disturbs my whole routine and my friends don't like to pop in any more with him here . . .

Mrs Jone's comments reflect a feeling which was common among women, that the home is their personal environment, and the running of it something which they simultaneously resent and value. It is their domain and the location of their identity. The very presence of a husband at home during the day is seen as disruption, and his taking over their customary tasks as a threat to their identity.

### The search for a 'work' identity

It is because the identity of each gender is so much determined by their position in the domestic division of labour that any assumption by men of women's work within the home can constitute a further threat to male identity, already damaged by loss of the bread-winner role. The response to unemployment on the part of the man may therefore be an extreme reaction against any blurring of the traditional division of domestic labour within the household. This reaction is maintained by his creating some kind of surrogate job. Many men dealt with the problems of redundancy in the short term by undertaking major structural alterations to the home, a domestic task culturally defined as masculine. This was a popular use of redundancy payment, and one encouraged by the DHSS ruling on supplementary benefit which denied eligibility to anyone with £2000 or over in savings, regardless of the source of the money (the amount has since been raised).

A number of men also became involved in household repair and conversion for friends and relatives. Such activity is non-domestic and analogous to 'an occupation', shading over into carrying out tasks for individual clients, for which some form of payment - not necessarily in cash - will be made. Alternatively, a man may accept paid employment which is not declared to the DHSS. In a few rare instances work will be full-time and long-term, but in most cases such bouts of employment are short-term and unpredictable. Slightly more common were cases which showed a pattern of fairly regular, though insecure and unpredictable, odd-jobbing for an employer, or for an individual client. The following case illustrates this sort of arrangement.

### A case of surrogate occupation

Aged respectively 29 and 27, Mr and Mrs Francis have two children, aged 4 and 8, and live on a large council estate. Apart from one spell of employment lasting 2 months, Mr Francis has been unemployed ever since his redundancy 18 months ago. Initially he spent a good deal of time completing alterations to the house. Now he spends as much of his day as possible out of the house - gardening, or welding in a small garden shed, doing odd jobs for relatives, neighbours and other contacts, and occasionally taking on a job jointly with a friend from school-days who lives nearby.

Mr Francis has a wide range of contacts in the area and a particular crowd of friends whom he sees regularly at a sports club. The only contribution he makes to the day-to-day running of the home is occasionally to prepare food and to provide transport when his wife goes shopping, although he maintains that if his wife could find a well-paid full-time job, he would gladly take over the running of the home. Mrs Francis, on the other hand, maintains that she could never consider a full time job:

> He's hopeless. Not domesticated at all. With some it would be all right, but not Jim. He just couldn't manage. My work takes longer now he's home because somehow if he's there he's always in the way and never helps.

Mrs Francis has recently taken on a part time job in her uncle's shop. During these afternoons at work she relies on a friend to collect the youngest child from nursery class, along with her own son, and to mind him until tea-time. In return, Mrs Francis takes her friend's child for the full day each Thursday while his mother works in her grandfather's shop.

What is remarkable about this case is that despite the recent change in the woman's employment status, and the long period of unemployment experienced by Mr Francis, the division of labour within the home has not been in any way affected and Mr Francis continues to organize his life as far as possible as if he were still in a full-time job. This arrangement maintains the gender identities of both spouses.

## The role of the social network

I have already noted that men who are involved in 'informal' economic activities tend to have a highly developed network of social contacts. I have also argued that with an extensive local network of acquaintances, among whom there is a high degree of mutual trust and regular contact and a collective code of behaviour, there will also be informal exchange of information and services, producing opportunities for economic activity, in both the formal and informal spheres. The secrecy which these networks facilitate is particularly important for those types of informal activity which are on the borders of legality.

The field data also suggest that different orientations to domestic labour coincide with different patterns of male social activity. Bott's work (1957) has suggested that there is a connection between the nature of a married couple's social networks and the degree of 'marital role segregation'. Role segregation, she maintains, will be most marked where the couple are deeply embedded in close-knit social networks. Harris (1969) has developed this idea and drawn attention to the vital importance of whether or not spouses, after marriage, retain membership of a single-sex primary group outside the family. Although there are aspects of Bott's work which are both confused and confusing (see Harris, 1969: 162–75; Morris 1985a), her central insight has been extremely valuable and has influenced more recent writing on similar issues (see Edgell, 1980). On the specific issue of the division of domestic labour, there are a number of questions which arise out of the field study in connection with Bott's hypothesis and its later development by Harris.

The most obvious question concerns the readiness or reluctance of a married man to assume tasks within the home which are culturally defined as women's work, and the extent to which his attitude may be reinforced by belonging to a predominantly male social network. We found a marked association between rigidly defined attitudes and behaviour regarding domestic labour where single sex groupings emerged and patterns of male social activity had a collective dimension (see Morris, 1985a).

The attitudes of women may, of course, be similarly influenced by the nature of their local social networks, but here the issues are not so clear-cut. On the one hand, a highly developed network of female friends and/or kin could provide domestic assistance, usually child care, which would free a woman to take on paid work outside the home. These contacts may also provide the information necessary to help women secure employment which accommodates domestic obligations. Nevertheless, as with men, there was a strong association between rigidity in the organization of domestic labour and the existence of a collective pattern of social contact.

Our findings suggest what one might intuitively expect to be the effect of different types of social contact. An individualistic pattern with a low level of internal connectedness, permitting no sense of group identity, and with no obvious means of bringing group pressure to bear in sanctioning behaviour, appears to leave people freer to *negotiate* a personally appropriate pattern of domestic organization, and is likely to reduce the incidence of couples rigidly conforming to the traditional division.

## Finance management and male unemployment

An important element in the response to redundancy, and one which again is closely related to social activity patterns, is the management of money within the home. When income falls, established systems for the control and management of money within the home will be challenged, and some re-negotiation of levels of need – both collective and individual – will be necessary. The result may well be marital conflict, which can perhaps be best understood in terms of the disjunction between two aspects of income: *household income*, the total income received by household members, and *domestic income*, that part of household income available for spending on collective items such as food, fuel and accommodation. Reductions in income require a reassessment of individual priorities against a notion of collective need, about which household members may not agree.

The traditional division of labour described earlier, which leaves the woman largely responsible for domestic affairs, together with a local normative tendency to attach priority to essential items of collective household expenditure, means that as household income falls the *proportion* devoted to these basic needs will rise. In other words, the vast majority of household income has to be made available for domestic income.

One result of this has been that in low-income households the control, management and budgeting of household income tends to be left to one person – usually the woman (see J. Pahl, 1983). In contrast, households with a higher disposable income, for example where both partners are employed and/or there are few children, a pooling of resources to which both members have notionally free access is more likely.

For many of the households studied in the field enquiry, even where the man found new employment, redundancy has meant a fall in income. At the Wave 1 interview, 53 per cent of all redundants in the sample claimed their standard of living had fallen. The way in which any particular household adjusts to these circumstances, and the effect on the marital relationship, will depend greatly on the man's pattern of social activity and the extent of his previous orientation towards the home and domestic activity. This is the case because the lower the household income falls, the less likely is the man to have an allowance for his own personal spending.

As we have seen, the Port Talbot area is characterized by a tradition of male social activity, engaged in independently of his wife, which revolves around pubs, and social and sports clubs and it is rare for married couples to share much of their social activities and contacts. This is not to suggest that women enjoy no independent social activity themselves, however. On the contrary, many women are located in a web of interlocking contacts with friends and/or relatives, but in contrast to the men this contact tends to focus on the home and rarely involves financial expenditure.

The point is that not only is there a strong tradition of independent male social activity which requires money, but also that for the most part women regard this as necessary for men, though not for themselves.

> Well, I've got the home and the children. I'm not one for gadding off out, but it's different for a man.

> I never go out myself, except for a special do. But men need to really, don't they? It's different for a woman. She sees her friends anyway. If he couldn't go out he just wouldn't see anyone.

The immediate response to a fall in household income is to cut back on the amount available for social spending, which will mean a curtailment of the man's social activity. Where the household income is controlled by the woman, as is usually the case when income is low, then the decision about how much money can be made available to maintain the man's social life is usually left to her.

A number of women make a considerable effort to ensure that there is a small amount of money so their husbands can go out for a drink, though usually without any explicit arrangement about a regular allowance of personal spending money to be made available to him. One woman explained her position: 'The Giro [Social Security cheque] came once a fortnight and I'd always try to make sure he'd get at least one night out of it. Even if it was only £2.' Or as another woman put it: 'I don't mind going short. I manage somehow. But I don't like to see him without money in his pocket. He's worth it.' Some men unquestioningly accept the decision, and take a pride in limiting their spending:

> There's many a time in the week I could do with a pint but I know if the wife gives it to me it comes out of the housekeeping so I make do with a cigarette – and that's not out of our budget either. I buy them from the bit my father gives me. I'd rather give up smoking than take it out of the house.

Others, however, will bring pressure to bear in a number of different ways. One woman clearly felt under considerable strain: 'If you're a good manager they think you're the Bank of England. It's not a question of me deciding if we can afford it. If he wants it he's got to have it . . . ' Even one woman whose husband would not consider making such demands remarked: 'I couldn't have gone on like that much longer. I didn't like to have all the financial responsibility when money was so short, and I worried about it all the time. I just used to wish I could hand it all over to someone else.'

One emphasis in much writing on domestic labour has been on the increased domestic burden for women where the money available for spending on domestic items has been reduced. Clearly, if a household continues to have a low domestic income, then the effort a woman must put into producing meals and repairing clothes will increase.

As well as the stress resulting from increased domestic labour, however, women are subject to the psychological pressures as a result of responsibility for according priorty to the various demands on the household purse. The task will be hardest where the man is unemployed, and where the absence of any money for his personal spending could eliminate all social contact and hence place a strain on the marriage.

## Social activity and household finance

So far this chapter has argued that an extensive pattern of social activities with companions of the same sex will lead to peer group pressure to conform to traditional gender roles. It is also the case that the higher the degree of male involvement in domestic life before redundancy, then the lower the potential for marital conflict. This is largely because home-centredness on the part of the man minimizes his personal spending requirements, encourages familiarity with collective needs, and thus, where income is low, reduces one major source of disagreement.

Different patterns of social contact will have implications for spending requirements which are more marked among men than women, because male social activity is dependent on spending taking place in the public rather than the private sphere. Thus, in the case of male unemployment the nature and extent of marital strain will vary according to a number of other factors, but can be linked to patterns of male social activity. We have suggested that a critical factor in contributing to marital harmony during male unemployment and/or low household income will be a high degree of home-centredness on the part of the man, and a low priority given to activities which require expenditure outside the home. This basic orientation will, in turn, be related to the degree of male involvement in extra-household social networks, and the characteristics of those networks.

## Three contrasting case studies

These general points about the management of household resources and variety in male spending patterns can be clearly illustrated by the use of case material.

*The Profligate Spender* Since his redundancy, Mr Lane has been in and out of work three times. His longest period in work lasted 6 months and so did his longest spell of unemployment. Mrs Lane gave an account of their financial wranglings:

> When we first married we just started out the way my mother had. He'd put his pay on the table, then keep asking for money . . . Then I said I just wanted an allowance. I worked out what I needed for rent and bills and food and a bit extra. I thought it would be better on my nerves . . . course, the redundancy pay just went straight off. But I knew the HP [hire purchase] would all be paid off so I got in quick and ordered some stuff from my mother's catalogue . . . It was the same when our make-up money came through. I struggled along till then, he was only bringing back £50 a week, and when the back pay finally arrived of course he just blew the lot. The corner shop and the pub were cashing him cheques, you see.

Mr Lane's life appears to revolve around a tight knit group of male friends who all congregate around the same pub. According to his wife:

> They all look after each other down there. If you go in and you're out of work the boys will buy you a drink. Even when he was working I've known Kev come back short because he's lent so-and-so money because he's out of work. Even if they go in with no money it's a good night. There's always credit for the regulars and the crowd there have built a little life together.

Clearly, Mr Lane's social commitments are largely independent of, and a threat to, his home life. This is not always the case.

*Delineation of Responsibilities* We mentioned Mr and Mrs Francis earlier in this chapter, and noted that apart from 2 months' work Mr Francis had been unemployed since redundancy. The domestic income in this household is made up of certain regular amounts of money, all of which go to Mrs Francis. These are supplementary benefit, child benefit for two children, and Mrs Francis's earnings from 4 afternoons a week in her uncle's shop. Mr Francis concedes that this financial arrangement offers men an easy way out but that he's hopeless with money. He receives no regular amount for his own spending, and occasionally will ask for money for tobacco or a newspaper. The decision lies with his wife about whether or not they can afford this: 'Well, I more or less accept what she says, though once in a while I might say to her, "Well, what the hell have you done with the money?"' Mrs Francis puts money aside regularly to cover the bills and allows herself a fixed amount for food, one big shopping expedition when the Giro (fortnightly benefit-payment cheque) arrives and a small one the following week. This amount will be reduced if there is an extra expense: 'I had to get the boy some shoes, they were in holes. But that left me short the next week. You just manage somehow. With my job I can just about do it.'

The small amounts Mr Francis receives for odd jobs or as 'expenses' finance his independent social life. Mrs Francis is sympathetic: 'I think it's more important to a man than to a woman. It doesn't bother me not going out.' Any larger payments for occasional work which Mr Francis might receive are usually divided equally between himself and his wife. The joint social life they had – a night out every two months – has been sacrificed.

This case illustrates a number of points which have already been made in this chapter: the woman has increased financial responsibility and with it greater strain because of the need to budget carefully, to make certain decisions about her husband's spending, and to meet irregular demands from an income which is barely sufficient to cover daily needs.

Mr Francis for the most part seems able to maintain a social life, though he has clearly reduced his spending substantially. Without his additional income, which remains separate from the domestic income, there might be considerably more tension in relations between the couple.

*The home-centred husband* Mr Amis has had a somewhat chequered work history since redundancy. He and his wife have three children aged 2, 6 and 9. Since they first married, the couple have found that Mr Amis is the better manager of money and Mrs Amis receives no regular allowance from him. They go shopping together and either he pays at the checkout or he leaves the money with his wife and goes off with the children. All other expenditure is handled by him, which of course means he has an effective veto over his wife's spending. Mrs Amis relies on child benefit to cover small items of daily expenditure, or she will ask her husband for money as a particular need crops up. Mr Amis commented that he has noticed a gradual change in his social life over the last 5 years or so. He now goes for a drink on a Sunday evening whereas earlier in married life he went out with male friends more often and spent more money with them. He has come increasingly to prefer a drive with his family, and perhaps with another married couple. In part because of a need to economize, and in part because of a wish to spend more time with his wife and children, Mr Amis's independent social activity has been significantly reduced.

Although the majority of households had adopted a pattern of female control of income, we found that control by the man was more successful, less stressful and more common where he had no highly developed pattern of independent social activity. This pattern was also found to coincide with the greatest degree of male involvement in the domestic sphere. Correspondingly, our findings suggest that the need for female control of household income is highest and the potential for marital conflict greatest where male social activity requires extensive and unpredictable spending. Such a pattern also coincides with a low degree of male involvement in the domestic sphere.

### Social support and additional income

Speculation about the possibility of the informal sector of the economy providing an alternative to formal employment (R. E. Pahl, 1980) has long been abandoned. There are nevertheless a variety of ways in which informal aid and association can play an important role for households confronted by falling income.

A number of couples received aid of various kinds from the relatives on both sides, each source of aid and the use to which it was put acknowledging the differences in gender roles already detailed in our discussion. For example, where a woman's mother provided assistance it was usually when her son-in-law was unemployed and took the form of some contribution towards collective needs, whether in cash or kind, or money or clothes for children. Where there were cases of a man receiving financial aid from his father it took the form of fairly small amounts of money for personal spending, for example: 'I always put a bet on for him on Saturdays and he gives me a couple of pounds to put on for myself. I put a pound on and keep the other for a pint.'

Similar points can be made about other 'informal' sources of income. Jan Pahl (1983) has drawn attention to the importance of earnings from the informal sector of the economy in connection with the allocation and control of income earned by different household members. Certainly there are men for whom informal economic activity provides a source of income which is at their disposal in a way that benefit, at least normatively, is not. Money earned in the informal sector may be used to finance some kind of male social activity; it may be earned with a view to meeting particular domestic costs, such as bills; it may be handed over entirely to the wife, who would almost invariably hand some back; or may simply be divided in half. We stress, however, that full-time long-term employment while receiving benefit was rare.

Sources of additional income for unemployed men varied from odd jobs for neighbours in return for a 'flagon of beer', assistance from male relatives, payment for odd-jobbing, occasional days or weeks of work for a local employer off the cards, or, much more rarely, longer-term undeclared employment.

We have already noted that opportunities for occasional earnings are usually distributed within a network of social contacts who enjoy a high degree of mutual trust. Where these conditions obtain it is possible that a man's social activity will become self-maintaining, being both a demand on personal spending and a possible source of income.

For women, the use of additional income tends unquestioningly to be used to increase housekeeping money, or to spend on children's needs. Common sources involve selling of some kind: being a mail order catalogue agent, organizing buying parties, selling Christmas hampers, or child-minding for an employed friend or relative. As with men, a network of contacts is necessary for such activities, but in contrast to men, women's earnings are more consistently put to domestic uses. Mr and Mrs Francis provide a good illustration of this arrangement.

It is clear that some of the tensions identified earlier in connection with male social activity and patterns of expenditure may be eased by additional income. The financial strain of social spending by the man can be relieved either by the woman's access, through her own network, to additional income for domestic spending, or the man's access through his own network to additional income for personal spending. Conversely, the home-centred man with less access to such resources will have less need of personal spending money and generally be more likely to be involved in domestic budgeting and domestic labour.

## Conclusion

This and the previous chapter have outlined the relationship between position in the labour market, access to employment and patterns of social activity, and have argued that these factors, acting together, will influence central aspects of domestic organization whose nature can be seen most clearly in household responses to male unemployment.

In chapter 6 the experience of broken employment histories in the wake of redundancy was discussed and related to the increased use of contractors by large-scale enterprise as a means of reducing the permanent workforce. It was also noted that men whose work histories were characterized by regular spells of short-term employment were most likely to be those with highly developed social networks.

In the present chapter we have noted that traditional attitudes towards the sexual division of labour also tend to be found among men with extensive social contacts. The coincidence of these two tendencies – resistance to change in the domestic sphere and the experience of intermittent employment – will make questioning the principles underlying the traditional sexual division of labour unlikely. Any erosion of established gender roles and the cultural patterns which have grown up around them will be inhibited as long as a man is able to perceive his unemployment as temporary, especially where full-time employment opportunities for women are also shrinking. Under these conditions a couple will be slow in adapting to the new reality of their situation.

Maintaining the kind of highly developed social network which is likely to lead to short-term waged work will pose a problem during periods of unemployment or low income. A man may endeavour to keep his social contacts by placing a higher priority on his own personal spending than on collective household expenditure, leaving his wife to cope alone with the problems posed by an inadequate income, while she also tries to curb her husband's spending.

A number of writers (see Molyneux, 1979, for review) have made the point that living standards can only be maintained in the face of falling income by an intensification of domestic labour. Where the sexual division of labour follows the traditional pattern, the burden will fall most heavily on the woman. Ironically, her labour will be intensified just at the time when the man, if unemployed, has lost his central sphere of activity.

An alternative response would be for the man to maintain an extensive social network with aid from friends and/or relations, or through opportunities for informal economic activity provided by that network. Indeed, aid from others, and work in the informal sector of the economy, can become a surrogate for waged employment. The contacts thus maintained may lead eventually to a new job.

Men with a less developed network of acquaintances seem likely to have a more flexible approach to the sexual division of labour. They may be more flexible in their response to unemployment but may also be more likely to experience long-term unemployment. The paucity of their social contacts will mean they have only minimal access to informal means of job acquisition. Conversely, a long period of unemployment for a man with a more extensive social network may diminish that network and, in doing so, eventually erode his resistance to assuming an increased share of domestic work.

In either case, home-centredness could have the effect of reducing the demands the man might make on the household income, and lead to his taking some share in domestic labour, thus reducing the strain on the woman. Equally, his presence in the home may disrupt her social and domestic routine, placing her under pressure from another source. Where the couple have had a largely segregated pattern of activities and contacts, the man's confinement to the home will be viewed by both spouses as an intrusion into the woman's sphere.

In sum, it seems that extensive social contacts, based on predominantly male social activity revolving around local social institutions, can not only act as a source of pressure which militates against the renegotiation of gender roles, but can also become a source of job information, a means of exerting influence in getting a job, and a way of finding opportunities for informal economic activity. These resources represent the means by which the redundant, with moral and material support from those who have retained secure employment, can continue to live with cultural premises which were established in a different era. Men with no such system of support may be the first to question these premises.

Because the recession of the 1980s was combined with a change in the level and character of labour demand, redundancy and unemployment constitute something more than a temporary, cyclical phenomenon at the aggregate level or personal misfortune for the individuals involved. They represent an assault on that way of life or culture which developed around the establishment of labour-intensive industrial production in the nineteenth century and which has persisted during the twentieth. Because, however, these changes in the labour market do *not* represent a collapse of the economic base, this assault is experienced only by some, even among the redundant, and will induce change only among those who lack the resources to resist it. Even here, however great the pressure, change is relatively slow. But simply because it is slow and partial, this does not mean that we are not witnessing the beginning of profound changes in a pattern of daily life which both our respondents and contemporary students of social life have come to take for granted.

# 8

# Getting By without Employment

The previous two chapters were based on field interviews with a random sample of all those in the main survey sample who were contacted in the second wave of interviewing in the spring of 1982, and who were under 55 and married. The findings of the previous two chapters have therefore concerned people who were in the process of adjusting to life outside BSC and among whom was to be found the whole range of market outcomes.

This chapter, in contrast, is based on 35 field interviews with a random sample of married men under 55, who were registered as unemployed when contacted in the second wave of survey interviewing. The focus of this chapter is therefore *unemployment* rather than redundancy. It concerns the domestic arrangements of those experiencing a long period of continuous unemployment.

By the time these men were interviewed in depth about their circumstances, sufficient time had elapsed for the cushion effect of the redundancy payments to have worn off, and since none was over 55 or was employed (except for 2 men recently employed), make-up pay was not an issue; there were no wages or pension to be made up. Almost all men had had stable pre-BSC work histories and reasonable service at BSC, so their experience of protracted unemployment was new. In fact the experience of protracted unemployment in a climate of economic recession was completely alien to them.

At the time the interviews were held, 32 husbands were unemployed, 2 had just resumed employment after a considerable period, and one had become a full-time student. Since leaving BSC the labour market experience of men had been varied, with 9 continuously unemployed, 11 unemployed

This chapter is based on research being prepared for submission as a doctoral thesis to the University of Wales. The research was supported by a linked studentship funded by the Economic and Social Research Council, grant award number L81 20861 SOC. The studentship was supervised by Professor C. C. Harris.

apart from participation in BSC-sponsored retraining, 10 having experienced unemployment, retraining and limited sporadic employment, and only 5 enjoying any stable employment (lasting up to one year) followed by continuous unemployment. The patterns of labour market experience after redundancy had consequences for the financial conditions of households, affecting the rate at which redundancy payments and savings were spent, as well as the period of eligibility for unemployment benefit. Exhaustion of entitlement to unemployment benefit, usually after a year of receipt, meant that households had to claim supplementary benefit. This caused difficulties for many households, not only because of the fall in income involved but also because of the complex regulations governing the claiming of benefit. Any attempt to understand what goes on inside the household in terms of its relations to its social environment must recognize that, for the unemployed, one of the most salient features of that environment is their relation to the *state* rather than to the *market*.

## The state apparatus

There are three main categories of state benefit which may be claimed in the United Kingdom: non-contributory benefits, such as child benefit; contributory benefits, such as unemployment or sickness benefit; means-tested benefit, such as supplementary benefit. It is the last of these which has received most criticism because of the complex framework of regulations governing its operation and application, which usually requires claimants to reveal very personal details of their private and domestic lives so that an assessment of their 'need' may be made. This process has been described as humiliating and demoralizing for all household members.

The legal framework for supplementary benefit, which in this study was the main benefit claimed, was established by the Supplementary Benefit Act 1976 as modified by the Social Security Act 1980.[1] The vast array of rules and regulations make full understanding of the system beyond the ability of the average person. This, together with the stigma associated with many elements of means-tested benefits, deters many from making claims.

The amount of supplementary benefit awarded to a claimant is calculated on a formula relating requirements to resources and the net award is the former minus the latter in most cases. The overal assessment of a claimant's requirements is based on three specific types of assessment: normal requirements (or scale rates) for basic daily needs of household members; additional requirements which may be granted for special needs of household members arising from ill-health or disability; and housing requirements which cover rent, rates and assistance with repayment of mortgage interest, but not capital. For most supplementary benefit claimants the basic scale rates apply for the first year, after which a long-term addition is payable. The only exceptions to this are households headed by an able-bodied person who is long-term unemployed. This actually makes the long-term unemployed less well-off than others reliant on supplementary benefit for income.

On the resources side of the calculation, consideration is given to income and capital. What constitutes income is complex. It includes many non-contributory benefits (notably child benefit) as well as any earned and unearned income, contributions such as maintenance payments, and regular income from kin towards living expenses (except the first £4 which is ignored). Occasional gifts of up to £100 are usually disregarded but one-off payments by charitable organizations or relatives towards clothing and fuel bills may be treated as capital. Capital includes money savings, title to money, valuables acquired for investment purposes, and property apart from the claimant's home, though not usually cars. However, the aggregate total of all household capital assets must be less than the maximum set by legislation, which at the time in question was £2,500. (It is reviewed annually.) In addition, the DHSS operates with a concept of 'notional capital', meaning that should a claimant be believed to have 'unreasonably disposed' of capital for the purposes of claiming, it can be treated as capital unspent.

With respect to housing costs, the system of operation was complicated by the introduction of the new Housing Benefits Scheme in November 1982 (Social Security and Housing Benefits Act 1982: the Partial Start). This initially applied to council tenants reliant on supplementary benefit but by April 1983 was extended to all claimants. The new scheme, administrated by local authorities in conjunction with the DHSS, usually operated to allow a 100 per cent rebate on the rent/rates of council tenants and was administered in such a way that the portion of benefit award included as 'housing requirement' was deducted from the final award payable to claimants who were no longer responsible for the payment of rent or rates.

Although the 1970s had witnessed some bitter debates over the injustices of the system, the inadequacy of basic scale rates and the operation of additional requirements and exceptional needs payments (a discretionary award payable for the replacement of bedding, clothing and domestic items),[2] the newly returned Conservative government of 1979 embarked on a series of changes which were to cause concern for the future. The provisions of the 1980 Social Security Act (and the effect of the 1982 Social Security and Housing Benefit Act) were particularly harsh for the long-term unemployed. Despite the debates and official reports of the 1970s, scale rates were in fact reduced in 'real' terms by the 5 per cent abatement clause (November 1980), there was no extension of the long-term addition to the unemployed, and no apparent simplification of the procedures for claiming exceptional needs payments. The net effect was to make the long-term unemployed worse off than other claimants and to tighten the conditions governing exceptional needs. These were severely restricted by the 1980 Act, payments for clothing and footwear being considered only if the need had arisen 'otherwise than by normal wear and tear' or by children outgrowing them. Hence, the benefit income received by claimants was now required to meet all expenses except housing costs, although purchasing power had been eroded.

## The impact of the social security system on households

Some 23 of the 35 households studied were reliant on supplementary benefit for income, and due to the modifications in legislation faced certain difficulties. All but 2 households had experienced problems claiming discretionary exceptional needs payments, especially for clothing and footwear for themselves and their children and for the replacement of domestic items such as cookers or beds. Enquiries relating to claims had often been automatically dismissed by benefit officers with no explanation given to the claimant of the new regulations of the 1980 Act. Respondents were left feeling bewildered and with no idea of their rights. In order to meet needs, many relied on shopping from mail order companies (with careful budgeting), Provident Society loans, credit from small local retailers and aid from family and friends, repayment of which caused considerable additional financial strain. The lack of explanation by benefit officers and the lack of understanding by claimants meant that few formal appeals were made, and there was therefore little challenge to policy decisions made by local DHSS officers. Many respondents were concerned about the way DHSS inspectors/visitors used their discretionary powers and claimed they made judgements about the needs of claimants which were often based on unsound and unjust assumptions. Indeed, the whole issue of 'discretion' had been one raised forcibly in the 1970s (Donnison, 1977) and was a focus of the legislation embodied in the Conservative government reforms of the early 1980s.

The determination of need is an extraordinarily difficult matter for both DHSS staff and the social scientist. All the families in this sample, whether or not they accepted the decisions of benefit officers, perceived the benefit they received as barely adequate. Financial survival in most cases involved 'robbing Peter to pay Paul'. This caused severe pressure, especially for women who, since the total flow of income into the household (household income) usually equalled income spent on collective needs (domestic income), assumed increasing responsibility for the management and control of income at a time when there was little scope for mistake or choice. Although the payment of housing costs before November 1982 was a high priority for all households (as shown in the following section), many admitted that rent or rates payments had been forgone on occasions to purchase items such as shoes for the children or to pay a fuel bill. Reduced purchasing power and the effect of the housing benefit scheme deprived households of this option as well as denying them the right to arrange the disposal of income as they saw fit or as necessity dictated. Thus, the cumulative effects of both the 1980 and 1982 Acts served to reduce the freedom of households in the allocation of an already limited household income and to reduce the official and legal avenues by which exceptional needs payments might be claimed.

In consequence, aid from friends and relations, although not involving large sums of money, was vital to many households. However, as previously noted, financial help can be treated as either income or capital to the household by the DHSS. The aid received by many households (usually for food, fuel, clothing/footwear, tobacco and confectionery) should have been in some instances declared. Those not declared could strictly have been deemed illegal exchanges. Unemployment is associated in both literature and the popular mind with lack of structure, an in some ways unwelcome *freedom*, a movement of the unemployed person from the world of formal regulation associated with work to the informal world of family and neighbourhood. For those dependent on supplementary benefit, however, what we find is an intrusion of the formal into the informal, an increase in regulation, a means by which the state can, in Donzelot's phrase, 'police the family' (1979).

It was fashionable at the beginning of the 1980s to hypothesize that higher rates of unemployment would lead to the substitution of informal for formal economic activity, some of which would be 'black' (illegal) as well as informal. Here we have a case of an increase in illicit activity as the result of the extension of the formal sphere, in an attempt to control exchanges along exactly those networks thought to be important for informal types of work. Such attempts are not likely to be wholly successful, since in the event of a crisis, especially over the needs of children, kin and friends would lend support and provide 'gifts'. From the standpoint of those giving and those receiving the aid, any reporting would detract from its value both in real terms and in terms of the cultural prescriptions and values that surround the act of giving and receiving within the context of a personal (that is, private/informal and not public/formal) relationship.

State intervention and control also affected households' use of the money they received in redundancy payments. Due to the capital ceiling above which claimants are debarred from drawing supplementary benefit, anyone in receipt of substantial redundancy awards (three-quarters of this sample received between £1,000 and £5,000) faced the problem of being ineligible for benefit at the time of redundancy. If, however, they had been deemed to have disposed of the 'capital' in order to become eligible to claim benefit, the concept of 'notional capital' could have been brought into play. The onus of proof lay with the claimant to show that the money was 'necessarily and well spent' and to account for it by receipts whenever possible, especially for large items of expenditure. Difficulties were experienced here. Few respondents had realized the importance of keeping receipts and correspondence for inspection, and all were angered by the necessity of accounting for expenditure of money to which they believed themselves entitled as compensation for lost jobs. Households often experienced considerable delay in receiving their benefit entitlement as a result and one household was actually refused benefit. A common feeling among respondents was that the maximum capital ruling was a great injustice when applied to redundant workers, who through no fault of their own found themselves reliant on supplementary benefit for income. It seemed to them that their redundancy payments were treated by DHSS officers as social security payments in advance, rather than compensation for loss of employment.

## Patterns of household consumption

For 70 per cent of the sample, the only source of income was from state benefits, especially supplementary benefit (around 65 per cent). The net effect of reliance on such benefit evens out the income available to households possessing the same objective attributes. Those who had higher working incomes had potentially the most to lose, but no household living on supplementary benefit could express satisfaction at their level of income nor be described as well provided for.

We have noted that there is an inherent difficulty in defining 'need'. The degree of difficulty lessens, however, the lower the standard of living becomes. It was not surprising, therefore, that data supplied by respondents on their financial priorities showed a considerable degree of agreement. As a result it was possible to construct a model 'hierarchy of needs' in which items of expenditure were ranked according to the respondents' priorities. This hierarchy is set out below. Each item was considered of great importance by households; items of daily consumption towards the bottom of the hierarchy are still important, but become *relatively* less so as available income falls.

The rationale underlying the model suggests that the items accorded greatest priority are those related to the basic collective needs of the household, that is, shelter, warmth and food. Once these are supplied, priority is given to safeguarding certain individual or partially collective needs, especially those of children, and then to the more peripheral aspects of collective need. It is interesting that the collective needs of households are generally given higher priority than individual needs, with the exception of children, and those of the parental generation are accorded relatively low priority. It follows that the lower the order of priority, the greater the extent to which expenditure on each item can be curtailed without causing too great a disruption or threat to the household as a collectivity. The higher the order of priority of an item, the greater will be the effect of the need going unfulfilled.

| Priority | Ability to live without | |
|---|---|---|
| High | Low | Rent/mortgage/rates. |
| ↑ | ↓ | Fuel bills. |
| | | Food and day-to-day living expenses. |
| ↑ | ↓ | Childrens' needs (school, clothes, entertainment). |
| | | Clothing and footwear. |
| | | Hire purchase and other outstanding debts/commitments. |
| ↑ | ↓ | Emergencies or unforeseen expenditure. |
| | | Replacement or repair of household items. |
| ↑ | ↓ | Household repairs. |
| | | Personal spending money. |
| Low | High | Leisure, entertainment and holidays. |

One must assume that choosing to reduce expenditure in the more peripheral areas was a rationally motivated action with the principles of household survival prompting the choice between options available. It can be argued that in reality such options are restricted and that household survival rather than freedom to choose how to consume becomes the foremost objective. Almost all households had cut down on most categories of expenditure. Households differed not so much in *what* they curtailed or cut, but in the degree to which this took place. As a consequence, some households experienced greater difficulties in budget management than others. To analyse the nature of these experiences, the following typology of hardship categories was constructed.

1 *Persistent needs crisis* – a continued battle to make ends meet which is never quite won.
2 *Intermittent crisis* – occasional but recurring crises making financial management difficult.
3 *Severe curtailment* – significant reduction in almost all areas of expenditure, especially severe in the peripheral aspects of consumption.
4 *Relatively minor curtailment* – curtailment is limited to the categories of expenditure with lowest priority; or has slightly affected the less important areas; or has not made any real changes which affect the household overall, or financial management has been aided by access to ancillary income, reducing the need for major cutbacks.

It appears that households least affected have certain identifiable characteristics. These households tend to be at a later stage in the developmental cycle (often containing independent offspring), include at least one person in full-time employment and/or have access to ancillary forms of income. Some 17 households were allocated to categories 1–3 and may be regarded as facing *very* real hardship: 1 faced persistent needs crisis,

2 intermittent crisis and 14 severe curtailment. The remainder varied from those experiencing moderate forms of hardship to those having apparently few problems but all had experienced some renegotiation of priorities. Table 8A2 (appended to this chapter) shows the distribution of those experiencing problems and worsening situations in relation to different types of expenditure among those classified as in hardship and those not. The table reveals the expected patterns of distribution: difficulty and deterioration appear more frequently in the overall category of hardship.

Why some households should suffer more than others depends upon a range of mediating variables which correlate with each other, as well as upon the level of household management skills displayed. Hardship results from a constellation of factors including the amount of redundancy award, length of BSC service, level of BSC income, age of husband, household composition and the ages of dependent children, skill level, post-BSC labour market experience, reliance on supplementary benefit as sole income and hence the length of time unemployed. It was also associated with housing tenure, since council tenants appeared to suffer more hardship (a possible transitional effect of the Social Security and Housing Benefit Act 1982 in its Partial Start phase).

The most striking fact to emerge from the analysis was that hardship appeared to be associated with households headed by younger men with shorter BSC service and lower levels of employment income. Hardship was also associated with the presence of dependent children in the household, the period of time spent unemployed, reliance on state benefits (particularly supplementary benefit) and was related to post-BSC labour market experience, especially to retraining offered to BSC employees on redundancy. Those who had acccepted retraining, especially if it led to employment, had fared better on the whole than those with continuous unemployment and/or sporadic employment with no retraining.

The issue of hardship cannot be analysed in absolute terms. Distinctions between categories must be tempered by the recognition that the quality of life had been eroded to some degree for all households. What constitutes hardship is a function of a particular historical moment coupled with a unique set of individual experiences. However, it is possible for subjective accounts to be translated into general categories for analysis to produce objective measures. This has been attempted by the development of the 'hierarchy of needs' and the classification of hardship experiences, which has been validated by relating it to the incidence of expressed difficulties in meeting certain critical household survival needs.

## Income allocation and control

Needs cannot be viewed as constant since they can change over time and in response to external events. Authors such as McIntosh (1981), following the formulations of Leiss (1978) and Grevet (1976), discuss the objective and subjective moments which influence our perceptions of need. The development of a theoretical approach in the study of poverty which is sensitive to the problems raised by the attempt to define needs and to deal with the wider issues of power and influence associated with any study of the allocation of resources, would be a mammoth task; yet it is possible to see signs of progression towards such a system in the work of Scanzoni (1979), Scanzoni and Polanko (1980), Scanzoni and Szinovacz (1980), Straus (1978) and Cromwell and Olsen (1975) in exchange and negotiation theory, and in the work of authors such as Safilios-Rothschild (1976) and Edgell (1980) on family power, as reflected in studies of resource allocation within the household (J. Pahl, 1980, 1983; McIntosh, 1981). These have influenced the model of income allocation used here.

Analysis of the allocation of household income between uses revolves around the complex theoretical issues noted above. Since it is difficult to combine all elements into one model, the majority of income allocation studies have derived models from observations and accounts of what happens to household income. Although including analytic elements they do little to account for the social processes which produce these patterns of income flow. The models of Gray (1979), J. Pahl (1980, 1983), McIntosh (1981) and Morris (1984b) were all found to be inadequate for this study, principally because of their failure to distinguish and combine the elements of both income allocation and power/decision-making. Nonetheless, previous models provided the *basis* for the formulation of a theoretical model, though this basis only became apparent through an analysis of their aetiology.

It became evident that consideration had to be given to the number of income sources, who gave the household access to income sources, the principles upon which money was allocated to different uses, the type of disbursement, who took responsibility in decision-making, who was principal in disbursement and who was principal on a mundane day-to-day level. Explanations of the processes involved made it necessary to make fine distinctions between different types of allocation and disbursement system which had been hidden in the previous models by the term income 'flow'.

A summary of the elements embodied in the model used in the present study is set out in table 8.1. A permutation of these elements yielded 432 logically possible types of system of allocation and disbursement, but only 13 of these types were found among the households under study. These 13 types were capable of combination in a way that enabled this classification to be used in analysis. Full details were obtained from each household on past (pre-redundancy) and present (post-redundancy) systems of income allocation and disbursement. The relevant types together with the pre- and post-redundancy distributions appear in table 8.2.

Comparison of the pre- and post-redundancy pattern revealed that 14 households had not changed their patterns of income management. The

Have

category experiencing least change involved single allocation and unitary control by someone other than the only income recipient (type Aii: see table 8.2).

Patterns of income management had altered in 19 households. The types of change involved are set out in table 8A1. (This table is appended to this chapter and must be read in conjunction with table 8.2 in the text below.) Of the 16 *types* of change involved, 13 were specifically attributable to the effects of unemployment.

The distribution between types in the *pre-redundancy phase* reveal that the predominant pattern was type A, especially Aii. Type Aii indicates a situation where the husband is chief income recipient, there is single allocation, unitary disbursement and the wife has responsibility as principal in both or, as our respondents would have put it, 'the Mam is Chancellor of the Exchequer'. The next most frequent type was Bi: the husband is the main breadwinner, there is single allocation, two people are separately responsible for different types of disbursement (dyadic segregated), the husband having overall control and establishing the *modus operandi* for the household, the wife having day-to-day responsibility and control.

*Post-redundancy* modifications reveal that type A was preferred, especially category Aii (which increased from 10 to 16 househlds). Types D and E also increased slightly. The most striking feature of the post-redundancy distribution was the total disappearance of type C households, that is, of those with joint allocative and dyadic-segregated disbursement functions.

There were two main kinds of *movement* within and across types. Movements from type B were all from Bi to Aii, illustrating a change from husband to wife in the 'orchestration' of power. The limitation of income (especially felt in households with young children) promoted recognition that greater 'unitary' control was needed to make most efficient use of household income, and thus the pattern of wife control emerged. As household income approached domestic income the room for manoeuvre decreased and emphasis on the careful management of resources increased in importance. As a result there was an accentuation of the household manager role of the wives and their status within the household was enhanced; although husbands still expressed interest in financial matters, they no longer took responsibility. This was also the case in the changes from type C. Here the main movements were to type Aii and to types D or E, illustrating a change in the ethos of partnership in budgeting to a more 'corporate' type of control.

Across the board some changes were in themselves minor but sufficient to cause identifiable differences. Not all individual movements can be analysed here but, in the context of diminished income resulting from unemployment, two paterns emerged after redundancy. First, a movement to unitary control usually by the wife, and second, a movement towards increased corporateness: to more joint access, control and/or distribution. It seems

TABLE 8.1 The key elements of the typology of income allocative and distributive functions

| | | | *Who is principal?* | | |
|---|---|---|---|---|---|
| *Number of income sources* | *Allocation* | *Disbursement function* | *in allocation* | *in disbursement* | *in day-to-day control* |
| One *or* Many | Singe (S) *or* Joint (J) | Unitary (U) *or* Dyadic segregated (DS) Dyadic joint (DJ) | Orchestration: Administrative/ policy level. One who sets *modus operandi* for household | Person in overall charge of control in outlay of collective expenditure | Implementation: Executive officer level - person follows established boundaries and spirit of house-hold policy as already laid down |

TABLE 8.2 Income allocation and disbursement models

| Type letter | | Number of income sources | Allocation | Disbursement function | Who is principal? in allocation | in disbursement | in day-to-day control | Incidence pre-redundancy | | post-redundancy | |
|---|---|---|---|---|---|---|---|---|---|---|---|
| | | *1* | *2* | *3* | *4* | *5* | *6* | | | | |
| A | i | 1 | S | U | CIR | CIR | CIR | 2 | | 2 | |
| | ii | 1 | S | U | Alter | Alter | Alter | 10 | 12 | 16 | 18 |
| B | i | 1 | S | DS | CIR | CIR | Alter | 6 | | 3 | |
| | ii | 1 | S | DS | None | None | Both | 0 | 6 | 1 | 4 |
| C | i | 1 | J | DS | CIR | CIR | Alter | 2 | | 0 | |
| | ii | 1 | J | DS | CIR | Alter | Alter | 3 | 7 | 0 | 0 |
| | iii | 1 | J | DS | None | None | Both | 2 | | 0 | |
| D | | 1 | J | DJ | None | None | Both | 1 | | 3 | |
| E | i | 2 | J | DS | CIR | CIR | CIR | 0 | | 1 | |
| | ii | 2 | J | DS | CIR | CIR | Alter | 0 | | 1 | |
| | iii | 2 | J | DS | CIR | Alter | Alter | 2 | 5 | 0 | 6 |
| | iv | 2 | J | DS | None | None | Both | 3 | | 4 | |
| F | | 2 | J | DJ | None | None | Both | 2 | | 2 | |

Key: column 2: S = single, J = joint; column 3: U = unitary, DS = dyadic segregated, DJ = dyadic joint; columns 4 to 7: CIR = chief income recipient, Alter = other than CIR

that, in their capacities as orchestrators of household policy, husbands lost influence after redundancy, as well as losing some responsibility for disbursement. Yet in some fashion they gained more say on the day-to-day level, perhaps due to their presence in the home which enabled them to influence aspects of domestic operation in which they had previously been unable to intervene.

Under 'normal' circumstances, spouses would accept each other's expertise in their respective spheres of responsibility. Income-producing work and being the chief earner were sources of power to husbands, but redundancy involved an attrition of this power base. The established gender ideology of male superiority persisted none the less.

Before redundancy, women exercised considerable control within the domestic sphere but the *de facto* superiority of the wife did not detract from the *de jure* superiority of the husband, based on his role in the public area of paid work. The wife's dominance was only real within the sphere of her responsibility, the home. Post-redundancy, protracted unemployment allowed husbands greater access to the home and gave them the opportunity to realise the level of their wives' power and autonomy in the use of income and the allocation of their time. Financial limitations made the wife's role more visible at a time when the husband had lost his primary function as bread-winner and was reduced to receiving state benefits at a fixed and low rate over which he had no control. Gender ideology prevented men from taking over control of the domestic sphere, however, and they were therefore forced to accept a situation in which the person who determined living standards was not the chief income recipient since the primary income disburser and the person with day-to-day control was increasingly the wife. However, although in a situation of unemployment the status of wives is enhanced, it also places them under severe pressure by increasing the burden of responsibility for financial management as well as for 'tension management' in the marital relationship.

Overall changes across categories reflected the necessity for increased control in the form of either unitary control or joint responsibility. Changes of the latter type suggest a movement towards a different conception of jointness, a movement away from 'both mucking in' to a more corporate form of control. The movement to both unitary and corporate control required the existence of a strong and stable relationship between the spouses if those movements were not to generate conflict.

Often the very foundations of relationships required renegotiation (conscious and otherwise) to ease the changes in power relations indicated by changes between the types. This undoubtedly caused great stress for women in particular, since, through the housewife role, women add to the very means by which households survive in the long term. It is a paradox, not a contradiction to argue that although material deprivation strains the relationship between spouses, it can act to strengthen it. (See McKee and Bell, 1985.)

## Consequences for the roles of spouses and the division of domestic labour

If there is a movement under the pressure of subsistence living at the level of both priorities and budgeting control, to a sort of 'familial collectivism', that is, to individuals co-operating to achieve collective goals at the expense of the realisation of individual interests, then one might expect the division of domestic labour in *these* families had also been the subject of substantial renegotiation. Such a prediction ignores, however, the strength of the traditional domestic division of labour and the connection between it, gender ideology and the division of household tasks.

The sexual division of labour in society operates to allocate primary responsibility in accord with what would generally be considered traditional values; the separation of the public sphere of paid employment from the private sphere of the home, and their allocation to husbands and wives respectively. Along with this division go all the attendant differences in access to resources and hence in the distribution of power. Despite some evidence of change at the ideal level, feminists writers are correct in their fundamental premise: however one accounts for the sexual division of labour in society, the fact of patriarchy cannot be denied.

It is not merely a question of what domestic tasks men and women actually do but what responsibilities they accept. It is very uncommon to find a working man with high levels of responsibility for the home but very common to find a working woman with such responsibility. Previous studies have devised sophisticated checklists of domestic tasks and shown who performs them. Their results have been cited, depending on theoretical perspective, to support or deny particular points concerning the debate on the nature of modern marriage and the sexual division of labour. If, however, we keep distinct the sexual division of labour in society and the sexual division of *domestic* labour in the household, it becomes evident that it does not really matter whether husbands actually do dust or shop; what *does* matter is whether or not they conceive any form of domestic labour as their responsibility. The answer must be that they neither can nor do accept such responsibility, even during long-term unemployment when actual involvement in task performance often increases. In the present sample female economic activity was limited in the pre-redundancy period, most wives being housewives and responsible for the domestic sphere. Help by husbands tended to be peripheral and most regular in the more 'masculine' areas of repair and maintenance, otherwise being restricted to assistance with washing dishes and child care. The shift system in operation at BSC affected both the availability of husbands to undertake domestic tasks and the routines of wives; it provided husbands with the choice of whether or not to participate in domestic work but imposed certain restrictions on the wives' routines.

An examination of who performed each domestic task indicated that, after redundancy, there was generally increased participation on the part of men, particularly in cases where wives were employed full-time. Otherwise, participation was still peripheral or masculine in its nature. Significant increases in participation in cooking, cleaning and laundry took place only in households where the woman worked, or in households where the health of household members so dictated (infirm mother, ill health of the wife and a handicapped child). Otherwise, the division of primary responsibility continued as before. This was further substantiated by the analysis and classification of households, using the types of domestic organization developed by Morris (1983) and referred to in chapter 7. Morris's classification – traditional, traditional rigid, traditional flexible and renegotiated – provided a most valuable corroboration of the continued existence of a division of responsibility between spouses. After redundancy, some 13 households displayed traditional patterns of organization, 9 displayed traditional rigid, 7 traditional flexible and only 6 renegotiated, which included 2 'role reversals'. (Morris found a distribution of 16, 14, 6 and 4 respectively.)

Thus 21 of the 35 exhibited either a traditional or traditional rigid pattern, *despite* the fact that in an itemized account of male participation after redundancy, there was evidence of increased task participation and performance. The surface contradiction, exposed in many previous studies, can be easily reconciled when the distinction is made between the *fact* that domestic tasks are often undertaken by men on a regular basis, and the *degree* to which any open or conscious movement has been made towards male identification with domesticity and the assumption of domestic responsibility.

In this study only 2 households described their situation as a 'role swap' but full analysis of those households revealed that this was not strictly accurate, a point also made by Morris in her study. The cognitive and normative leap from the traditional framework had not been made and what was described as a role swap was really the most extreme point on the behavioural continuum of male participation. Such a degree of participation arose from the need to preserve and maintain the household as a functioning unit with acceptable standards of living and was a style of organization viewed as a compromise, and as a temporary *expedient* only.

What appeared to be happening was a confusion of the culturally established patterns of activity of husband and wife, since occupational opportunities were becoming even more restricted for men than women. People were being pushed, therefore, by circumstances to make a cultural transition which could not be fully achieved in the short term. In the long term, the households of the unemployed face a crisis in that many assumptions appropriate to 'normal' circumstances are being challenged, and with them the assumptions underlying traditional marriage itself. Anything which encouraged the belief that things would one day return to normal was enthusiastically received, and responses to the challenges of household predicaments tended to draw on pre-crisis patterns of living since these were familiar and unthreatening. Yet sometimes these patterns were not appropriate to the new context, which was not always as temporary as was at first believed. The 14 cases of modified organization, traditional flexible and renegotiated, represented considerable leaps forward for households and often brought novel problems for spouses, resolution of which was a matter of negotiation whose success was contingent upon the quality of the relationship and the personalities of those concerned.

Of course, certain features of unemployment can cause problems in all households, whether household organization has been modified or not, especially for wives. The degree to which households were affected depended on the wives themselves, on the degree of sharing already established in the relationship and on the existence of surrogate 'employment' (see chapter 7). Increased husband participation on a day-to-day level did not include increased responsibility or control. This caused an uncomfortable situation between spouses, especially for wives who remained responsible for certain things yet felt they were losing direct and full control. In a traditional/traditional rigid context with restricted husband participation, the wife retained control at the cost of having to carry out her role with reduced resources (often intensifying task performance) with a husband continually 'under her feet'. Either way the wives incurred costs.

Oakley (1974) views housewife autonomy as theoretical rather than real but the constraints she illustrates are not incompatible with a considerable degree of housewife autonomy within the sphere of activity which they define. This is not to deny that women perform their duties under pressure but to emphasize that the doctrine of primary responsibility ensures the housewife's autonomy since she can choose how to meet the various demands made upon her. Having a husband at home interferes with this, as men often attempt to retain a sense of control by seeking participation in the domestic sphere, and in the process disrupt routines, question task performance and comment on methods. At the same time, they come to recognize the importance and value of good household management and the nature of housewife autonomy. Having been used to more formal work practices and being responsible to someone who monitors their work, men find this situation disconcerting and in view of the woman's greater experience within the home feel themselves to be at a disadvantage. The nature of the husband–wife domestic relationship under normal circumstances approximates to the provision of vital services. Husbands receive services and may praise or complain but usually do not 'buy-in' such services due to any poor performance on the part of wives. However, in the context of male unemployment, tensions abound as *he* stays clear of involvement but interferes and comments, or gets involved and is subject to being directed and monitored by *her*.

This was very marked in the households of shift workers since the shift system demanded considerable flexibility in domestic tasks and routines. The fact that some tasks can be performed independently while others impinge on and affect each other, gives men the impression of disorganization and can lead to their actually disrupting the situation by attempting to interfere, not realizing that by far the greatest disruptive element is their presence in the first place. When husbands do succeed in helping, they find themselves subject to unfamiliar standards of performance imposed by their wives. Yet these household standards are not like industrial ones, with accepted and specifiable elements, but seem subjective and personal, intrinsic to the wife's reputation as a housewife, constituting her chief source of identity. The man's apprehension of this situation is modelled on his work experience so the wife is seen as acting as 'boss', setting standards, monitoring activity; the pull–push of the situation produces tension in the relationship. Men *feel* they should have more say simply because of their gender (a legitimate source of authority on a traditional base), but traditionally women have normative and practical control in the domestic sphere because it is their primary responsibility. Here lies the heart of the whole problem. What was notable among unemployed steelworkers was neither any change in the nature or specificity of gender roles, nor any significant blurring of the boundaries between male and female spheres of responsibility, but a confusion of spheres and a disclosure of some of the pre-requisite conditions under which radical change could take place.

## Conclusion

This chapter has attempted to illustrate the consequences of long-term unemployment for households and the various ways in which they have adapted in order to survive in the circumstances thrust upon them. Analysis has developed on two levels. The first concerns the more visible areas of income (sources, dispersal, allocation), domestic consumption and organization patterns. The second level concerns the covert consequences of change at the first level: changes in marital role performance and power relations, compounded by the confusion created by attempts to safeguard not only the household but a traditional way of life under adverse and inappropriate conditions.

It can be seen that unemployment and reliance on state benefits has a profound affect on living standards, on priorities in consumption and on the material well-being of households. The implications of these modified patterns are perhaps even more significant when analysed from the perspective of the couples involved. Whether it be income receipt, allocation, decision-making practices or domestic role performance, there were considerable modifications in the balance of marital power and in the power bases of the spouses. Such changes serve to put more power and influence in the hands of wives, while at the same time placing on their shoulders an almost intolerable burden of responsibility for household survival.

## Notes

1 The law governing supplementary benefit is summarized in *The Law Relating to Supplementary Benefit and Family Income Supplement* (known as the Yellow Book), available at local DHSS offices and public libraries. All references to statute and regulations apply to the period under study and some aspects may have been modified by recent legislation.

2 See DHSS (1978). This report was hailed as a major post-war policy document. However, many recommendations were never implemented due to the change of government in 1979.

## Appendix

APPENDIX TABLE 8A1 Types of changes in models pre- to post-redundancy

| | *Model changes* | | | | |
|---|---|---|---|---|---|
| *Number of cases*[a] | *Pre-redundancy (from)* | | *Post-redundancy (to)* | | *Comment* |
| 1 | A | i | B | i | All due to particular changes in |
| 1 | A | ii | E | ii | situation - not necessarily related |
| 1 | A | iii | A | i | to employment. |
| 4 | B | i | A | ii | All realted to unemployment |
| 1 | C | i | A | ii | All households category 'C' |
| 1 | C | i | E | iv | disappear in post-redundancy |
| 1 | C | i | D | | phase. Very interesting feature. |
| 1 | C | ii | A | ii | Related to unemployment |
| 1 | C | ii | A | ii | |
| 1 | C | iii | D | | |
| 1 | C | iii | A | ii | |
| 1 | D | | F | | Additional income source |
| 1 | E | iii | E | i | Only slight modifications |
| 1 | E | iii | E | iv | |
| 1 | E | iv | D | | |
| 1 | F | | B | ii | Loss of income source |
| N = 19 | | | | | |

APPENDIX TABLE 8A2 Elements included in the hierarchy of needs against subsequent post-redundancy experience of hardship

*(a) Difficulties*

| | *In hardship* | | *Not in hardship* | | |
|---|---|---|---|---|---|
| *Category of expenditure* | *expressed difficulty* | *no difficulty expressed* | *expressed difficulty* | *no difficulty expressed* | *Fisher's exact probability value* <0.05 critical |
| Rent/mortgage | 11 | 6 | 2 | 16 | 0.0013 N = 35 |
| Fuel bills | 17 | 0 | 5 | 13 | 0.000006 N = 35 |
| Food purchasing economies | 15 | 2 | 4 | 14 | 0.0001 N = 35 |

*(b) Changed situations*

| | *In hardship* | | *Not in hardship* | | |
|---|---|---|---|---|---|
| *Category of expenditure* | *situation worse* | *situation unchanged* | *situation worse* | *situation unchanged* | *Fisher's exact probability value* <0.05 critical |
| Maintaining good standard of family meals | 14 | 3 | 3 | 15 | 0.0001 N = 35 |
| Quantity of fresh meat purchased and eaten | 15 | 2 | 7 | 11 | 0.0029 N = 35 |
| Standard of parents' clothing/footwear | 11 | 6 | 0 | 18 | 0.00003 N = 35 |
| Standard of children's clothing/footwear | 3 | 14 | 0 | 17 | 0.1136 N = 34 |

# *Part III*

# Labour Market Outcomes

# 9

# The Fate of the Redundant in the Market

We concluded the first part of this book by presenting the results of our investigation into the labour market outcomes of those redundant steel-workers who had remained in the market at the time of their first interview, 9 months or so after being made redundant (chapter 4), and argued that, when a labour market is very loose, it is extremely difficult to explain labour market outcomes simply in terms of supply side factors. The term 'supply side factors' refers to the standard variables used in the study of redundancy, which previous works have shown to affect outcomes in relatively tight markets: these are skill, age, timing of redundancy, and timing and method of job search. We also examined other factors, however, which can affect workers' behaviour: their experience of the internal labour market they have left, their previous experience of the external market, their labour market attitudes, their social attributes and their location in the structure of the labour market (understood as the network of relations linking the inhabitants of the settlements which constitute it). The second part of this book has attempted to show the importance of social identity and network location in job search with reference to both survey and field data (chapters 5 and 6 respectively). It has also investigated the location of the household in the market and its relation to the market, and examined aspects of the connection between household location, the market participation of its members and its internal organization.

Merely to widen the definition of supply side factors does not in itself improve our ability to predict labour market outcomes, however much it enlarges our understanding of worker action (by locating it in a fuller social context) and however much it enriches our understanding of the way labour markets operate. For we have also argued (chapter 4) and seen in our examination of the redundancy event (chapter 3) and from the field material in chapter 6, that in a loose market jobs are acquired as a result of employers' techniques in *labour* search as well as workers, techniques of *job* search. The redundancies studied here were accompanied by an important shift in the character of labour demand towards increased demand for short/fixed term or temporary labour, and part of this type of demand was associated with the use of contractors, a substantial part of whose demand for labour was generated by BSC's decision not just to make less steel but to make it in a new way.

Another important theme has also emerged: the problem of measuring labour market outcomes, or, put more popularly, of describing the fate of the redundant steelworkers. If a significant minority of our respondents embarked on labour market careers which involved constant oscillation between employment and unemployment, and if others were made redundant from permanent jobs they had acquired after leaving BSC then collecting data about their current labour market status, however long after redundancy, will not provide an adequate indication of the fate of the redundant in the market.

The solution to this problem is to measure outcomes not in terms of current status, but in terms of a typology of labour market histories. The second part of this chapter describes the fate of our respondents, or their labour market outcomes, in terms of such histories as opposed to their current status. We have used the term labour market history as opposed to work history, the conventional term in industrial sociology, because we are not concerned with a succession of jobs punctuated by periods of search or frictional unemployment, as that is not typical of the experience of our respondents. Their experience of the market was characterized by periods of unemployment between temporary occupations, by periods of sickness or other forms of withdrawal, by attempts at self-employment and periods of retraining, as well as by the acquisition of permanent employment after a period on the market. The analysis of such varied histories is a complex task, technically and conceptually, and even when the best that can be has been done it must remain inadequate. When people are struggling to 'get by' they are involved in a complex process of juggling income sources: pension, different type of benefit and income flows from different forms of paid work: whether jobs, that is, paid work 'on the cards', or 'hobbles', paid work ancillary to an income derived from a job or to a benefit. Such hobbles, as we have seen, may be formal or informal, licit or illicit. They are often of short duration, as both chapter 6 and Fevre's study of contracting work (1985; 1987) show. Market histories are therefore accounts of the complex and shifting experience of bewildered subjects striving to make sense of what is happening to them. They are also the product of a meaning negotiated between the respondent and the interviewer (see Smits et al., no date) and coded into machine-readable form, and the typification of labour market histories represents a further abstraction and systematization even from the coded data.

This is not to say however, that we regard such histories and their typologies as worthless. Indeed, we consider them infinitely superior as *indicators* of labour market outcome to those provided by current status measures, in whose terms the *initial* labour market outcome of the redundancies was described in chapter 4. The attention of the reader must, however, be drawn to one other inevitable defect which the history approach shares with the current status measures: histories end at an arbitrary point, the date of their collection. The day after the interview the permanently unemployed may have obtained a job and the employed may have been made redundant. Labour markets involve an endless series of flows; history can only be written 'at dusk'. Because even the statutorily retired may return to work, dusk in the case of any given worker is death or chronic incapacity.

## Explaining current status outcomes

If redundancy is followed by complex labour market careers it is these that need to be explained, not current status. None the less, we did attempt to explore the suitability of standard variable explanations of current status as measured at the first interview. The analysis of this Wave 1 data is presented in this section of the chapter. There are three preliminary points to be made about the results presented below. The first is that they show the inadequacy of the standard variables under loose labour market conditions in predicting *successful* outcomes as measured by *conventional* status scales. The second is that none the less this analysis does throw interesting light on the operation of a loose labour market and the process by which workers arrived at different outcomes, particularly when the conventional measures are improved to take some account of labour market histories. It is therefore no part of our argument that the standard variables are unimportant. The third point is that, in this section of the chapter, we shall be referring to data from the whole sample, not just those who remained in the market. Unlike the account given of the survey data in Part I, this section uses data which are not re-weighted to compensate for the over-sampling of the younger age groups, which was intended to reduce the numbers of those over 50 in the sample. No inference can be made, therefore, from any statement about sample percentages to percentages of the population under study unless otherwise stated. We are concerned here solely with the relationship between different variables in the sample, not with the size of categories in the population.

The analysis shows a relation between respondents' labour market experience prior to their employment with BSC and their initial labour market outcomes. There is a negative relation between being employed at first interview and their experience of unemployment: 28 per cent of those never having been unemployed were in work, compared with only 13 per cent of those classified as having experienced 'many spells, some long'. Conversely, the proportion formed by those who had been continuously unemployed rises from 20 per cent among those with little experience of unemployment to 61 per cent of those in the category with the highest experience of unemployment. Previous experience of unemployment seems to be a better predictor of ***unemployment*** than employment after redundancy. However, those who had never been unemployed experienced a higher rate of continuous unemployment (29 per cent) than those who had little experience. This suggests that prior unemployment experience is probably an indicator of two factors: experience of the market (which aids job search) and skill, lack of which increases the chance of unemployment both before and after redundancy. As we shall see, however, the relation between skill level and continuous unemployment is by no means as marked as the relation between past and present unemployment discussed here.

If we now turn to prior work experience, we find no relation between it and successful job search, nor between it and continuous unemployment. What we do find is that those who had worked *only for BSC* have a lower rate of continuous unemployment, largely because they have a higher incidence of non-continuous unemployment. These men are likely to have been the most successful in obtaining work with BSC contractors after redundancy, the assumption being that their experience as dedicated BSC workers provided them with some advantage in obtaining such employment. This can, however, be no more than a plausible hypothesis. An examination of the relation between market outcome and the type of BSC department in which the respondent had worked (see table 3.3), though showing no significant relationship, does suggest that those in indirect services are more likely to have experienced non-continuous employment. This suggests that 'indirect services' is the category where the greatest experience of contracting is to be found.

Discussion of the relation between skill, age and market outcome is complicated by the fact that skill and age are themselves related: older workers were also less skilled. In so far as this is so, the operation of both factors in the same direction might be expected to produce steep age and skill gradients, younger and more skilled workers having higher success rates than would be expected on the grounds of either skill or age alone. In fact, in both cases the success rates (defined as the percentage of each category who were employed) show nothing that could be described as a gradient, let alone a steep one. They do none the less show differences. Those with both qualifications and marketable skills have a success rate of 32.5 per cent compared with only 20 per cent for those with neither, and with a sample mean of 25.9 per cent. All other permutations of skill and qualifications, with one insignificant exception, are all within 3.5 percentage points of the mean. Differences between the qualified and the unqualified, and those with marketable and steel-specific skills, are in the expected directions, but the interval between them does not exceed 5 per cent.

This, it can be argued, is a product of the crudeness of our measures, or the lack of skill differentiation in the sample, or both. While not rejecting such arguments, however, their validity must be considered in the light of what the data show when we examine market failure rather than success, that is, when we examine the relation between skill and the incidence of *continuous unemployment*. Here we find a substantial difference in the failure rate between the qualified (26 per cent) and the unqualified (35 per cent), and also between those with negotiable skills (22.5 per cent) and those with steel-specific skills (34 per cent). The sample mean for failure - continuous unemployement - is 32.4 per cent. Moreover, the incidence of continuous unemployment shows a gradient in the expected direction when calculated for the hierarchy of categories of our constructed variable, which combines qualifications and type of skill; it starts at 20 per cent for those with negotiable skills and qualifications and reaches 38.3 per cent for those with neither. There may not be much relation between skill and market success, but there is a definite if not very strong negative relationship between skill and continuous unemployment.

This is not the end of the story, however. If we add in those who, though unemployed at first interview, had not been continuously unemployed, to create a standard 'unemployed' outcome category, the gradient disappears. As in the case of employment, there is a difference in the incidence of unemployment between the most advantaged (37.5 per cent) and the least (43.9 per cent). This difference is very small, however, and the rates for the intervening categories show no pattern and include one category - those without qualifications but with negotiable skill - which has a lower incidence of failure (29.3 per cent) than the most advantaged. This unsatisfactory result for those with current status unemployed in comparison with the much more intelligible one produced by the market experience category of continuously unemployed, is a finding of the first importance.

The incidence of non-continuous unemployment does not show a clear gradient, but the two most advantaged categories of the skill variable have higher frequencies of non-continuous unemployment (15 per cent) than the remaining less advantaged categories (5.8 per cent; sample mean: 7.6 per cent). This suggests that non-continuous unemployment is, under loose market conditions and when there is a steady demand for intermittent labour, *a form of market success rather than failure*. Non-continuous unemployment is positively related to skill while continuous unemployment is negatively related, which is why the relationship between skill and unemployment disappears when they are combined.

If we take the daring decision to classify non-continuous unemployment as a form of market success and then bring together the three forms of market success - employment, self-employment and non-continuous unemployment - to form a *global success indicator* and calculate its incidence for each category of the skill variable, we find that apart from one small exception (no qualifications but other skill: 21 cases out of 710), we have a relatively steep gradient from 57.5 per cent for those with qualifications and skill, to 29.1 per cent with neither (sample mean: 40.4 per cent). Removing the non-continuously unemployed diminishes the difference between the most and least skilled (40 per cent and 24.5 per cent) and upsets the pattern between these extremes. It appears therefore that the inadequacy of current status measures, and of at least one standard variable as a predictor of outcomes, are not separate but related issues. Inadequate outcome measures diminish the value of the explanatory variables as predictors.

In examining age we shall therefore use the global estimate of success mentioned above. The relation between the global success indicator and age is in the form of a curve with its highest point in the 30–5 age group, which has a success rate of 59 per cent; the youngest age group has a success rate of 46 per cent. The effect of age as a barrier to market success is stronger for those over 50. The success rate of those over 44 and under 60 is 50 per cent; for those in their early 50s 35 per cent, and for those over 54 a mere 10 per cent. This last figure is the result of market withdrawal; for the early 50s it is predominantly the result of an increase in unemployment which explains their lower success. The shape of the relation between age and each of the three forms of success is that of a curve. They do not, however, have the same highest point: success in the form of employment and self-employment is most frequently in the 35–44 age group, but, in the form of non-continuous unemployment, the highest incidence is in the 25–9 age group. The subtraction of the non-continuously unemployed, in contrast to the case of skill and unemployment, does not greatly alter the picture except in the younger age groups, where the success rate of the 25–9 age group (30 per cent) becomes substantially lower than that of the under 25s (38 per cent).

If we turn to age and labour market failure measured by continuous unemployment, we find that the pattern of incidence is the reverse of that of success, but here the lowest incidence is found in the 30–4 age group in contrast to the 35–9 age group where success was highest. The reason for the shift is that it is among the 35–9 age group that workers begin to withdraw from one market in significant numbers. In the younger age groups the failure pattern is the inverse of the global success measure when the non-continuously unemployed have been subtracted from it. In other words, in this age group men who, on the grounds of age, 'should' be unemployed have avoided that fate by intermittent employment, thus altering the symmetry of a failure incidence curve which has its highest points among the very young and the very old.

Job search commencement was also found to relate to measures of successful labour market outcome. Here, however, we are not justified in adding the three forms of success together. There is no reason to associate self-employment with early search, except in so far as early experience of the market may lead to a decision to become self-employed. Both employment and non-continuous unemployment are positively related to earliness of search and both show a gradient, though the non-continuous employment gradient (15.9 to 4.7 per cent) is much less steep than the employment gradient (44.9 to 24 per cent). Conversely, continuous unemployment is negatively related to early job search (gradient 23.2 to 55.6 per cent).

By widening the outcome indicators beyond current status to include labour market experience, skill has been rescued as an outcome indicator and the status of the other two standard variables confirmed. We have, however, serendipitously reached another conclusion: that non-continuous unemployment, which is an indicator of intermittment employment, behaves in the same way as success indicators, and in the opposite way to failure indicators. This is a finding of great methodological importance for the understanding labour market behaviour in loose markets. In the case of the BSC redundancies, however, it has additional significance. The existence of this category and its behaviour is, we know, at least in part the result of BSC's decision to increase the use of contractors, and one of the key issues posed by the emergence of this category is what factors determine entry to it. We know that there is an association between this type of history and having worked only for BSC: it is negatively associated with prior experience of unemployment and positively with skill, its incidence is highest in the 25–9 age group and it is weakly associated with earliness of job search. It is likely, however, that it is also associated with the location of the worker in BSC itself.

We have already noted that the incidence of non-continuous unemployment was highest among men who had worked in departments supplying indirect services to BSC, that is, in departments whose work could most easily be put out to contract. No relationship was found between outcome and the extent to which respondents had experience of BSC as an internal market. More managers become self-employed, retrained or became non-continuously unemployed than any other BSC grade, due to their higher educational level and age. Respondents were asked if they had had another job while holding their job at BSC, and from the sample we estimate that 5 per cent of those made redundant fell into this category. Its members were extraordinarily successful in the market, with a global success rate of over 73 per cent, a success rate higher than any age, skill or search category. They were also 3 times more likely than the sample as a whole to be non-continuously unemployed. Though no relation was found between size of BSC department and outcome, the non-continuously unemployed were significantly less likely to have worked in a large department. We can therefore add to our list of factors predisposing to intermittent work: having worked in indirect services, having held another job while at BSC and having worked in a small BSC department.

We shall further investigate the social location and identity of those who worked intermittently in the next chapter. We shall not do so here, however, since non-continuous unemployment is only a crude proxy for intermittent work, and the first interview (Wave 1) data only cover a short period of respondents' post-redundancy experience in the market. We shall conclude this section by examining two factors closely related to the issue of social identity.

The first concerns job acquisition. In chapter 5 the importance of networks and intermediaries as factors facilitating job acquisition in a loose market was discussed. However, since it is important that network members put in a good word for applicants if chances of success are to be increased, it cannot be the mere possession of a network, its interconnectedness, or its geographical extent that matters *but what the network connects the applicant with*. To put this point another way: networks as well as individuals may be thought of as having a location in the market in the social structural sense (chapter 4, pp. 99–100). If this is the case the use of informal methods of job search cannot strongly predict outcomes any more than possession or type of network can. Using networks of informal relationships will only be an effective method of job search if those networks connect the job seeker with employment opportunities.

We predicted that those who obtained their BSC job through a friend or relative working there would be more successful than those who obtained their BSC job through friends or relatives who were not working there, for two reasons. First, the individual who helped to find the BSC job cannot by virtue of that fact help the worker concerned to get a job after redundancy. Therefore there is no intrinsic reason why those who did have a friend or relative to speak for them at BSC should be more successful in their post-redundancy job search than those who obtained their BSC job through a friend or relative who was *not* working there. Second, if those who had a friend or relative in BSC are none the less more successful, an explanation which refers to factors other than the personal characteristics of a given network member must be found. Having had a well-placed contact in BSC can be regarded as an indicator of the character of the network itself, of the existence of a network whose points are people in a position to provide information about jobs and influence potential employers on behalf of other network members.

An examination of the relation between global success rates and the way in which the BSC job was secured shows considerable variation between the different types of job acquisition. Those who had obtained their BSC job by answering an advertisement had the highest success rate (50 per cent). The lowest rate, however, was found among those who had got their job through friends or relatives *not* working at BSC (37.5 per cent success). Those *with* a contact in BSC had, in contrast, a post-redundancy success rate of 48.7 per cent, close to the top of the range. The difference (among those who had used informal methods to get their BSC jobs) between those with and without contacts, could scarcely have been more marked (given the range of variation in BSC job acquisition types). Of those using informal methods, those who had contacts in BSC were more successful *after* their redundancy than those without. If, therefore, having a contact in BSC is the equivalent of respondents' networks being connected with job opportunities, then our hypothesis is confirmed. If, on the other hand, this interpretation is rejected, it is extremely difficult to find an alternative explanation for the finding. It is worth noting that this result is *not* due to those with BSC contacts experiencing more intermittent employment, since incidence of this outcome approximates to the sample mean. In contrast, it was those who had relied on friends and relatives outside BSC to obtain their BSC job who had the greatest experience of intermittent employment – over 3 times the sample mean.

This interpretation of the data is confirmed when we examine the relation between the modes of acquisition of BSC and current jobs. Of those who had acquired the BSC job through someone working there, the proportion who had acquired their present job through relatives and friends was almost at the top of the range. (Unfortunately the small numbers of successful respondents make further comparisons between BSC job acquisition types of dubious validity.) It seems that those with BSC contacts did make use of their networks after redundancy and it is, therefore, these network characteristics that are responsible for the high success rate in this category.

Networks extend over space, and the west Industrial South Wales labour market extends over a lot of space within which are a variety of settlements. The relation between success rates of respondents resident in different types of locality was examined on the assumption that settlements constitute the nodes of local social networks which are more dense within than between settlements. As there are differences between parts of the market in opportunity structure and in the timing of the recession, it is not unreasonable to expect differences in success rates between areas in the market, and between types of settlement, on the grounds both of variation in demand for labour, and how redundant workers were connected with job opportunities.

We estimate that 3.8 per cent of those made redundant lived outside the market when interviewed. Within the local market, employment rates varied between areas from 5 percentage points above the mean to 5 below it; continuous unemployment rates varied from 6 points above to 11 below. This last variation is the result of the low rate of continuous unemployment experienced in the Bridgend area. Intermittent employment was higher than the mean by a few points in those areas adjacent to Port Talbot, but not in the town itself. This suggests that over relatively short distances the social distance of workers from employment opportunities is more important than the geographical; the variation, however, was very small.

When we turn to settlement type we find little variation in employment, but continuous unemployment was highest in areas classified as 'urban sprawl' between settlements, and lowest in small isolated settlements with other types, major or minor, in intermediate positions. Perhaps the clearest feature of this analysis is the distinctiveness of small isolated settlements where, we estimate, 7 per cent of the redundants lived. Redundants with this type of residence had higher proportions of work, in self-employment and retraining and lower proportions who had withdrawn or experienced any form of unemployment, than among redundants from any other settlement type. Since we know that unemployment is higher in the small settlements characteristic of the Welsh valleys than on the coastal plain, it appears likely that the success of the small settlement redundants is a result of their advantaged position in terms of human capital, which has in the past meant that they live in desirable semi-rural areas within the market.

## Classifying outcomes on the basis of market histories

The preceding discussion of labour market outcomes and their determinants has, we hope, demonstrated the necessity of measuring outcomes in terms of market histories rather than current status, and the weakness of standard variables as predictors of successful outcomes in loose markets. This weakness is the result of the over-determination of outcomes, due to the mediation of the effects of market factors (in the economic sense) by others which are social structural. The fact that standard variables predict failure better than success is a result of the looseness of the market. Absence of attributes favoured by the market, poor timing and inappropriate search procedures can predict *failure*, but as there are not enough jobs for all those who have the right qualities and search effectively, they are less successful predictors of *success*. The difficulty here is that non-economic market factors, though crucial determinants of success, are likely to be even weaker predictors of outcomes than standard economic market variables, since it is useless being personally acceptable to employers, well connected to the source of job opportunities, having someone to speak for you and being efficient in job search, if you lack the attributes favoured by the market or come on to the market when no one is taking on, or both.

The next chapter will address this problem by examining the attributes of categories of redundants with different market outcomes. Before this can be done, however, we need to classify the labour market histories of the redundants. Data presented in Part I, in chapter 5 and so far in this chapter were generated by interviews with redundant steelworkers 9 months after the redundancy date. A sub-sample of the original sample was interviewed again in the spring of 1982 at the request of the ESRC, our sponsors, to confirm that no significant geographical movement out of the local labour market area had occurred in the year which had elapsed. Apart from confirming this negative result, the second added nothing to what we learnt from the first wave of interviewing. The original sample was interviewed again in the early winter (October–January) of 1982–3, approximately two-

and-a-half years after the majority of the redundancies took place (July–August 1980). The prime aim of this third and final wave of interviewing was to collect labour market histories. Outcomes classified in terms of histories therefore cover a two-and-a-half year period of market experience. Unfortunately but inevitably, interviewee exhaustion (some were interviewed four times) increased the rate of refusal and deliberate non contact, while mobility within the local labour market area increased the non contact rate. The result was a high rate of 'panel mortality', so that the achieved sample on wave 3 (n⅜473) was only 62.5 per cent of the achieved sample on the first (754). The data presented below were generated by this third wave of interviewing.

We have already referred to the current status measure of market outcomes. A labour market history outcome is a series or *string* of statuses classified in the same way as current status. An example of such a string would be:

> unemployed sick employed retraining unemployed self-employed unemployed

Strings were characterized by the number of statuses (the example above has 7) and the number of types of status (the example has 5). Analysis of the histories in these terms confirmed Dr Morris's conclusion from her field data that the labour market experience of the redundant was characterized by its variety 'not only with the employment experience of one individual worker, but also between the experiences of different workers' (see chapter 6). Table 9.1 shows the distribution of the number of statuses held by those remaining in the market and compares it with the distribution for the whole of the Wave 3 achieved sample. Data in tables 9.1–9.3 are unweighted and include women.

TABLE 9.1 Number of statuses held since redundancy: Wave 3

| *Number of statuses* | *Those 'in market' only* (%) | (*cumulative %*) | *Whole wave 3 sample* (%) | (*cumulative %*) |
|---|---|---|---|---|
| 8 or more [a] | 2.6 | 2.6 | 1.9 | 1.9 |
| 7 | 1.6 | 4.2 | 1.3 | 3.2 |
| 6 | 4.0 | 8.2 | 3.1 | 6.3 |
| 5 | 5.3 | 13.5 | 4.5 | 10.8 |
| 4 | 10.6 | 24.1 | 8.5 | 19.3 |
| 3 | 18.0 | 42.1 | 14.3 | 33.6 |
| 2 | 31.2 | 73.3 | 24.9 | 58.5 |
| 1 | 26.7 | 100.0 | 41.5 | 100.0 |
| Base | n = 316 | | n = 473 | |

[a] Only 4 respondents had more than 8

Even where those who withdrew immediately from the market (and who have only 1 status) are included, a third of all respondents had 3 or more statuses and a fifth 4 or more. Excluding those who withdrew, the proportions increased to two-fifths and one-quarter. Substantial proportions (two-fifths and one-quarter) had, however, only 1 status and as many as two-thirds of the total sample and well over half of those in the market had only 2. A large minority had highly variegated careers, therefore, but a small majority, even of those in the market, did not.

Table 9.2 shows the number of types of status held since redundancy. The variation both within strings and between workers in the number of types of status is markedly smaller than in the number of statuses, only 16.5 per cent of the whole sample and a fifth of those remaining in the market having 3 or more status types. Among those remaining in the market, however, the largest single category was that with 2 types of status. Respondents' labour market histories are, therefore, less varied than the case histories cited by Morris and the example used above may suggest. The point we wish to make is not that a majority of our respondents had careers which were highly variegated in terms of type, but that a large minority of respondents had such careers.

The reason for this aggregate lack of variation by type is demonstrated in table 9.3. Very substantial majorities of the respondents never experienced

TABLE 9.2 Number of status types held since redundancy: Wave 3

| *Number of types* | *Those 'in market' only* (%) | (*cumulative %*) | *Whole wave three sample* (%) | (*cumulative %*) |
|---|---|---|---|---|
| 5 | 0.3 | 0.3 | 0.1 | 0.1 |
| 4 | 3.2 | 3.5 | 2.5 | 2.6 |
| 3 | 17.5 | 21.0 | 13.9 | 16.5 |
| 2 | 50.1 | 71.1 | 40.1 | 56.6 |
| 1 | 28.9 | 100.0 | 43.4 | 100.0 |
| Base | n = 316 | | n = 473 | |

TABLE 9.3 Proportions experiencing each status (Wave 3: total sample)

| | *Ever* | *Never* | *Total* |
|---|---|---|---|
| Employment | 42.9 | 57.1 | 100 |
| Self-employment | 8.6 | 91.4 | 100 |
| Unemployment | 67.2 | 32.8 | 100 |
| Retraining | 17.0 | 83.0 | 100 |
| Withdrawal | 38.6 | 61.4 | 100 |
| Other | 1.7 | 98.3 | 100 |

self-employment or retraining, so the statuses statistically available to most workers were employment, unemployment and withdrawal. In view of this it is perhaps the substantial proportions of those having 2 (rather than 3) status types in their market histories that should be borne in mind when reading table 9.2.

Table 9.3 is, however, important in other respects. Only 17 per cent of the sample had any form of retraining, despite the efforts of the MSC, though when those who immediately withdrew are subtracted this proportion rises to 25 per cent (see Lee, 1985a). Only 8.6 per cent experienced self-employment in spite of the capital provided by redundancy payments and the encouragement given by the government to small businesses (see Lee, 1985b), though excluding immediate withdrawers this proportion rises to nearly 11 per cent. Of particular importance here is what table 9.3 tells us about labour market experience as opposed to outcome. Experience of both employment (43 per cent) and unemployment (67 per cent) differ from those suggested by either the current status measures at the Wave One interviews (23 per cent and 38 per cent respectively) or at the last, Wave Three, interviews (23.5 per cent and 28 per cent respectively). Unemployment experience is more extensive than any of these measures suggest, but so is that of employment.

This has important implications for the way Pahl's polarization thesis is interpreted (R. E. Pahl, 1984). Because different forms of work tend to be concentrated among the employed and because the unemployed are excluded from them, this does not mean that the population is polarized into the deprived unemployed on the one hand and, on the other, comfortable Britain (to use Bishop Sheppard's phrase), whose denizens have no experience of the harsh realities of the 1980s. Many of those who are, at any given moment, out of work have recently been in work and many of those in work have had recent experience of unemployment. Since this study is concerned with a sample of redundants the proportions quoted above are not indicators of the discrepancy between current status and market experience in the general population even in South Wales, let alone elsewhere.

If a substantial minority of respondents had variegated market histories, then to use these histories as outcome indicators meant that their patterns had to be coded, and this in turn involved a simplification of an elaborate current status set of codes to yield the 5 main types used in table 9.3. The coding of strings consisting of a single type of status posed no problem, nor did the coding of those with intermittent employment whose strings were composed solely of the statuses 'employed' and 'unemployed'. These 2 types accounted for two-thirds of the cases. It was with the remaining third that the difficulty lay. To solve it we developed the notion of 'T plus', that is, a string predominantly composed of a major *type* of status *plus* a minority of other statuses. This also posed problems, for further work by Brown on Lee and Harris's classificaiton showed that however the categories were juggled, there was a small but significant overlap between them. As a result the attempt to classify status strings purely on the basis of their components, without reference to the ordering of those components, was abandoned.

It is hoped that the reader will forgive this intrusion into the text of matter normally relegated to methodological appendices, but we consider it absolutely necessary. While we never supposed the position of a status in a string was unimportant, we had hoped to separate out the diachronic and synchronic, sequential and characterological aspects of the strings, analyse them separately and relate them. That is, we thought of the market history status strings as indicating the character of labour market experience, and wanted to explain experience types instead of outcomes which we still thought of in current status terms. (For a discussion of the problems in string analysis which reflects Lee and Harris's thinking at this stage see Lee, 1983.) This was a conceptual error. While the labour market histories provide the data for describing labour market experience in various ways by abstracting aspects of those histories, they are in the full sense *histories* and not just sets of statuses. They can only be understood as totalities, therefore, with reference to their end-points, and any classification of such histories, while it need not refer to the sequential pattern of statuses, must take note of the final status that is, the one at time of interview. Any status type in this position in the sequence must be accorded a logically privileged position over those in other sequence locations. Labour market experience is not the opposite of a labour market outcome, but is a way characterizing that outcome. The use of histories which reflect that experience is not an escape from the problem posed by the fact that we do not know what will happen immediately *after* the interview, but a way of providing a more adequate description of the outcome by including reference to what went *before* it.

Table 9.4 sets out our final classification and shows the distribution of the Wave 3 achieved sample over its categories when re-weighted to permit inferences from sample to population. Categories 2 with 3, 5 with 6, 8, 10 and 12 are Lee and Harris's 'T plus' categories, modified by Brown's introduction of *last status* as a differentiating criterion to make them exclusive.

Table 9.4 is in many ways very remarkable. It demonstrates the variegated character of labour market experience by the dispersal of our respondents across the categories of the outcome measure. No category has more than a fifth of the sample within it; the two largest categories are types of withdrawal, and the largest categories of those remaining in the market (4–12) are 'continuous unemployment' (4) and types of intermittent employment (11 and 12).

A word needs to be said about the term 'chequered'. It was first used to describe what we have called the *variegated* character of the post-redundancy market career of our sample, but was later restricted, and is used here to refer to careers characterized by 'intermittent employment' whose

TABLE 9.4 Labour market outcomes measured by a classification of labour market histories

| | *Category name* | *Number of statuses* | *Category description* | *Percentage* | *Collapsed category and percentage* |
|---|---|---|---|---|---|
| 1 | Withdrew | 1 | Withdrawn only | 20.5 | Withdrawn 35.9 |
| 2 | Withdrew. no employment | at least 2 | Unemployment and/or retraining; *last status* withdrawn | 15.4 | |
| 3 | Withdrew: experience of employment | at least 2 | Employment and *last status*: withdrawn; or as above plus other status types | 2.7 | Indeterminate excluded from analysis |
| 4 | Unemployed only | 1 | Unemployed only | 13.8 | Unemployed 20.0 |
| 5 | Unemployed plus | at least 2 | Unemployed as *last status* preceded by withdrawal or retraining | 4.9 | |
| 6 | Employment to unemployment | at least 2 | First status employed or self-employed; *last status* unemployed | 1.3 | |
| 7 | Self-employed | any number | Self-employed only or employed and *last status* self-employed | 2.9 | Self-employed 4.5 |
| 8 | Return to self-employment | at least 2 | Any status other than employed and *last status* self-employed | 1.6 | |
| 9 | Employed | any number | Employed only | 8.2 | Employed 16.2 |
| 10 | Return to employment | at least 2 | Any status and *last status*: employed | 8.0 | |
| 11 | Chequered 'pure' | at least 3 | Employed and unemployed only | 10.5 | Chequered 20.7 |
| 12 | Chequered 'plus' | at least 3 | As above but with at least one other type of status | 10.2 | |

*Source*: Wave 3 interview data, total sample less women; n = 456

indicator on the first wave of interviewing was 'non-continuous *un*employment'. As can be seen from the table, unemployment and intermittent employment (chequered) are the most frequent outcomes. Indeed, category 10 probably includes some respondents who had embarked upon a career of intermittent employment late, and for this reason and because of the length of their spells of employment or unemployment were excluded from the chequered category. Even so, a chequered career is the most frequent market outcome apart from withdrawal.

As we have seen, it would be quite illegitimate to add the chequered to the unemployed, because 'chequeredness' (intermittent employment) is a form of market success, not failure, since it is positively related to variables which have predicted success in global terms, and which, in tight labour markets, have been associated with a return to employment. If, when regarded as an effect, chequeredness is a form of success, it is, at the level of personal experience, akin to failure; for those for whom intermittent employment had become a way of life, it is a way of getting by in the absence of a permanent job after leaving BSC. It involves a struggle to manage on a lower income, and juggling income sources which cross the line between the formal and informal and, possibly, legal and illegal. Chequeredness, in terms of 'lived experience', is more akin to unemployment than to employment.

The chequered constitute, therefore, a distinct category which cannot be assimilated to conventional outcome categories. Table 9.5 compares the current status and labour market history outcomes at the last interview (Wave Three). However, it also shows the relative importance of chequeredness when only those in the market are considered.

It is clear that using current status measures inflates the proportion of both the employed and unemployed. Shifting to a history measure of outcome reduces the proportion of those still in the market classified as employed from 37.5 to 26.4 per cent, and of those unemployed from 45 to 32.4 per cent. Though the size of all the conventional categories changes when histories rather than current statuses are considered, the chief result of adopting the history measure is that it permits the appearance of the chequered as a distinct category.

When the 61.4 per cent of the redundants who remained in the market are considered (see columns 2 and 3 of table 9.5) we find that column 3 shows that chequered outcomes form (at 34 per cent) a larger proportion of those in the market than any other single category, marginally larger even than the two other successful outcomes (employment and self-employment) which together total 33.6 per cent.

There is a sense, then, in which the 'discovery' of the chequered is the most important result of this study. It is, like all findings, a product of the method of classification which is, of course, purely phenomenal. It is a classification of cases on the basis of a common pattern of experience, not on

TABLE 9.5 Current status and labour market history outcomes (Wave 3)

| *Current status* | 1 *All redundants* *(n = 456)* | 2 *In markets only* *(n = 281)* | | *Labour market history* | | 3 *In markets only* *(n = 281)* | 4 *All redundants* *(n = 456)* |
|---|---|---|---|---|---|---|---|
| Withdrawn | 38 | - | | (See table 9.4) | | | |
| Employed | 23.5 | 37.5 | 1 | Withdrawn | | | |
| Self-employed | 5.5 | 9.0 | 2 | Withdrawn plus | withdrawn (1–3) | - | 38.6 |
| | | | 3 | Probably withdrawn | | | |
| Total with work | 29.0 | 46.5 | 4 | Unemployed only | | | |
| | | | 5 | Unemployed plus | unemployed (4–6) | 32.4 | 20.0 |
| Unemployed | 28.0 | 45.0 | 6 | Employment to unemployment | | | |
| Training | 1.6 | 2.5 | 7 | Self-employed | | | |
| Sick | 2.6 | 4.8 | 8 | Return to self-employment | self-employed (7–8) | 7.2 | 4.5 |
| Other | 0.8 | 1.2 | 9 | Employed | | | |
| | | | 10 | Return to employment | employed (9–10) | 26.4 | 16.2 |
| | | | 11 | Chequered 'pure' | | | |
| | | | 12 | Chequered 'plus' | chequered (11–12) | 34.0 | 20.7 |
| Total | 100.0 | 100.0 | | Total | | 100.0 | 100.0 |
| % | 100.0 | 61.4 | | % | | 61.4 | 100.0 |

that of a common propensity to intermittent employment; that is, cases were not classified on the basis of their labour market position, in the sense of their chances of obtaining irregular employment. Nor is it an aetiological classification: cases were not classified as the same because we had identified a set of conditions sufficient to produce a chequered labour market career. If chequeredness be thought of as a propensity to generate a history of intermittent employment, then that propensity is not shown by some we have classified as chequered (on the basis of their history), the chequeredness of their career being the result of chance factors. Equally, as we have noted, some respondents who have such a propensity could well appear under a different heading, especially category 10. The label 'chequered' is, like most social survey codes, an indicator rather than a measure, and this point must be borne in mind when we turn to examine, in chapter 10, the distinguishing characteristics of those with different types of labour market history outcome.

Are the chequered merely the creation of our coding procedures? We do not believe they are. The attempt to distinguish this category was based on field data – it is not simply the result of playing around on the computer. Moreover, we have abundant evidence from field data on redundants' experiences, on BSC's new mode of operation (cited in chapter 3), and from Fevre's study of contracting in Port Talbot (1987) of the existence of a type of labour demand which would constitute a causal factor in the generation of chequered careers. However, the discovery of a new category only sharpens the question raised by this chapter: what, in addition to the standard variables determines labour market outcomes in a loose market? To the question: 'what makes one man "employed" and another "unemployed"?' must be added, 'and a third "chequered"?'

We showed some of our respondents these results and asked them this question. They didn't know any more than we did, though they made some suggestions which we have followed up in this chapter. No one doubted, however, the reality of the category. They even liked the name. As one of the shop stewards involved in the redundancy process remarked, 'I think it's very suitable – a sort of harlequin character, half black, half white, neither one thing nor the other, spinning around not knowing whether he's coming or going. That's just what it's been like for some of these boys.'

# 10

# The Determinants of Labour Market Experience

We noted at the beginning of chapter 9 that the standard explanatory variables predict current status outcomes more powerfully when status is modified to take account of a labour market experience element. The first question we wish to address in this chapter is: does reclassification of labour market outcomes in terms of the labour market experience categories described at the end of chapter 9 improve the predictive power of the standard variables? Briefly, the answer is that in one sense it does not. In no case can the chequered be added to the self-employed or employed and the total used as a measure of global success. Our detailed analysis of the components of the chequered category in the second section of this chapter will make it evident why this is.

However, the standard variables do operate as predictors of labour market experience outcome. Using the membership of the employed or self-employed categories as a criterion of success, we find higher success rates among non-manual workers, those of prime age, with qualifications, with marketable skill, who looked earlier, those made redundant before the peak flow on period and who had held pre-redundancy jobs. We also found that those made redundant on the LIFO (last in, first out) principle had been more successful than other redundants. These variables also predict failure measured by membership of the unemployed category, with the exception of marketable skill and the manual–non manual variable.

The chequeredness rate was lowest among the older workers, among those who were in non-manual occupations at BSC, possessed a marketable skill, had experience of long periods of unemployment prior to redundancy, who came on to the market early and who looked late. It is highest among those made redundant on the LIFO principle and shows no relation to qualifications or the number of pre-redundancy jobs. The chequered combine, therefore, attributes which in the sample as a whole are associated with both success and failure. This means that it is only by separating out the chequered from the successful (self-employed and employed) and the unsuccessful (the

TABLE 10.1 Standard variables as outcome predictors (percentages)

| | Failure | | Difference | Success | | Difference |
|---|---|---|---|---|---|---|
| Age | 12.0 (prime) | 46 (old) | 34.0 | 48 (prime) | 22 (young) | 26 |
| Search commencement | 7.0 (early) | 27 (late) | 20.0 | 41 (early) | 28 (late) | 13 |
| Number of pre-redundancy jobs | 16.0 (few) | 26 (many) | 10.0 | 46 (few) | 34 (many) | 12 |
| Qualifications | 15.0 (yes) | 26 (no) | 11.0 | 44 (yes) | 35 (no) | 9 |
| When made redundant | 18.0 (early) | 26 (late) | 8.0 | 48 (early) | 34 (late) | 14 |
| Non-manual/manual | 23.0 (n-m) | 24 (m) | 1.0 | 53 (n-m) | 32 (m) | 21 |
| Marketable skill | 19.5 (yes) | 24 (no) | 4.5 | 44 (yes) | 37 (no) | 7 |

*Source*: Wave 3 data, those in market only. Unweighted n = 339

unemployed) that the standard variables act as predictors. Even then, only age acts as a strong predictor. Table 10.1 shows the rates of the polar categories for each variable in terms of both success and failure.

Only two of the variables appear to have a substantial effect on outcomes: age and search commencement. The rest 'produce' relatively minor differences: the non-manual–manual dichotomy is a good predictor of success, but useless as a predictor of failure; marketable skill is a poor predictor of both success and failure. The weakness of the standard variables as predictors and the anomalous character of the results for the skill variables suggest the intervention of other factors. This raises the question of whether any other variables (by themselves) are better predictors of labour market experience outcomes.

## Other predictors of labour market experience outcomes

We have claimed that outcomes are the result of the relation between the two sides of the market. They are therefore as much a result of changes in the type of labour demand and in the recruiting behaviour of employers as of the characteristics of workers and their job seeking behaviour. These demand side factors cannot be directly measured by examining a population of workers. However, we have also suggested that, at least in loose markets, the social location of a worker – his or her social identity and social relationships – is (with the standard variables) also a determinant of labour market experience outcomes, given the importance of information, moral suasion and the ability of the employer in loose markets to choose applicants with acceptable characters. We have noted, however, that non-formal methods of recruitment can only operate if the employer and applicant already stand in some relationship to one another. Therefore we would predict that belonging to a network and its type are factors likely to determine outcomes. However, they can only do so weakly since it is also necessary that the network in question *connect the job searcher with employment opportunities*. We would therefore expect outcome to be related to both network type *and* geographical location. At the same time, if employers are choosing what are from their point of view 'tidy lads' (see chapter 6), then there should be some relation between outcome and respondents' attitudes.

We have attempted to test the importance of social location by analysing outcomes according to four locational variables: network type, settlement type, geographical location and religious denomination. This last choice was determined by the analysis reported in the last two sections of this chapter. The results are summarised in table 10.2.

The first point to make about this table is that the differences between the highest and lowest rates on each line are in most cases substantial, 7 out of 12 being over 15 per cent, a proportion which compares favourably with the

TABLE 10.2 Locational variables as outcome predictors

| *Outcome type* | *Variable* | | | | | | *Difference (highest–lowest)* |
|---|---|---|---|---|---|---|---|
| | NETWORK TYPE | | | | | | |
| | *Collective* | *Dispersed* | *Independent* | | | | |
| Failure | 22 | 26 | 23 | | | | 4.0 |
| Chequered | 38 | 39 | 47 | | | | 9.0 |
| Success | 40 | 35 | 30 | | | | 10.0 |
| | SETTLEMENT TYPE | | | | | | |
| | *Main* | *Minor* | *Sprawl* | *Isolated* | | | |
| Failure | 18 | 23 | 33 | 29 | | | 15.0 |
| Chequered | 45 | 40 | 31 | 29 | | | 16.0 |
| Success | 37 | 38 | 36 | 42 | | | 6.0 |
| | GEOGRAPHICAL LOCATION | | | | | | |
| | *Port Talbot* | *PT environs* | *Neath* | *Swansea* | *Maesteg* | *East fringe* | |
| Failure | 26 | 27 | 15 | 13 | 30 | 24 | 17.0 |
| Chequered | 46 | 22 | 39 | 52 | 32 | 27 | 30.0 |
| Success | 27 | 51 | 45 | 35 | 38 | 48 | 24.0 |
| | DENOMINATION | | | | | | |
| | *RC* | *Anglican* | *Eng. Nonconformist* | *Welsh Nonconformist* | | | |
| Failure | 19 | 26 | 27.5 | 7 | | | 20.5 |
| Chequered | 53 | 33 | 40.0 | 54 | | | 21.0 |
| Success | 28 | 41 | 32.5 | 39 | | | 13.0 |

*Source*: Wave 3 data, those in market only. Unweighted n = 339.

4 out of 14 differences of over 15 per cent shown by the standard variables in table 10.1. All except network type predict failure by this criterion; only geographical location indicates success, and all except network type predict chequeredness. Conversely, there are only two differences which are so small as to diminish the usefulness of the variable as a predictor: network type does not predict failure, and settlement type does not predict success. *Prima facie* there seems to be good reason to accord locational variables at least the same predictive force as standard variables.

Is the same true of attitude variables? Questions designed to test attitudes on tax evasion, capitalism, union pay restraint and militancy, political preference, global pessimism, belief in individual drive and initiative and preference for high pay as opposed to job security, were all tested as predictors. Generally the attitude variables did not predict outcomes. There were, however, the following minor exceptions: those preferring high pay to job security had a higher failure rate (32 per cent) than those who did not (20 per cent); those voting in 1979 for a party other than Labour or Conservative had a higher success rate (47 per cent) than Conservative (41 per cent) or Labour (36 per cent) voters.

There was, however, a major exception. Responses to the statement: 'it is the job of a trade union to get as much as it can for its members' predicted the incidence of failure (agree: incidence 35 per cent; disagree: incidence 17 per cent) and, less strongly, success. They also weakly predicted chequeredness (agree: incidence 33 per cent; disagree: incidence 42 per cent). Fevre (1987) and Morris (chapter 6) have both argued in their studies that contracting employers (whose workers had chequered outcomes) seek to exclude 'militants and trouble-makers', and this hypothesis is weakly supported by the data. Chequeredness is, however, an inadequate proxy for contracting (see below). The figures cited immediately above do more strongly support the general contention that information about trade union militancy of applicants is taken into account by employers in a loose market when taking on labour.

At this point the traditionally minded but methodologically sophisticated student of labour markets may well object that there is a major epistemological difference between the standard variables and others: the standard variables have been selected on the basis of a commonsensically grounded but formally *rational theory* of how labour markets work. To this it may be replied that locational variables have been selected on the basis of an understanding of how labour markets work which is grounded in social theory and commonsensically informed.

It may be objected that no rational connection can be made between the formal categories of market outcome and, say, Anglicanism, which is perfectly correct. However, these are not both theoretical variables. Nominal denominational allegiance is an index of social identity which issues in different patterns of social action. To attribute importance to the meanings of members as well as those of the observers of social life, as most sociologists would do, necessitates using members' meanings as categories in analysis. This results in particularizing description alone only if such analysis is not concerned to explore hypothesis couched in general terms. In this case it is being used to test just such a hypothesis: that social identity and location are important factors affecting outcomes in loose markets.

At a more mundane level, our critics may object further that the only reason why location and (occasionally) attitude variables predict outcomes is that these variables themselves correlate strongly with the standard variables, chiefly age and skill. In reply, three things must be said. First, while the standard variables do vary across the categories of locational variables, they do not do so in such a way that one could predict the results from their differential distribution between the categories of the location variables. Second, the standard variables are not themselves particularly strong predictors: their relation to the locational variables cannot itself, therefore, be responsible alone for the locational variables' greater predictive power. Third, we take it for granted that the standard variables play a crucial part in explaining differences in outcome between the categories of the locational variables. Our argument is not that locational variables are *theoretically* more important than standard variables, nor that the former have causal powers independent of the standard variables, but that locational variables structure their operation at the aggregate level because they constitute the context of social action at the individual level. We are unable to parcel out the 'effects' of standard and locational variables, if indeed it would make any sense to do so. It should be noted in this regard that the standard variables themselves interrelate both theoretically and empirically in a manner which makes estimating the causal efficacy of each equally difficult.

It is for this reason that we shall, in the last two sections of this chapter, *not* explore the determination of labour market outcomes by examining the efficacy of each hypothetically influential variable as a predictor while holding others constant. The importance of the location variables results from their acting together with other variables; it is not to be expected that they have causal power independent of the 'context of causality' in which they operate. Rather, we shall explore the pattern of characteristics associated with each market outcome type.

The general conclusion that may be drawn from table 10.2 is, then, that it demonstrates the importance of locational variables. It also provides information as to the way those variables affect outcomes. Success is negatively and chequeredness positively related to living in a large settlement and failure associated with urban sprawl. Neath and Swansea appear to be the large settlements where failure is least likely, Port Talbot and Swansea the large settlements where chequeredness is most common, followed by Neath. Chequeredness was found least frequently in areas peripheral to these settlements.

The success rates according to religious allegiance suggest that those occupying positions in the traditional social structure (Anglican–Welsh Nonconformist) are at an advantage compared with the non-traditional categories (English Nonconformist and Roman Catholic). Both Roman Catholics and Welsh Nonconformists have much higher chequeredness rates, however, with the result that it is the English non-Catholic denominations that have the highest failure rates.

Lastly, the network data do not support the hypothesis put forward early in our study that belonging to a collective or dispersed network was associated with a career in contracting. These types of network would appear to produce success rather than chequeredness and it is the latter category that contains the contracting men. Chequeredness is associated, instead, with individualistic network types.

It must be admitted that network type is the most disappointing of our locational variables. However, it is the most crude of all our hypothetical predictors. In the case of chequeredness a more serious problem arises. Chequeredness, is, in part, the result of the shift of BSC (and of other firms) to policies involving the employment of fixed term or contract labour. However, it is not the case that all of those who had chequered types of labour market experience embarked after redundancy on careers in contracting. Hence it is a mistake to test hypotheses derived from field data which refer to contract workers on outcome data which submerge these workers in the larger category of chequered.

This raises the central issue of how far the chequered category, whose existence is one of the major conclusions of the outcome analysis, can be regarded as any more than just a category. Do the chequered share any substantive, as opposed to formal, market and work characteristics? When compared with other categories on a whole range of variables they do not show marked differences from the sample mean. Should the chequered outcome category not be disaggregated? 'Better not try and disaggregate them,' one of us remarked, 'they might disappear.' The question of the heterogeneity of the chequered cannot be avoided, and resolving it is the task of the next section.

Before beginning that task something must be said about the procedure followed in the rest of the chapter. If the problem of the operation of the locational variables is posed as a question of how social identity relates to outcomes, then the question is what differences in social location/identity exist between those with different labour market experience outcomes, conceived as distinct sub-populations. That is, we shall abandon the classic method of using variables as predictors and shall attempt instead to answer the question, *who* are the unemployed, self-employed, etc.? Technically this means producing tables with labour market outcome across the top, *as if* outcome were an independent variable. However we are not going to treat it as such. Rather, the different categories of outcome will be used to identify different sub-populations of redundant steelworkers whose respective characteristics will be described and compared. Unweighted data have been used in the analysis throughout. Except when otherwise stated, any percentages quoted cannot be used to estimate population parameters. Our concern is with the relation between categories in the sample.

## Who are the chequered?

One of the central problems of this research was not to explain the *emergence* of the chequered, which is clearly the result of greater use of fixed term and contract labour, especially by BSC itself, but to identify what determined its *membership*. Preliminary analysis suggested that the category chequered, that is, those who have experienced intermittent employment and unemployment is socially heterogenous and needs to be disaggregated, that is, divided into sub-categories. Ideally it would have been desirable to distinguish those whose chequeredness was the product of demand side factors – fixed term employment or work with contractors – as opposed to supply side factors, such as willingness to change jobs. Unfortunately we only have data on respondents' involvement in contract labour and not on fixed-term employment. Demand side chequeredness was probably much more extensive than that generated by contracting, particularly in settlements other than Port Talbot. The chequered were divided, therefore, first into those who had experience of *contracting* and those who did not. Second, there were those who had not been involved in retraining or self-employment (chequered pure) and those who had (chequered plus). The chequered category was evenly split between the pure and the plus, while those workers with experience of contracting constituted 32 per cent of all those with chequered careers. It is clear that it is the size not the existence of the chequered category that is a result of contracting; the importance of the chequered would have been one of the conclusions of this study even if there had been no contracting.

By permutating these two distinctions it is possible to divide the chequered into 4 sub-categories. The largest was the non-contracting plus at 40 per cent. The smallest was contracting plus at 9 per cent. Intermediate were the two pure chequered categories, contracting (23 per cent) and non-contracting (28 per cent). Differences between the sub-categories were then examined along a number of dimensions including those constituting the standard variables and a broad range of social identity/locational variables. These comparisons are set out in table 10.3. Of 29 comparisons made there, 17 showed the contracting sub-categories to be more like each other than like the non-contracting sub-categories. These comparisons have been indicated by printing the variable names concerned in bold type.

Briefly the contractors, as contractors' men are termed locally, occurred in higher proportions in the prime age and younger (under 30) age group, who were advantaged in terms of qualifications, transferable and marketable skills, who had largely been made redundant on the LIFO principle with a smaller proportion who volunteered for redundancy. An above average proportion of those who had retrained had done so early and had used informal or direct methods of job search. The contractors had the highest rates of job acquisition by informal means. Below average proportions had received make-up pay. More of the contractors than non-contractors had spent an average or below average proportion of their time after redundancy unemployed. Above average proportions lived in the Port Talbot area and belonged to dispersed or collective networks with relatively low levels of interconnectedness.

The non-contractors, in contrast, were over-represented in the older and younger age groups and were either average or disadvantaged in terms of skills and qualifications. Above average proportions had volunteered for redundancy but the incidence of LIFO redundancies was only average. Those who retrained had done so later rather than earlier. The non-contractors preferred formal to informal or direct methods of job search and they had the highest rate of job acquisition by formal means. Most had spent above average proportions of their time since redundancy unemployed and when in work an above average proportion had received make-up pay. Above average proportions of non-contractors came from areas other than Port Talbot, and the non-contracting pure had dispersed or individualistic networks. The non-contractors had, however, higher rates of network connectedness.

If we examine the variables which do not distinguish the contracting from the non-contracting chequered we do not find that their distributions allow any other grouping of the four sub-categories. What we do find is the existence of at least three distinguishable social identity groups.

The *contracting pure* have average proportions who are Alliance voting, are Nonconformist, have low levels of religious observance, and whose social life is centred in public places which supply some of their network members. This sub-category was most successful in terms of current status.

The *contracting plus* have above average proportions who are Labour voting, Roman Catholic and religiously active, which suggests that the 'other' location where a relatively high proportion say they got to know network members is the Roman Catholic Church. Though first encountered in a public place their contacts are seen in their own homes. This sub-category was least successful in terms of current status.

The *non-contracting pure* include above average proportions who are older, have traditional denominational but non-traditional political allegiances, high levels of religious activity and social networks to which kin are central, and thus high levels of interconnectedness and home centredness. This sub-category has above average proportions living in Swansea and Bridgend. It is nearly as successful as the contracting pure in terms of current status.

TABLE 10.3 Who are the chequered?

| | Contracting | | Non-contracting | |
|---|---|---|---|---|
| *Characteristic* | *pure* | *plus* | *pure* | *plus* |
| Market variables | | | | |
| **Age** | Prime (30–44) | prime and young | old (45 + ) | young ( <30) |
| **Qualification** | average | advantaged | average | disadvantaged |
| **Marketable skill** | advantaged | average | average | average |
| **Transferable skill** | slightly advantaged | advantaged | average | slightly disadvantaged |
| **Make-up** | below average | below average | average | very high |
| **Trained late** | – | below average | – | above average |
| **Voluntary redundancy** | low | very low | high | above average |
| **Hard, LIFO redundancy** | average | high | average | average |
| When looked for work | late | later | later | earlier |
| When made redundant | late | peak | peak and late | early |
| **Job search (current status unemployed)** | informal | informal/direct | formal | formal |
| Search to acquisition shift | formal to direct/informal | formal to informal | formal to direct | formal to informal |
| Current job acquisition (see foot of table) | | | | |
| **BSC job acquisition** | direct | direct | informal | informal |
| **Retraining spells** | – | high | – | average |
| **Time unemployed** | average | low | above average | average |

| | | | | |
|---|---|---|---|---|
| Locational Variables | | | | |
| How voted 1979 | Alliance | Labour | SDP/Welsh Nationalist | Conservative/Labour |
| Denomination | Nonconformist | Roman Catholic | Anglican/Welsh Nonconformist | no pattern |
| Church attendance | low | high | above average | low |
| **Geographical location** | Port Talbot | Port Talbot | Swansea/Bridgend | Maesteg/outside market |
| Settlement type | minor | main | minor | sprawl |
| Network | | | | |
| **Self-ascribed** | dispersed | collective | dispersed/individual | no pattern |
| How contacts known | relatives/social | other (?church) | relatives | work/social circle |
| Where contacts met | club or pub | own/contact's home | own home | club or pub |
| Rate of contact | low | high | low | average |
| **Interconnectedness** | low | low | high | high |
| Job acquisition (current status: employed) | | | | |
| **Formal** | 20 | - | **62** | **53** |
| **Informal** | **40** | **80** | 8 | 35 |
| Direct | **30** | 20 | 23 | 12 |
| % employed at interview | 52 | 33 | 45 | 35 |
| % distribution (weighted) | 23 | 9 | 28 | 40 |
| Number of cases (unweighted) | 29 | 15 | 29 | 49 |

The remaining sub-category, the *non contracting plus*, is composed of two further sub-categories. One is relatively advantaged in terms of its market capacity, includes people who reside on the edge of or outside the local labour market, have individualistic networks and have tried (unsuccessfully) to become self-employed. The other sub-category resides predominantly in the urban sprawl in the core of the local labour market area, is relatively disadvantaged in the market and unsuccessful in searching for employment; formal means of job search are favoured despite membership of collective local networks centring on public institutions.

Examination of the sub-categories of the chequered cannot, by itself, determine the distinguishing characteristics of the category. What this investigation has done, however, is to demonstrate the distinctiveness of the contractors. We have already seen that the incidence of the chequered is highest in two settlements, Port Talbot and Swansea (table 10.2). The present analysis has made it clear that experience of contracting is associated with Port Talbot and the implication must be that fixed employment is associated with the Swansea sub-market, where the non contracting pure are over-represented. If we compare the contractors with the non-contractors, it appears that age, skill, geographical location, network type and job search behaviour operate together to ensure the acquisition of contracting employment. That the contractors have a prospensity to a distinctive job search pattern independent of market conditions, is shown by the fact that they obtained their BSC jobs by different means from those of the non-contractors.

The significance of network type in the provision of contracting work requires some clarification. Morris has suggested (1984a) that there is an association between network type and contracting employment, the acquisition of contracting work being facilitated by the possession of a collective network type. Collective networks are large, local and interconnected and members maintain contact with each other in a public place. Dispersed networks are similar but the respondent sees his network members individually rather than in collective settings. In contrast to both these types is the individualistic network which is not interconnected and whose members are geographically dispersed (Morris, 1985a). This, Morris suggests, is associated with long periods of search unemployment but the eventual acquisition of permanent rather than temporary employment (1984a).

It is extremely difficult to devise survey measures which can detect network types. Morris's types appear in table 10.3: respondents were asked to choose which of the network descriptions approximated to their own type. By this measure ('self-ascribed' network in the table), more *contracting* workers had dispersed or collective networks than non-contracting workers, although as we have already noted, it is the independent type of network that tends to predict *chequeredness*. The present analysis therefore confirms Morris's hypothesis about *contracting* work. It is because the *contractors* are only a minority of the chequered that membership of a collective or dispersed network fails to predict chequeredness.

Other measures of network type (interconnectedness, frequency of contact and contact setting) also showed differences between the sub-categories of chequered. The contractors' networks were not highly interconnected, suggesting that a contracting career requires a network with a high level of penetration into the market. Contractors with high rates of contact fared worse than those with low rates, thus tending to support Granovetter's weak tie hypothesis (see chapter 5). Among the non contractors also it was those with low rates of contact that had the highest success rate in finding jobs.

When we consider the setting of network contact we find that the contracting pure included an above average proportion who met their network members in a public place, as predicted by Morris's hypothesis. The non-contracting plus were, however, also over-represented among those who met fellow network members in a public place. The failure in this case of public settings to be associated with contracting work, can be explained in terms of residence of non-contractors in areas not associated with demand for contract labour. Public setting would appear to be a condition of contracting employment only in locations giving access to contracting work. The non contracting pure, included a high proportion of those with individualistic networks, also had a greater than expected proportion who had spent substantial amounts of time since redundancy unemployed, but this category enjoyed a relatively high success rate as measured by current status. This is consistent with Morris's hypothesis of an association between individualistic networks, long search and eventual success.

We may conclude, therefore, that the chequered are, as we suspected, a heterogeneous category in terms of employment type (contracting/other), in terms of social identity, labour market behaviour, geographical location and network type. Only the contracting chequered share characteristics which constitute an intelligible pattern. We can distinguish three groups of non-contracting chequered. The chequered pure survived in the market by means of fixed term employment associated with Swansea and Bridgend. This elderly, traditional and not particularly privileged group seems to have succeeded by a combination of persistence and the use of kin-based networks. Some advantaged redundants in desirable but remote market locations unsuccessfully tried self-employment. Other disadvantaged redundants in types of geographical location associated with unemployment tried retraining but failed to obtain work. These two sub-groups constitute the chequered plus. Since the geographical location of both sub groups is unfavourable to employment, the key characteristic of the network is the extent of its geographical penetration of the market. In the absence of kin connectedness and the presence of public interaction settings, an interconnected network type suggests lack of penetration. Unfavourable geographical location and lack of market penetration by networks characterize the non-contracting chequered plus.

It seems possible, therefore, that the existence and take-up of retraining and self-employment opportunities may increase the size of the chequered category, independent of the demand for contracting or fixed-term workers or the predisposition of workers to change jobs; that is, the very factors designed to induce employment may, in a loose market, be associated with chequeredness instead.

But what about social identity? We have demonstrated major differences in identity between sub-categories, but not that they are relevant to differences in labour market experience, except in the case of the non contracting pure. Generally, identity differences cannot be related to labour market experience outcomes except through network type and job search behaviour. The hypothesis must be that identity in the categorical sense is related to identity in the relational sense which affects network type, and network type affects both job acquisition and job search. This issue, too, cannot be explored without a comparison of the contractors with the group that they failed to join (the employed) and the non-contractors' with the group they have avoided joining, the continuously unemployed. That is our final task.

## The market and network characteristics of labour market outcome categories

It is obviously impossible to present or discuss comparisons between 8 categories (employed/self-employed/chequered/unemployed, each divided into 'pure' and 'plus'), let alone to take account of the further division of the 2 chequered sub-categories into contracting and non-contracting, which would yield 10 categories in all. We shall therefore deal with the 4 main categories of labour market experience outcome, making reference to sub-categorical differences only when absolutely necessary.

There is no difficulty in ranking 3 of the main categories according to the classic variables of age, skill and search timing. The employed are over-represented in the prime 30–44 age group, the unemployed among the old (45 plus), the chequered among both the prime and young (under 30) if contracting and among the young if non-contracting. The self-employed, however, are over-represented among both the prime and the old, and this will not be the last occasion on which we shall note their distinctiveness.

In terms of skill, the employed are over-represented among non-manual workers, the self-employed among the non-manual and skilled, the chequered among the skilled (due largely to the advantaged position of the contractors) and the unemployed among the semi- and unskilled, as classified by a collapsed version of the Goldthorpe-Hope scale. Our own combined qualification and skill measure shows however the self-employed to be ranked above the employed in terms of qualifications, followed by the chequered and unemployed. An examination of marketable skills shows the self-employed to be at a slight disadvantage in comparison to both the employed and the chequered, with the unemployed least advantaged. Marketable skill, however, shows least variation; across all the categories of the combined measure both employed and chequered exhibit the same pattern. What distinguishes the self-employed is the proportion possessing both a qualification and a marketable skill, and what distinguishes the unemployed is the above average proportion possessing *neither*.

As regards search timing, the employed are over-represented among those who looked for work as soon as redundancies were announced, the self-employed among those who waited until told and the unemployed who waited until after they had left. The chequered are average, because the late search of the majority is balanced by the earlier search of the largest and least successful sub-category, the non contracting plus. Though the employed and self-employed keep changing position in the above measures, the ranking employed, chequered, unemployed is clearly established in terms of all three factors.

If we consider the pre-BSC labour market experience variables, certain continuities between pre- and post-redundancy experience can be noted. The self-employed and the employed had experienced least unemployment before redundancy and the unemployed most, with the chequered as an intermediate category. Our more sophisticated measure, which takes into account the number and length of spells, requires us to rank the self-employed as the most advantaged since none had experienced any long spells of unemployment. Next in rank came the chequered, fewer of whom had experienced long spells of unemployment than the employed or unemployed, among whom the experience of long spells is very similar. Incidence did not vary between sub-categories of chequered. On the grounds of age alone we should expect the unemployed to have the highest number of pre-redundancy jobs, followed by the self-employed, and employed and the chequered. However, though the unemployed did have the highest proportion of those with two or more pre-BSC jobs, the predicted pattern did not emerge; next in order are the chequered, followed by the employed and self-employed. The exception to this statement within the chequered is the elderly, traditional non-contracting pure category whose involvement approximates to that of the employed. They have no more business to be in the chequered category on the grounds of their pre-redundancy labour market experience than on the basis of their social identity.

While at BSC it was the self-employed who were more likely than other categories to have had an additional job, not the chequered. Hobbles (ancillary employments) while at BSC are not associated with chequeredness but with self-employment. It is the self-employed (not the chequered) who were disproportionately from indirect service departments in BSC, only the 'traditional' non-contracting pure being over-represented in this type of department.

When we consider the redundancy process, we find that the self-employed had most and the unemployed and chequered the fewest voluntary redundancies, with the employed occupying an intermediate position. In terms of hard (LIFO/department closed) redundancies, however the chequered occupy the highest position and the self-employed the lowest, with the employed and unemployed falling between the two. This is easily explicable in terms of the age composition of the different categories. In terms of timing, the employed were most advantaged, followed by the self-employed, while the unemployed and the chequered were equally disadvantaged. In addition, the employed looked for work sooner, followed by the self-employed and then the chequered, the unemployed including by far the largest proportion who looked late – whether that is defined as after being told or after leaving. Once again, the expected ranking (employed, chequered, unemployed) is confirmed by the redundancy process variables, with the exception of the hard redundancy rate.

The methods by which respondents obtained their BSC job are also related to labour market experience type. Markedly fewer chequered and hardly any of the 'contracting chequered' obtained their BSC jobs by formal means, a characteristic the chequered share with the self-employed. The employed favoured formal methods most with the unemployed in an intermediate position. Informal methods were used most frequently by the chequered and unemployed, followed closely by the employed. The self-employed used formal methods least of all, direct acquisition being more favoured by this category than any other.

In terms of search method after redundancy, those chequered with current status unemployed had used formal methods more frequently than the unemployed category, at the expense of informal methods. When we turn to the job acquisition methods of those with the current status employed, however, we find that there is no appreciable difference between the methods used by the employed and chequered. What we do find is a marked difference between the search methods of the unsuccessful and the acquisition methods of the successful: only 40 per cent of the successful used formal methods, compared with 60 per cent of the unsuccessful, and 19 per cent of the successful used direct methods against only 9 per cent of the unsuccessful. Two-and-a-half years after redundancy, therefore, direct methods, as well as informal methods and the good word, seem to differentiate those who secured jobs from unsuccessful seekers.

If, however, we compare methods of job acquisition at BSC with methods used to obtain current jobs we still find what we noted with regard to the Wave 1 data: a massive movement away from direct methods in favour of both formal and informal methods (see chapter 5). This confirms two arguments developed in this book. First, job acquisition methods depend on the state of the market and are not the unique result of job seekers' choices. They represent a relation between the two sides. Second, the looser the market, the less reliance will be placed on direct methods. Hence the further we move away from the peak redundancy point, the greater the number of people who will have gone off the register and therefore (other things being equal) the *less* loose the market and the *greater* the number of jobs acquired by direct methods. Since, however, the market was (in absolute terms) still very slack, formal and informal methods still predominated. We calculate that within the redundant population about 30 per cent of all respondents who were currently employed had obtained their job by informal means, and that the proportion of those using such means who had had a good word put in on their behalf by their contact was greater for the successful (69 per cent) than for the unsuccessful (47 per cent).

In spite of a small shift back to the direct method, it is therefore still worth examining the network types of the labour market experience categories and their relation to search and acquisition methods and (where relevant) to current status. This is done in table 10.4.

The first point is that either our crude network measures (rows 2 and 3) fail to discriminate or there is little difference in contact and interconnectedness between outcome types. Self-ascribed network type (1) focuses on the setting of the interaction as do variables 4 and 5, and all of these do show differences. The unemployed have a more restricted and privatised social life than the employed, and in this they resemble the chequered contracting plus. This group describes its networks as collective but the measures suggest that the dispersed type predominates. This is the Catholic sub-category and the apparent discrepancy must reflect a contrast between the collective setting in which they meet acquaintances and the private setting of their encounters with intimates. They have the highest unemployment rate.

The employed have social lives largely dependent on contact made through social activities centring on club or pub and work. In this they resemble the contracting pure sub-category of the chequered. The emphasis on collective networks among the employed is not found among the contracting pure, who describe their networks as dispersed, because, unlike the employed, relatives as well as social contacts are an important part of their networks. This sub-category also have the highest of all the chequered sub-categories currently working.

We have already noted that the characteristics of the non contracting pure lend some support to the hypothesis put forward by Morris on the basis of her field study, that those with independent networks spend longer unemployed but are more likely to end up with jobs. This group, the 'elderly and traditional' from the last section, appear to be classic 'stickers'. In terms of its success rate this category also might be regarded as approximating the employed, yet its social life seems to differ. The reason

TABLE 10.4 Labour market experience categories and network characteristics

| | | | | | Chequered | | | |
|---|---|---|---|---|---|---|---|---|
| | | | | | *Contracting* | | *Non-contracting* | |
| *Characteristic* | | *Unemployed* | *Employed* | *Self-employed* | *pure* | *plus* | *pure* | *plus* |
| Self-ascribed network type | 1 | no pattern | collective: not independent | dispersed | dispersed | collective | dispersed + ind | no pattern |
| Interconnectedness | 2 | average | average | less connected | less interconn-ected | less interconn-ected | more interconn-ected | more interconn-ected |
| Contact rate | 3 | average + | average | average – | average | high | average – | average |
| How known | 4 | neighbours | social | work | relatives; social | neighbours; 'other': ?church | relatives | work; social |
| Where seen | 5 | home | club/pub, work, varies | work; church/chapel | club/pub | contacts' homes | own home | club/pub |
| Current status | | all unemployed by definition | all employed by definition | all self-employed by definition | employed: 52% | employed: 33% | employed: 45% | employed: 35% |
| Search method (unemployed) | | informal relative to chequered | - | - | informal | informal/ direct | formal | formal |
| Acquisition method (employed) | | - | same as chequered | - | informal/ direct | informal | formal | formal |

*Source*: Wave 3 data, those in market only

for this, we suggest, connected with its greater age. Its members are visited in their own homes by younger relatives who are scattered throughout the market, and this category has above average proportions describing their networks as dispersed and individualistic. Their networks include kin members and should therefore be more connected than other categories; and, being older, their kin should be scattered geographically and this is presumably the reason for their lower rates of contact. While their network type increases market success, their age is against them. In social terms they are therefore *elderly employed* as their high rate of employment suggests.

The non contracting plus are, as we have already argued, heterogeneous and cannot be assimilated to any other group.

## Outcome, identity and location

We have already demonstrated that the outcome categories can be ranked in terms of their labour market position. In these terms the ranking is employed, chequered, unemployed. The ranking of the self-employed is more ambiguous but their superiority to the employed in terms of qualifications, terminal education age, non-manual occupation, transferable skill, under-representation among the semi-skilled at BSC and household income at Wave 3 justify (we believe) ranking them 'above' the employed.

In terms of identity–location variables the differences between the outcome types can be summarized as follows: the self-employed are over-represented in the prime and older age groups, but only slightly among the over 50s. They have no Catholics among them and are markedly over-represented among the Welsh denominations and are under-represented among those with single and widowed marital statuses. They stand in marked contrast to the unemployed who are over-represented in the oldest age group (45 and over) and even more noticeably among the over 50s, who are markedly under-represented in the Welsh denominational category in spite of their age, which increases the members of this religious category in the sample as a whole. In terms of marital status, they have the highest proportion of widowed. The empoyed and chequered fall between these polar categories, the employed being over-represented among the prime, and the chequered among the prime and young age groups. As a result, the chequered are over-represented among the single. Compared with the employed, the chequered are over-represented among both the Catholics and the Welsh Nonconformists, chiefly at the expense of the Anglicans.

Each category has a distinctive location within the local labour market area. In terms of settlement type, the employed are distributed in the same way as the sample as a whole. The chequered are, however, over-represented in the main settlement category, which emphasizes the importance of availability in gaining short-term employment. Fewer of the unemployed, in contrast, live in main settlements, but are over-represented in 'urban sprawl'. There are above average numbers of the self-employed in small isolated settlements on the periphery of the manufacturing core; this should not be thought of as a cause of their 'self-employment' but as a result of their superior status position.

If we examine attitudes to moving as indicators of attachment to the local social structure, we find that a higher proportion of the unemployed and chequered (in spite of their very different age distributions) regard moving as a hardship, while the self-employed are more likely than any other category to dispute this statement, and to agree that workers should move to employment opportunities elsewhere. Though change of residence was low across the whole sample, the chequered were twice as likely to have moved – though within the local labour market area – as the sample as a whole.

Attitude measures can also be used to throw light on the relation between social identity, location and labour market behaviour. There is little of interest to report about the psychological attitudes. On a number of measures the degree of optimism/pessimism about the future relates positively/negatively with the labour market position ranking. There were, however, two important exceptions. It was the chequered, not the unemployed, who claimed most frequently to have felt degraded by the experience of unemployment, and this suggests a motivational component in this particular outcome. The second exception was that it was the self-employed who disagreed least frequently with the statement 'I *sometimes* think things will never get better for me', thus spoiling what otherwise would have the predicted gradient. This finding nicely points up the insecurity involved in self-employment, but might also have been expected to be associated with chequeredness. It was not, however, suggesting that significant numbers of the contracting chequered experienced contracting as a way of life rather than a predicament.

In their response to the economic attitude questions, the self-employed stand out from the other categories. They were more likely to believe in the importance of personal drive and to disfavour government support of ailing industries, less inclined to blame economic difficulties on the capitalist system and less likely to be pessimistic about the state of the country. In their responses to the industrial attitude questions, the self-employed were again distinctive, being more hostile to management and more in favour of curbing union pay claims.

The indusrial attitude questions did, however, show differences over all the outcome categories. The employed were most inclined to value job security over high pay and the unemployed least (the chequered and self-employed occupying intermediate positions), which suggests a motivational component in the determination of labour market outcome as well as being a result of labour market experience, especially as this result, though statistically significant on Wave 1, ceased to be so on Wave 3. The employed less frequently emphasized the importance of maintaining the standard of living on Wave 1, suggesting (together with their high pay versus security score) a willingness to trade down to obtain employment. On Wave 3, they emphasize the importance of maintaining living standards more than any other group. While the unemployed included higher proportions who believe that a trade union's job is to get the most that it can for its members on both waves of interviewing, the employed who most frequently failed to agree with this statement on Wave 1 ceased to be distinctive on Wave 3 and the proportion agreeing increased slightly. The chequered, on the other hand, who tend to be like the unemployed in their militant conception of the role of trade unions on Wave 1, move closer to the employed on Wave 3. The shifts between waves by the employed are clearly the result of their experience: they have moved to a position where hanging on to what they have achieved becomes more important than improving it, and towards a more militant view of the role of unions. The chequered, in contrast, become much more concerned with maintaining their standard of living and less likely to see the role of the unions as highly significant.

It was to be expected, therefore, that these differences in identity, motivation and attitude will be reflected in political allegiance. However, since in South Wales an overwhelming majority of every social category voted or intended to vote Labour, it is difficult to establish significant patterns of variation. The first wave of interviewing took place shortly after the formation of the SDP ('Who are they? Oh, I know, that new lot' – in the words of one respondent). Nearly half of the sample expressed a positive attitude to 'the new lot' on Wave 1, but by far the most positive was that of the self-employed, two-thirds of whom saw this new development as a good thing. Enthusiasm had diminished 18 months later, less than a quarter agreeing with the positive attitude statement, but once again the self-employed stand out from the other categories, most of them continuing to view the new party favourably.

When asked how they would vote tomorrow the majority said Labour, but the incidence of intended Labour voting across the outcome categories showed the expected gradient, with the self-employed having the lowest proportion of Labour votes, the unemployed the highest, the employed and chequered occupying an intermediate position. Those uncertain how they would vote (14 per cent of the unweighted sample) were asked how they thought they *might* vote. Here the employed stood out as having the smallest category who thought they might vote Labour, an above average proportion considering voting for every other political party. This finding accords with the industrial attitude shifts which suggest a general move towards conservative attitudes among those who had been successful in the market. Allegiance to Labour does not, however, seem to have wavered among the employed and unemployed between Waves 1 and 3, when current voting intentions, excluding those who were uncertain, are compared with the past voting behaviour. The chequered and the self-employed had both, however, shifted away from Labour when present intention is compared with past voting.

## Conclusion

It is difficult to sum up the differences revealed by the analysis in any way which does justice to the complexities of the data, except by resort to the use of pure types. The unemployed seem to approximate to the traditional collectivistic solidaristic working class beloved of sociologists of the 1960s. Their polar opposites are the self-employed, whose attitudes and identity approximate those associated with the petty bourgeoisie. The employed and the chequered represent subdivisions of a new working class, but they are not the affluent and instrumental workers of Goldthorpe and Lockwood's 1969 study. The employed who have 'made it' in the market are more concerned with security than high pay – with preserving their relatively privileged position in employment. At the same time they are most opposed to trade union militancy, though less so than when first interviewed nearer the redundancy point.

The chequered, as we saw in the previous section, are not socially homogeneous, and comprise the 'failed' employed (the contracting chequered pure), two different types of 'successful' unemployed (the non-contracting chequered pure and the contracting chequered plus) and a residual heterogenous category (the non-contracting chequered plus). The contracting chequered pure constitute a genuinely new category within the working class in terms of their labour market position and have emerged as a result of changes in the pattern of demand for labour. The defining features of this new and very important category appear to be motivational factors which predispose them to snatching rather than sticking; a relatively privileged labour market position and a social location which gives them access to contract work.

There is, however, another way of conceptualizing the results of labour market history data analysis, and that is in the terms which Brown has used to interpret a different body of material (Brown, 1987). The activity of workers in the market may be seen as a struggle to *retain or reproduce*, under unfavourable conditions, *a traditional social identity*. Those who fail in market terms cling to the political and social models which in the past have been associated with their class. Those who have been successful in market terms do not have to cope with the problems of spoilt identity and can afford to move to a modified traditional set of attitudes which reflects the state and their experience of the market. The contracting chequered, likewise, are successful in maintaining their working-class identity. Their spells of unemployment notwithstanding, they are continually successful in selling their labour power on the market, which they interpret as the result of individual drive and initiative. There are, therefore, indications in the data that this new category may be moving in the general direction of the self-employed, that is, emphasizing pay above job security, having a greater willingness to move, being distrustful of collectivities on both sides of industry, with a corresponding shift in political allegiance to the Alliance and Conservative parties and away from Labour.

The basis of this shift has long been laid in the decline of traditional working-class communities, in South Wales as elsewhere. The working class character of South Wales consists in a strong sense of belonging to both regional and class categories, and of interconnection through a network of ties focused on locality and spatially extended through kinship. Intra market geographical mobility, public housing, and urban planning and redevelopment, together with the influence of the media have, however, destroyed the traditional pattern of social life focused on local communal institutions: club/pub, church/chapel and various forms of associational life. These public institutions still exist, and the participation and non-participation of people in them is important in differentiating the characteristics of their networks. They have ceased, however, to be *common* features of the networks of individuals. Indeed the location data suggest that it is in the commuter villages (small isolated settlements on the eastern periphery of the market in the attractive Vale of Glamorgan) that social life shows the 'traditional working-class pattern' centred on public institutions.

'Networks' have replaced 'community'; they define identity and location and are an important element in determining market access. The reproduction of identity therefore involves network maintenance and participation and it is here too that the unemployed, whose social life is confined to neighbouring in the urban sprawl have failed to reproduce their identity. Network and the struggle to maintain identity are two notions which link the survey studies of the workers with the field studies of their households and they will therefore constitute a theme of the final chapter.

# 11
# Redundancy and Social Transition

## Conclusions

### *The effect of the redundancies on the market*

We are now ready to conclude, not the histories of our respondents, but the story of the BSC redundancy with a final consideration of its impact on the market. Two questions were posed in chapter 2 and only partially answered. How did the market manage to absorb such a massive flow on of redundants without unemployment levels rising to and remaining well above the national average? Why did the post-redundancy market, instead of becoming stagnant, become more dynamic after the redundancies, that is, characterized by an increased number of flows on and flows off the register?

The answer to the first question is in part that a large proportion of those made redundant withdrew from the market and, of course, that a large proportion of the remainder left the register within a relatively short space of time. This raises the second question. The timing and speed of flow off was partly the result of the movement of workers into retraining and self-employment. However, as we have seen, take up of retraining was not high and the self-employed constitute our smallest outcome category. This cannot be the whole reason, therefore.

The other and crucial part of the explanation is connected with a change in the character of labour *demand* which coincided with the redundancies. BSC decided not merely to make less steel, but to make it in a new way, using contractors to do work previously done by direct labour. At the same time the plant, instead of being run down, was steadily modernized throughout the post-redundancy period, thus generating contracting employment in construction. As a result the proportion of the demand for fixed, short-term labour in the Port Talbot market increased, resulting in a rise in the number of flows off or on the register far beyond that generated by the movement in and out of retraining and self-employment.

Though we are unable to study the whole of the west Industrial South Wales market as Fevre (1984) studied the Port Talbot market, it is clear from the survey data that fixed-term labour is associated with main settlements, principally Port Talbot and Swansea. The increase in demand for short-term labour is not therefore purely a result of changes in the labour process and capital investment in BSC, but is a more general market characteristic associated with the recession which arrived later in the rest of the local labour market than it did in the Port Talbot sub-market.

The redundancy event, by causing a flow on to the market of workers whose pay would be made up to 90 per cent of their BSC earnings, created a supply of labour highly attractive to contracting firms at the very moment that the demand for contract work was increasing. Changes in the pattern of demand generated changes in the conditions of supply of labour which satisfied the new pattern and encouraged its establishement.

From a slightly different perspective the change in the market caused by the redundancies can be described as a fall in the demand for permanent labour, which did not result in an equivalent rise in unemployment because it was balanced by an increase in demand for temporary labour. As a result the market, understood as a market for permanent employment, was far looser than the unemployment statistics suggest; that is, it was much more difficult for redundant workers to get back into permanent employment than it would appear. We have spoken throughout of loose labour market conditions. If we consider *permanent employment* only, the market was very loose indeed. Conversely, however, the unemployment statistics do not over-estimate the non-availability of all forms of paid work, since although some of those out of work at any given moment are between contracting jobs, some of those in work are between spells of unemployment.

### *The effect of the new market on workers' labour market experiences*

The effect of the changed pattern of demand in the market as a whole did not of course affect all workers currently in the market. The burden of adjustment to the new pattern had to be taken on by those who came on to the market during this period, that is, those entering it for the first time and those made redundant from permanent employment. By far the largest sub-category of the latter were the redundant steelworkers themselves.

The flows on and off due to retraining and self-employment are reflected in the market experience categories originally suffixed by the term 'plus' (categories 5 with 6, 8, 10, 12) in table 9.4. The increased demand for short-term labour resulted in a large number of work histories composed of the status types employed and unemployed to which we responded with the purely phenomenal notion of chequeredness. Chequered careers are not all necessarily the result of increased demand for short-term labour – they include that sub-category of 'the frequent job changers' of earlier studies, whose members were unemployed between jobs. Not all sequences of short-term jobs punctuated by unemployment are due to experience of contract work. However, it is the changed character of labour demand that is responsible for the size of this category, and the most distinctive component of this type of demand appears to be for labour by contractors.

If we consider only those who remained in the market, therefore, the most common labour market experience outcome has turned out to be not continuous employment or unemployment but chequeredness. There is no doubt that working for contractors (locally 'being a contractor', that is, a contract labourer) has become a way of life for some men. For others it is a way of 'hanging in there' until permanent employment can be obtained. Those for whom it is a way of life are market men, adept at working the market and cobbling together benefit, wages from short-term employment and hobbles (ancillary employment). These men are exercising essentially entrepreneurial skills: they are surviving by combining different types of resource in response to market conditions. Others are reluctant contractors driven by the fear of continuous unemployment to snatch at any opportunity for employment, however unsatisfactory.

### *Matching two sides in loose markets*

To specify something as a market warrants, for the economist, the applicability of supply and demand theory as a means of explaining outcomes. For the student of economic institutions, whether an economist or not, a market is essentially a mechanism for bringing buyers and sellers of a commodity together for the purpose of exchange. There is therefore a tension between theoretical and institutional economic explanations of market outcomes, although it is not a tension between the perfect market of the theorist and the imperfect market of reality. It is rather one between the explanation of outcomes, given the existence of a market, and the study of social processes which *result* in the existence of a market. If one side offers labour for sale and the other side seeks to purchase it and neither knows of the existence of the other, a market cannot be said to exist, only two sets of unreconciled wants. Public institutions can bring the two sides together: employment exchanges and the mass media. The same effect can, however, be achieved by private (individual) enterprise: the canvassing of potential employees by employers, and employers by workers. These private methods may or may not involve social mediation, which can be either technical (the transmission of information) or moral (the intermediary uses 'influence' on the applicant's behalf) or both. Theoretically, mechanisms which relate those people who supply and demand a commodity and thereby constitute a given population as a market in the concrete, rather than abstract/theoretical sense, are of three kinds, as Lee has argued in chapter 5: public; private direct; private indirect. It has been our finding and is our contention that the looser the market, the greater the importance of public and private indirect methods of market constitution and the lesser the importance of private direct methods.

The reasons are as follows. In tight (sellers') markets uninformed direct application to employers is likely to be successful since most employers will have unfilled vacancies. Employers too may attempt to poach workers from other employers by approaching them directly. In such markets workers will have a stronger market position than employers, and will select employers on the basis of not only the reward package they offer but also their reputation for fair dealing with their workforce. In tight markets, workers can choose employers on the basis of their reputation taking into account both suitability and acceptability.

In loose markets none of these considerations applies: direct application will be fruitless since no one is taking on, and the worker's primary concern is with minimizing drops in income: eking out unemployment benefit, not maximizing rewards in employment. In loose (buyers') markets employers will be the superior party and will be able to choose. However, there are always many workers and relatively few employers, and the latter cannot directly recruit workers on the basis of their public reputation. Employers cannot therefore adopt the direct methods of workers. They can only exercise their newly-acquired ability to choose employees if they have access to information which is only available in the worker's social circle. Hence employers can only exercise their choice if they are members of the same social circle as applicants, which is unlikely, or have access to information transmitted by intermediaries, that is, if they are connected to an applicant by membership of the same social network.

Loose market conditions provide the possibility of choice by employers, which they must exercise since in a loose market there is an excess of supply over demand for the commodity being exchanged. This means that some of the commodity will remain unsold unless or until equilibriating mechanisms effect the equation of supply and demand. Buyers therefore *have* to choose, and to choose, moreover, between different units of the commodity which are identical in formal terms. This can only be done by recognizing other characteristics which differentiate them.

In labour markets the other characteristics which are recognized will, however, be unique, for what buyers of labour power get (a potentiality) is not what they want. What they want is actual labour. Potentiality has to be transformed into actuality by the activity in the labour process of the carrier of the labour power which the employer has bought. Judgements about 'acceptability' will therefore have to be made by persons (employers) about other persons' (applicants') *character*. This was well recognized by informants, both employers and applicants working with the purely formal category of 'tidy lad' (see chapter 6). Tidiness is a relational attribute and refers to the appropriateness of the person's character to the job in question. The tidiness of an applicant's character is inferred from information about his or her social identity (social category membership) as mediated by a network of social relations, and the character of his or her social circle. Hence employers must choose, and on the basis of information which can only be provided by intermediaries as a result of the employer's private initiative.

From statements about the tightness or looseness of a market, it may, therefore, be inferred that the market is constituted *as* a market in a particular way, and from statements about its constitution we may deduce further facts about job search behaviour of workers and job recruitment behaviour of employers. Each must be seen as correlative to the other and as responses both to the market level and the behaviour of members of the other side. The behaviours are not simply the result of the individual characteristics of the workers/employers concerned.

## *Predicting and explaining outcomes*

It follows from the argument of the preceding section that job search and acquisition behaviour should be seen as indicators of the state of a collectivity (a market) rather than measures of a causal determinant of outcomes. Acquisition data in particular are unreliable indicators of modes of acquisition since they only involve data deriving from the knowledge of the applicant. For example, direct recruitment by the employer – a category that increased between Waves 1 and 3 as the market became less slack – must have involved another informal (non-market) relation between employer and applicant, or the activity of intermediaries, otherwise the employer would not have been able to approach the applicant directly. In addition, as Lee has noted in chapter 5, all possible elements may be and often are involved in a single job acquisition episode. Search methods cannot, we suggest, be seen as independent causal factors in market outcome, and their survey proxies are crude in the extreme.

In this study (even if for somewhat special reasons) we have excluded those withdrawn from the market from analysis of its operation. Withdrawal is closely related to age and to sickness which is also age related. Once the withdrawn have been excluded, the power of age as an outcome predictor is weakened and that of the skill measure enfeebled. This result is predicted by the preceding argument. The distinction between the prediction of market success and failure is crucial here. No one in a loose market wants unsuitable workers, that is the elderly, sick, unskilled, hence these factors predict failure. But since there are not enough vacancies for suitable workers, a relatively privileged market position cannot by itself be a strong predictor of success. Search commencement and redundancy point remain strong predictors since they are related to the *relative* looseness of the market – the excess of supply over demand – at the point of entry to it. Hence the causal and explanatory factor is market state at search commencement rather that search timing itself. The relation between early timing and success depends on the market becoming looser in proportion to the total number made redundant at any given point, a condition that only holds *ceteris paribus*. In the instance studied here other things were not equal but the arrival of the recession reinforced the temporal relation between earlier time points and tighter market conditions and did not reverse it.

It has been the argument of this book, therefore, that in addition to the standard market variables, other social structural factors are important determinants of market outcome in loose markets, and we have referred to these as 'social location' or 'identity'. While the operation of these factors can be seen during fieldwork and reported in ethnography, such methods of investigation cannot explore their predictive power or assess their relative explanatory weight. Survey methods are, however, even less satisfactory tools for the examination of these factors than of those indicated by the standard variables. It is not that it is in principle impossible to devise identity and location indicators from survey data. The basic problem is a practical one: a research instrument which incorporated labour market history, network, location and identity data, standard variables, and job description data for both applications and acquisitions would probably be so long that it could not be administered in one interview.

We sought to demonstrate in chapter 10 that proxies of identity, location and network type are as well related to labour market experience and outcomes as are the standard variables, and that outcome types show differences in terms of their social composition along these dimensions.

The identification of identity proxies requires local knowledge; it is not being suggested, for example that denominational allegiance would necessarily be a useful indicator outside Wales. The use of geographical location indicators also requires local knowledge of the kind supplied in the present case by the review in chapter 2 of the changing character of the west Industrial South Wales labour market.

Geographical location gives some indication of what a particular network is likely to connect with, and in any full analysis of outcomes both variables would need to be used in conjunction with one another as predictors. The classification of networks posed a problem throughout the research and we were, I think, blinded to a degree both by Granovetter's 'weak tie' hypothesis which informed much of Lee's job acquisition work, and by the traditional anthropological focus on network interconnectedness, which was particularly important to Harris. To these dimensions of analysis Morris added setting type, size and geographical dispersion, and included all three dimensions in her models. However, we now believe it was a mistake to have used these holistic types as nominal measures *in survey work* and would seek in future to measure size, density, dispersion, contact and setting to construct empirical network types constituting the categories of a constructed nominal variable to be used in analysis in conjunction with identity and location measures.

We may sum up our contention concerning outcome prediction in the following way. The looser the market the more important are social identity and location as determinants of market outcome, and the weaker the power of market variables in predicting success. In addition we repeat, for the sake of completeness, that these relations must be explored among those currently in the market (withdrawers should be excluded); and whether or not outcomes are measured by labour market experience or current status, chequeredness must be distinguished as an outcome and the chequered not assimilated to either the employed/self-employed or unemployed categories if the effect of any type of variable is to be discerned.

## Labour markets and social transitions

In the preceding section we have not devoted any space to those conclusions of the field studies which concern the domestic division of labour. The reason for this is, we hope, self-evident. If the field data had shown that redundant workers were withdrawing from the market and households were moving from having single (or single and ancillary wage) economies to households dependent on the wife's wages and the husband's benefit (and hobbles) because of the husband's effective withdrawal from job search and the renegotiation of the domestic division of labour (role reversal), then market behaviour and outcomes would not have been intelligible unless the domestic division of labour was included as an outcome determinant. However, the field data show that this is not the case, the prime responsibility of the man for income generation and of the woman for domestic organization being largely unquestioned by both husbands and wives. Moreover, wives' employment is positively related to the labour market experience hierarchy, 60 per cent of the 'pure' self-employed category having a working wife compared with only 18.5 per cent of the unemployed 'plus' category. Hence role swap is least likely precisely where it is most necessary.

We originally supposed that this 'polarization' (Pahl, 1984) was a result of households' market location in the social structural sense, some households' networks facilitating job acquisition and others diminishing it for both spouses. An alternative hypothesis is that of marital homogamy in terms of level of marketable skill and 'tidiness'. These remain interesting hypotheses for further research. They were not explored in this study, however, because the field data show them to be unnecessary to explain the relation between the employment and unemployment of spouses which is a result rather of the interaction of three factors: gender relations within households; the relation between the households and the 'local' state; and the relation between gender and the market. Both Morris's and Leaver's studies (chapters 6 and 7 and chapter 8 respectively) reveal the absence of role reversal and no more than a blurring of the division of domestic labour, the division of primary responsibility for traditionally defined masculine and feminine tasks remaining intact.

Once again one of the things at issue here is social identity, in this case that associated with gender. Membership of gender categories is ratified by the taking part in appropriate and avoiding inappropriate *activities*. The loss of employment by the husband threatens his gender identity, which can only be further weakened by the assumption of domestic tasks, while any intrusion by him into the domestic sphere threatens the wife's identity and erodes her autonomy. At the same time, as both studies show, a fall in disposable income is associated with the unitary control of finance, usually by the wife, thus depriving the man of any independent source of income to finance those social activities associated with male identity. This can also involve the attrition of the husband's social network, which is significant in determining his chances of job acquisition. The wife in contrast experiences an intensification of her domestic responsibilities as the whole burden of ensuring household survival now rests upon her.

The importance of hobbles is not simply that they provide an alterantive to employment but that such forms of ancillary income supply men with money for personal spending which facilitates network maintenance and hence job acquisition. However, membership of an appropriate network is likely to be a precondition of operating a hobble, so that a network can both provide access to employment and the ancillary income necessary to maintain contacts during employment, while network absence is associated with the attrition of life outside the households. It is in the light of this ethnographically based understanding that the discussion of the relation between networks and outcome categories in the survey data in chapter 10 must be understood.

Whereas Morris's study develops our understanding of the relation between the internal organization of the household and its mode of articulation with the local social structure, Leaver's study documents the effect of long-term unemployment on domestic organization and the operation of the social security system. With regard to the latter, her most important finding is the way in which benefit regulations prevent flows of aid from the employed to the unemployed and constitute a bureaucratic intervention and control of family life. In this context the remark of one of our informants, cited in the Introduction: 'I used to be working class, but I've fallen below that now', takes on a more profound significance. Unemployment in the case of these formerly privileged members of the working class is associated with the decline of communal sociability and reciprocal flows of aid which were once the very essence of working-class culture and solidarity.

Leaver's other central finding reinforces this conclusion. The struggle to get by on supplementary benefit does not result in an increased individualism. Quite the reverse: there is a subordination of the needs of family members, including those of the man, to the survival needs of the household. But it is the household that is the collectivity, not the locality ('community') or the class. Hence poverty, unemployment and geographical stability push in the same direction as affluence and mobility insofar as they both increase the tendency to the isolation of the nuclear family and the child-centredness it already exhibits. The net result is the segregation of the unemployed from the social life of their own locality and class, a theme subsequently being pursued by Morris in the North East of England. There is a sense in which the unemployed have 'fallen' *out* of the local social structure. This is different from claiming that the unemployed as a category tend to be segregated. That argument concerns the causes of unemployment, but here we are concerned with its effects, since we are dealing with workers with relatively stable work histories who have *become* unemployed.

### *The transition and the social response*

There is no space here for an extended discussion of the state of advanced industrial economies in the 1980s and the implications of the changes they have experienced for the operation of the labour market. We must be content here to specify the transitional character of the 1980s as seen from the standpoint of the market studied. It has been characterized by massive falls in the level of labour demand which have not been adequately accommodated by increased rates of withdrawal and have been exacerbated by increased rates of labour market entry by young people. There has however been an increased demand for short service workers. Two other features are also of central importance. First, as is now widely recognized, there is no longer any simple relation between changes in the rate of growth of GDP and the volume of employment. Hence it is possible for the recession to have ended according to the former measure and not according to the latter. This circumstance is closely related to the second feature: capital investment is no longer associated with increases in the demand for labour.

These features may be illustrated by the unfulfilled expectations of the BSC redundants. First, the market did not pick up after the first shock of the redundancies; it recovered, but employment never returned to pre-1980 levels. Second, the recession came to an end, as other recessions have, but unemployment did not fall. Third, the faith of the steelworkers in the possibility of 'saving steelmaking at Port Talbot' was justified. It even got the investment it needed, and production climbed back to levels approaching those of the 1970s. But steel was now made with much lower manning levels. As a result BSC did not start taking workers back on as production climbed; it simply stopped making even more of them redundant.

This study has not therefore been simply concerned with redundant steelworkers in a loose labour market, but with workers living through a profound economic and social transition which reverses one of the two changes discussed in Harris's first book on the family and social change in Swansea (data, 1960): the transition, via the Second World War, to a full employment economy (Rosser and Harris, 1965; abridged edition, 1983).

The present study is therefore concerned with redundant steelworkers in a loose market during a peirod of profound economic and social transition. All the evidence available to us underlines how slow the response, at the cultural level, has been to economic change. After two-and-a-half years on the dole with no expectation of work the long-term unemployed are beginning, Leaver's study suggests, to renegotiate their marital relationships and their whole attitude to life as they come to realize that the supports of the old way of life have gone. The period since redundancy has been a struggle, but it has not been a struggle to adapt to new market conditions. For all our respondents it has been a struggle to preserve social identity and social relationships by maintaining their position within the working class and they have used that very identity and those very relationships to do so. What the unemployed are adjusting to is *failure*. The majority have avoided long-term unemployment but the unemployed only form a minority because some of the rest have responded to the demand for short-term labour. Joining the ranks of the chequered, though it removes them from the traditional arena of class struggle, the shop floor, does not entail their falling *out* of the working class in the cultural and relational sense. Rather, their chequered labour market careers attest their continued membership of the working class and their determination to remain within it (for discussion, see Harris and Lee in Rose, 1986).

Two questions remain. Will chequeredness persist as a way of life for a significant proportion of the labour force in west Industrial South Wales? Is chequeredness a phenomenon peculiar to South Wales in the 1980s? The frank answer to both these questions is that we do not know. There are field indications that the 1980s boom in contracting in the Port Talbot labour market is already (by 1986) falling off and that as BSC starts recruiting again to replace natural wastage, the contracting firms are beginning to lay off even long service employees. These two facts are of course connected. BSC Margam's ten year modernization 'plan' is complete and with its conclusion one of the largest and hitherto most stable components of demand for construction contracting in the market has disappeared. It is probable that the reduction in this demand after summer 1986 will more than offset BSC's increased need for contract labour in the making of steel in the first part of the decade. If so, we may expect that proportion of the redundant population who can succeed in retaining their status and identity through contracting to decline. The variegated pattern produced by movements on and off the market to try self-employment and for industrial retraining must of course have long since disappeared. We may expect therefore the numbers of chequered to decline in the local labour market studied here, rather than to increase.

The particular type of post-redundancy labour market experience described in this book is, however, the result of a more general process in which labour demand calls forth its own supply, whose characteristics then condition the way the labour process is structured. (For discussion, see Lee and Harris, 1985.) Which has to adapt to which, labour process to labour force or force to process, will depend on the relative power of employees and employers *in the market*. It was the loosening of the market and the consequent power shift that made possible the restructuring of the labour process and resulted in the transformation of the lives of both remaining and redundant workers and involved the creation of a new 'class' of chequered worker. This study has been concerned therefore with a particular case of a more general phenomenon.

When we turn to consider whether chequeredness as a phenomenon is unique to the market studied, however, there are good reasons for supposing that it is not. In the first place the increased use of contracting in the steel industry is not confined to Margam and would seem to have spread throughout BSC's operations (see Fevre, 1987). In the second place one of the reasons actually stated in the Redundancy Agreement was the need for *flexible* manning. Research by the Institute of Manpower Studies has led to the conclusion that firms are responding to the present transition by a movement in the direction of what Atkinson (1984) has described as the 'flexible firm'. 'This new structure involves the breaking of the labour force into increasingly peripheral, and therefore numerically flexible groups of workers clustered about a numerically stable core group which will conduct the organisation's key, firm specific activities.' He claims that 'so widespread have aspirations for greater flexibility become that many employers now expect to introduce changes which will restructure the work experience of some or perhaps all of the labour force'.

These are large claims but they are supported by an increasing volume of evidence. Not only is there IMS's own study, published by the National Economic Development Office (July 1986) but an increasing amount of anecdotal evidence in the press. One of these newspaper reports stands out because it parallels so closely the findings of the present study. It is of particular interest to the sociologists of redundancy since it concerns UIE, the successor to the John Brown shipyard, once an elment in the ill-fated Upper Clyde Shipbuilders, redundancies from which were studied by Frank Herron in *Labour Market in Crisis* (1975). According to a report in the *Guardian* (1 September 1986), that labour market would now appear to be undergoing the same *transition* as the South Wales market which has been described here:

Large engineering companies . . . are turning to temporary labour to meet peaks in demand. 'It's a clinical solution,' said one personnel manager who confessed some misgivings about the practice. 'Demand falls and out they go and you don't have to carry any surplus labour.' . . . Currently [UIE] has a workforce of over 1300 made up of 850 on short-term contracts and 530 'core' workers. 'We never liked this situation, but it was forced on us by circumstances – accept contract workers or there'll be no UIE,' said the yard's union convenor . . . 'When I came into the industry over twenty years ago we had just won the battle over casualisation – at a moment's notice you could be sacked – and now it's all coming back again.'

The present study seems therefore to have, quite fortuitously, chronicled one case of the beginning of a much wider trend. Hence we may reasonably expect a movement towards short-term employment in other areas than South Wales and other industries than steel in the rest of this decade, if indeed this shift has not already occurred unnoticed. In so far as the character of labour demand does change in this direction we may expect to find an increased proportion of workers having chequered labour market careers across the country, while in west Industrial South Wales the fall in the proportion of short-term employments engendered by the end of the boom in contracting in Port Talbot is likely to be partially offset as local enterprises other than BSC seek ever greater flexibility in manning.

Atkinson, following the tradition of both industrial sociology and management studies, fails to emphasize that changes in the direction of the flexible firm will not merely restructure the *work experience* of the labour force but increase the proportion of the working class who have experience of *the market*, that is to say of those who actually experience their class position as sellers of labour power, subject to what Marx termed 'the play of chance and caprice in the market' as well as the 'despotism of the workplace'. The consequences of such a shift, in terms of political consciousness and action, could be far-reaching indeed. We do not claim that they will be, but the results of the research reported here do, we believe, require that this issue be placed firmly on the political and research agenda.

These agenda coalesce when we restore to the notion of 'the working class' its original social and political significance. If sociology is about class (as opposed to anthropology, which is 'about' kinship) it is because of the centrality of the problem posed by the emergence of class relations as a central structuring principle of social life. This problem originally posed itself as that of the proletariat: a class of civil society which is outside civil society, in the words of Marx – who is himself, of course, merely echoing Hegel. This anomic mass, without rights or duties, perpetually poses an anarchic threat to encultured social life. More generally the predominance of class as opposed to status relations spells the end of civilized society or quite possibly the end of 'society' itself. Can there be a stable social order which is based upon purely categorical relations by which people relate to each other in a purely instrumental and calculative fashion?

At a practical level this problem has only two solutions - the abolition of the society from which the proletariat is excluded or the incorporation of the proletariat into civil society. The enormous popularity of Goldthorpe et al.'s *Affluent Worker* study derives from its having equal significance to those who favour each solution. 'Embourgeoisement' is a modern form of 'incorporation', and (from one perspective) is to be welcomed as neutralizing an ever present threat to the social order. From the other perspective it is the result of the increasing hegemony of the dominant class at both material and ideological levels, and is to be resisted.

However, the incorporation of the working class at the cultural level has already been accomplished a good while back. It is quite some time since the working class could be called an anomic mass. On the contrary, it has become an encultured group whose own culture has absorbed elements from that of the society as a whole and has contributed to that common culture. It is also a long time since it has been outside political society; it has steadily been incorporated in this sense also, as Marshall claimed in *Citizenship and Social Class* (1950). Moreover, as this book has implicitly argued, the working class does not confront the agents of the opposing class as anonymous members of a category but as persons with qualities other than those intrinsic to their class position. And this is so because labour power is bought and sold not on *the* market but on *a* specific local labour market which is constituted by a population whose social life is structured by membership of a plurality of categorical relations and a network of interpersonal ties.

Incorporation at the relational, cultural and political levels is, however, only partial. Working-class culture is in part one of resistance; interclass personal relations are inherently unstable and can slip into categorical ones and political rights can be used against the political order itself as well as to promote class interests within it. Incorporation will remain incomplete so long as the working class lacks economic rights to parallel its political ones. Both the major political parties recognize this fact by seeking to extend economic 'citizenship' to the working class. The Labour party attempted, with the Redundancy Payments Act of 1965, to give workers rights in their jobs. The Tory party has consistently attempted to extend home ownership, and the present administration share ownership, to working-class people.

The working class is not, however made less working class by its acquisition of property as long as its non-ownership of productive property, ensures that it is forced to sell its labour power on the market. Full incorporation requires, if not the restoration to its members of the ownership of productive property, then at least that they be accorded rights in employment. The movement in the direction of the flexible firm is, however, a movement away from economic incorporation, away from status relations back to contractual, that is, class relations. It requires that an increased proportion of the population continually comes on to the market to sell their labour power, thus increasing their consciousness of their class position as sellers of labour power and their dependence on those controlling or owning productive capital. It is a move towards the disincorporation of the working class. It may or may not be that such a move is morally desirable. It may or may not be that such a move will create a leaner, fitter and more competitive economy. But whether it is technically or morally desirable it must tend to exacerbate, not ameliorate, the problem posed by the working class since it will push a significant proportion of that class further out of society.

Who are the chequered? Are they a new negatively privileged class fraction whose position entails that they have fallen out of the encultured working class? Or are they, on the contrary, destined to become a new breed of proletarian: individualistic market-oriented individuals, whose social and political values will approximate to those of economic individualism rather than to those associated with the class solidarity born of struggles to control the labour process? Do permanent and peripheral workers have opposing economic interests (as the *Guardian* report referred to above suggests)? Will the increasing affluence of the permanent workers and the economic marginalization of peripheral workers create two distinct categories of workers, a subdivision of the proletariat into two classes having quite different chances in the market for goods and services? These are only some of the questions for the research agenda. The central theoretical question is, however, a profound one. Will the development of the forces of production under capitalism permit continued incorporation of the proletariat through 'affluence' (that is, consumerism), citizenship and mass culture? Or does its own logic of development require a continual re-creation of a class or class fraction excluded from participation in the legal and material benefits which the development of those forces of production makes possible? This is the central question posed by the transition of the 1980s.

# Appendix 1
# Samples and Response Rates

## Main sample

The sampling frame for the redundancy survey was a list of steelworkers who had been made redundant from BSC Port Talbot in 1980 compiled with the help of MSC. The MSC list was, however, governed by the Official Secrets Act and could not be divulged to the researchers. MSC very kindly drew a sample from this list, on our instructions, and contacted members of the sample by post, asking them to return a pre-addressed postcard if they did not wish to participate. Because of the high proportion of the original sample who indicated they did not wish to participate, it became necessary to draw a supplementary one. It soon became evident that the information supplied to MSC which had made possible the constitution of the original framework was defective, involving a higher than expected number of incorrect addresses and persons not actually made redundant. This necessitated compiling a second supplementary sample while field work was in progress. The drawing of this sample was delayed as a result of an industrial dispute affecting MSC, and the net result was that the period of interviewing was extended beyond the two months originally planned. This had consequences for the survey agency (Gallup) whose field force had other commitments during the period into which the interviewing extended. This further protracted the interviewing and complicated the administration of the survey for both the agency and the researchers, which in turn resulted in delays in the processing of the data into machine readable form. The net result was that data did not become available until eight months after the point at which the field work on Wave 1 of interviewing had been planned to terminate.

## Response rates

There were three waves of interviewing and the response rates are given in tables A1–3. The interviewing rates are tolerably satisfactory (80 per cent; 82 per cent; 77.5 per cent). The problems relate to those who did not co-operate: 36 per cent of the effective drawn sample on Wave 1, 3.5 per cent on Wave 2, and 19.5 per cent on Wave 3. The first rate was the result of the postal canvas by MSC; the second and third comprised respondents who indicated at the previous interview that they did not wish to be contacted again, and represent pure 'panel mortality'. Since this is related to the number of interviews experienced it is significantly higher on Wave 3 than on Wave 2.

## Representativeness

The substantial amount of non response, generated by the two stage contact procedure, necessarily raises questions about the representativeness of the sample. MSC carried out a small investigation involving the comparison of a random sample of 100 redundants interviewed on Wave 1, with 100 who had not wished to participate. This was designed to test the hypothesis that the decision to co-operate was related to the labour market status of the respondent. The enquiry failed to falsify the null hypothesis that there was no significant status difference between co-operators and non-co-operators. In respect of age, however, the data showed the participating unemployed to be slightly younger than the others.

The sample was compared also with BSC data on age and departments and the weighted sample distributions showed it to be representative of the redundant population on both these dimensions.

## Age weighting

To increase the number of economically active respondents, the original sample was disproportionately sampled by age, the sampling frequency of the over 50s being one-third that of other age groups. The analysis was based on unweighted data. For making inferences from the sample to the population sampled, weighted distributions were used.

Wave 1 data were weighted by multiplying cases where respondents were over 50 years of age by 10/3 and then multiplying the resultant distribution by a constant:

$$\left(\frac{\text{unweighted N}}{\text{weighted N}}\right)$$

Wave 2 data are not reported in this work. Wave 3 data were reweighted to produce an age distribution with the same shape as the Wave 1 distribution.

## Field study samples

A systematic sample of one-fifth of the achieved Wave 1 sample was drawn to provide respondents for Morris's study of households and networks, the residuum forming the Wave 2 interviewees. Morris's respondents were a random sub-sample of this fifth and included only married respondents who, following Wave 1, were male, aged between 24 and 54 and not resident on the periphery of the local labour market area. Leaver's initial sample was a one in two sample of all those married males under 55 who were unemployed or retraining at the time of the Wave 2 interviews, later supplemented by a one in two sample of those not selected at the first sampling stage.

*Timing of the field periods*

| | *Months elapsed since peak redundancy period: July – August 1980* |
|---|---|
| Wave 1: April – August 1981 | 9–13 |
| Wave 2: April – June 1982 | 21–3 |
| Morris's study (economically active males): April – December 1982 | 21–9 |
| Wave 3: October – December 1982 | 27–9 |
| Leaver's study (unemployed males): September 1982 – May 1983 | 26–34 |

**Interview schedules**

The interview schedules were designed by Lee in conjunction with Social Surveys (Gallup Poll) Ltd. Copies of the schedules may be obtained from the Department of Sociology and Anthropology, University College of Swansea, Swansea, SA2 8PP.

**Data deposit**

All machine readable data have been deposited in the ESRC data archive at the University of Essex.

TABLE A1.1 Response rates: Wave 1

*Sampling response*

| a Drawn | b Duplicates | c Ineligible | d Effective drawn a–(b + c) | e | Effective sample (d–e) | Sampling response rate |
|---|---|---|---|---|---|---|
| 1716 | 15 | 111 | 1590 | 570 | 1020 | $\frac{1020}{1590}$ 64% |

*Interviewing response*

| a drawn | b ineligible | (a–b) effective drawn | moved or not traced | emigrated | other non-contact | refused | other | total non-contact | interviewing response rate |
|---|---|---|---|---|---|---|---|---|---|
| 1020 | 63 | 957 | 57 | 17 | 17 | 76 | 37 | 204 | $\frac{753}{940}$ 80% |

*Gross response*

| a original drawn | b duplicates | c ineligible | a–(b + c) effective drawn | refusals/ non-co-operation | other non-contact | total non-contact | gross response rate |
|---|---|---|---|---|---|---|---|
| 1716 | 15 | 174 | 1527 | 646 | 128 | 774 | $\frac{753}{1527}$ 50% |

TABLE A1.2 Response rates: Wave 2

| *a* *Wave 1 respondents* | *b* *Non-co-operators* | *c* *Women respondents* | *Available population (a–(b+c))* | *Drawn sample (81%)* | *Moved: no trace* | *Emigrated* | *Away* | *Other non-contact* | *Refused* | *Other* | *Total non-contact* | *Response rate* |
|---|---|---|---|---|---|---|---|---|---|---|---|---|
| 753 | 20 | 46 | 687 | 550 | 12 | 10 | 4 | 20 | 30 | 26 | 102 | 448/550 82% |

TABLE A1.3 Response rates: Wave 3

| *a* *Wave 1 Respondents* | *b* *Non co-operators* | *Drawn sample a–b* | *Moved: No trace* | *Emigrated* | *Other non-contact* | *Refused* | *Other* | *Total non-contact* | *Response rate* |
|---|---|---|---|---|---|---|---|---|---|
| 753 | 147 | 606 | 16 | 13 | 51 | 31 | 23 | 134 | 472/606 77.5% |

# Appendix 2

# Papers Arising from Research undertaken by the Redundancy and Unemployment Research Group

(unpublished papers available from the authors)

**Papers arising from ESRC grant GOO 230023: Redundancy in Steel**

*Authored or co-authored by C. C. Harris*
*(Professor of Sociology, Department of Sociology and Anthropology, University College of Swansea)*


Harris, C. C. (1981) 'Domestic organisation, informal economy and unemployment'. Paper presented to the BSA Urban Sociology Group.

Harris, C. C. (1982) 'The geographical definition of the labour market of west industrial South Wales'.

Harris, C. C. (1983) 'Social transitions and the deconstruction of the family: reflections on research into the domestic circumstances of the victims of economic change'. *Tocqueville Review*, V (ii).

Harris, C. C. (1984) 'The idea of a labour market'. *School of Social Studies Occasional Papers No. 4*, University College of Swansea.

Harris, C. C. (1986) 'Redundancy: a problem for class analysis', in R. M. Lee (ed.) *Redundancy, Layoffs and Plant Closures: the Social Impact*, Croom Helm, London.

Harris, C. C. (1986) 'What happened at Margam'. *Planet*, 59 (October/November).

Harris, C. C. and Morris, L. D. (1985) 'Households, labour markets and the position of women', in R. Crompton and M. Mann (eds) *Gender and Stratification*, Macmillan, London.

Harris, C. C., Lee, R. M. and Morris, L. D. (1985) 'Redundancy in steel: labour market behaviour, local social networks and domestic organisation', in B. Roberts, R. Finnegan and D. Gallie (eds) *New Approaches to Economic Life*, Manchester University Press, Manchester.

Harris, C. C. and Lee, R. M. (1987) 'Conceptualising the place of redundant steelworkers in the class structure', in D. Rose (ed.) *Social Stratification and Economic Decline*, Hutchinson, London.

*Authored or co-authored by Dr R. M. Lee*
*(Senior Lecturer in Sociology, St Mary's College, Twickenham)*

Lee, R. M. (1983) 'The job-search activity of unemployed redundant steelworkers'.

Lee, R. M. (1983) 'The job-acquisition behaviour of redundant steelworkers'.

Lee, R. M. (1983) 'Estimating shadow wage labour: the use of the randomized response technique'. Paper presented to the SSRC Workshop on Local Labour Markets and the Informal Economy, Manchester, December, revised November 1984.

Lee, R. M. (1985) 'Redundancy, labour markets and informal relations'. *Sociological Review*, 33 (3).

Lee, R. M. (1985) 'The entry to self employment of redundant steelworkers'. *Industrial Relations Journal*. 16(2) Summer.

Lee, R. M. (1985) 'Retraining following redundancy in steel' *School of Social Studies Occasional Paper No. 9*, University College of Swansea.

Lee, R. M. (1986) 'Introduction' in R. M. Lee (ed.) *Redundancy, Layoffs and Plant Closures: the Social Impact*, Croom Helm, London.

Lee, R. M. (ed.) (1986a) *Redundancy, Layoffs and Plant Closures: the Social Impact*, Croom Helm, London.

Lee, R. M. and Harris, C. C. (1985) 'Redundancy studies: in Port Talbot and the future'. *Quarterly Journal of Social Affairs*, I (i).

Lee, R. M., Morris, L. D. and Harris, C. C. (1983) 'Aspects of the everyday life of the redundant: the place of informal relations'. Paper presented to the SSRC Conference on the Urban Change and Conflict, January.

*Authored by Dr L. D. Morris*
*(Lecturer in Sociology, Department of Sociology, University of Durham)*

Morris, Lydia D. (1983) 'Renegotiation of the domestic division of labour in the context of male redundancy'. Paper presented at BSA meeting, April; also in B. Roberts, D. Gallie and R. Finnigen (eds) *New Approaches to Economic Life*, Manchester University Press, Manchester, 1985 and in H. Newby, J. Bujra, P. Littlewood, G. and T. Rees (eds) *Restructuring Capital,* Macmillan, London, 1986.

Morris, Lydia D. (1983) 'Structure, personality and technique in semi-structured interviewing of married couples'. Paper presented at seminar, University of Aston, Birmingham, May (revised October).

Morris, Lydia D. (1984a) 'Patterns of social activity and post-redundancy labour-market experience'. *Sociology*, 18 (3) August.

Morris, Lydia D. (1984b) 'Redundancy and patterns of household finance' *Sociological Review*, 32 (3) August.

Morris, Lydia D. (1984c) 'Research note: renegotiation of the sexual division of labour'. *British Journal of Sociology*, September.

Morris, Lydia D. (1985a) 'Local social networks and domestic organisation – a study of redundant steelworkers and their wives'. *Sociological Review* 32 (2) May.

Morris, Lydia D. (1985b) 'Responses to redundancy: labour-market experience, domestic organisation and male social networks' (September 1983). *International Journal of Social Economics* (special issue), 12 (2).

**Papers arising from ESRC grant GOO 230048: Social Response to Redundancy in Steel**

*Authored by Dr R. Fevre*
*(Lecturer in Sociology, Department of Social Theory and Institutions, University College of North Wales, Bangor)*

Fevre, R. (1984) 'Employment and unemployment in Port Talbot'. *School of Social Studies Occasional Papers No. 6*, University College of Swansea.

Fevre, R. (1984) 'A postal survey of employment in Port Talbot'. *School of Social Studies Occasional Papers No. 7*, University College of Swansea.

Fevre, R. (1985) 'Contract work in the recession'. Presented to the BSA Annual Conference on Employment and Unemployment. In S. Wood and K. Purcell (eds) *The Changing Experience of Work: Restructuring and Recession*, Macmillan, London.

Fevre, R. (1986) 'Redundancy and contract labour' in R. M. Lee (ed.) *Redundancy, Layoffs and Plant Closures: the Social Impact*, Croom Helm, London.

**Papers arising from ERSC grant number GOO 232031: Retirement through Redundancy**

*Authored by Dr W. R. Bytheway*
*(Senior Research Fellow, Institute of Health Care Studies, University College of Swansea)*

Bytheway, W. R. (1985) 'Induced voluntary early retirement: a research report'. Institute of Health Care Studies, University College of Swansea.

Bytheway, W. R. (1986) 'Redundancy and the older worker', in R. M. Lee (ed.) *Redundancy, Layoffs and Plant Closures: a Social Impact*, Croom Helm, London.

Bytheway, W. R. (1986) 'Making way: the disengagement of older workers', in C. Phillipson, M. Bernard and P. Strang (eds) *Dependency and Interdependency in Old Age: Theoretical Perspectives and Policy Alternatives*, Croom Helm (in association with the British Society of Gerontology), London.

# Bibliography


Acton Society Trust (1958) 'Redundancy: a survey of problems and practices'. (Two reports), Acton Society, London.

Ashton, D. M. (1986) *Unemployment under Capitalism*, Wheatsheaf, Brighton.

Atkinson, J. (1984) 'Manpower strategies for flexible organisations'. *Personnel Management*, 16(8) 28–31.

Aylen, J. (1984) 'Prospects for steel'. *Lloyds Bank Review*, April.

Baber, C. and Thomas, D. (1980) 'The Glamorgan economy, 1914–1945', in A. H. John and B. Williams (eds), *Industrial Glamorgan*, Glamorgan County History Trust, Cardiff, 519–80.

Balchin, W. G. V. (1971) *Swansea and its Region*, British Association for the Advancement of Science, Swansea.

Becker, C. (1932) *The Heavenly City of the Eighteenth Century Philosophers*, Yale University Press, New Haven.

Beveridge, W. (1909) *Unemployment: A Problem of Industry*, Longman, London.

Bott, E. (1957) *Family and Social Network*, Tavistock, London.

Bresnen, M. J., Wray, K., Bryman, A., Beardsworth, A. D., Ford, J. R. and Keil, E. T. (1985) 'The flexibility of recruitment in the construction industry: formalisation or re-casualisation'. *Sociology*, 19(1) 108–24.

British Institute of Management (1974) *Redundancy Policies – A Study of Current Practice in 350 Companies*, British Institute of Management, London.

Brown, P. (1987) *Schooling Ordinary Kids*, Tavistock, London.

Bryer, R. A. Brignall, T. J. and Maunders, A. R. (1982) *Accounting for British Steel*, Gower, Aldershot.

BSC (1981) *Annual Reports and Accounts*, BSC, London.

Bytheway, W. R. (1985) *Induced Voluntary Early Retirement: a Research Report*, Institute of Health Care Studies, University College of Swansea, Swansea.

Bytheway, W. R. (1986a) 'Redundancy and the older worker', in R. M. Lee (ed.) *Redundancy, Layoffs and Plant Closures: the Social Impact*, Croom Helm, London, 84–112.

Bytheway, W. R. (1986b) 'Making way: the disengagement of older workers', in C. Phillipson, M. Bernard and P. Strang (eds) *Dependency and Interdependency in Old Age: Theoretical Perspectives and Policy Alternatives*, Croom Helm, London.

Callender, C. (1985) 'Gender inequality and social policy: women and the redundancy payment scheme'. *Journal of Social Policy*, 14(2) 189–213.

Carmichael, C. L. and Cook, L. M. (1981) *Redundancy and Displacement in the Tyre Industry*, MSC, London.

Cartwright, W. F. (1952) 'Preliminary planning of the Margam and Abbey Works'. *Iron and Coal Trades Review*, special issue, 9–12.

Cartwright, W. F. (1964) 'The future of automation in the iron and steel industry'. *Iron and Steel*, 37, 1964, 637–43.

Cottrell, E. (1981) *The Giant with Feet of Clay: the British Steel Industry*, Policy Studies Institute, London.

Cromwell, R. E. and Olsen, D. (eds) (1975) *Power in Families*, Sage, London.

Daniel, W. W. (1972) *Whatever Happened to the Workers of Woolwich?* PEP Broadsheet No. 537, London.

Daniel, W. W. (1974) *A National Survey of the Unemployed*, PEP, London.

Daniel, W. W. and Stilgoe, E. (1977) *Where Are They Now?*, PEP Broadsheet No. 572, London.

Daniel, W. W. and Stilgoe, E. (1978) *The Impact of Employment Protection Laws*, Policy Studies Institute, London.

DHSS Review Team (1978) *Social Assistance: a Review of the Supplementary Benefits Scheme in Great Britain*, HMSO, London.

Doeringer, P. B. and Piore, M. J. (1971) *Internal Labour Markets and Manpower Analysis*, D. C. Heath, Lexington, Mass.

Donnison, D. (1977) 'Against discretion'. *New Society*, 22 September, 534–6.

Donzelot, J. (1979) *The Policing of Families*, Hutchinson, London.

Edgell, S. R. (1980) *Middle Class Couples*, Allen and Unwin, London.

Edwards, R. C., Reich, M. and Gordon, D. M. (1975) *Labour Market Segmentation*, D. C. Heath, Lexington, Mass.

*Employment Gazette* (1978) 'Age and redundancy'. September, 86, 1032–9.

*Employment Gazette* (1983) 'Statistics of redundancies and recent trends', June, 91, 245–59.

*Employment Gazette* (1985) 'Recent trends in redundancies', May, 93, 202–9.

Fevre, R. (1984) 'Employment and unemployment in Port Talbot'. *School of Social Studies Occasional Paper No. 6*, University College of Swansea.

Fevre, R. (1985) 'Contract work and the recession', in S. Wood and K. Purcell (eds) *The Changing Experience of Work: Restructuring and Recession*, Macmillan, London.

Fevre, R. (1987) *Wales is Closed*, Spokesman, Nottingham.

Fothergill, S. and Gudgin, G. (1982) *Unequal Growth*, Heinemann, London.

Fryer, R. H. (1973) 'The myths of the Redundancy Payments Act'. *Industrial Law Journal*, 1, 1–16.

Garraty, J. A. (1978) *Unemployment in History*, Harper and Row, New York.

Goldthorpe, John H. and Hope, Keith (1974) *The Social Grading of Occupations: a New Approach and Scale*, Clarendon Press, Oxford.

Goldthorpe, John H., Lockwood, David, Bechhofer, Frank and Platt, Jennifer (1969) *The Affluent Worker in the Class Structure*, Cambridge University Press, Cambridge.

Goodman, R. (1962) *Redundancy and the Affluent Society*, Fabian Tract No. 340, Fabian Society, London.

Gordon, D. M. (1972) *Theories of Poverty and Unemployment*, D. C. Heath, Lexington, Mass.

Granovetter, Mark (1973) 'The strength of weak ties'. *American Journal of Sociology*, 78, 1360–80.

Granovetter, Mark (1974) *Getting a Job: A Study of Contacts and Careers*, Harvard University Press, Cambridge, Mass.

Granovetter, Mark (1981) 'Towards a sociological theory of income differences', in Ivar Berg (ed.) *Sociological Perspectives on Labour Markets*, Academic Press, London, 11–48.

Gray, A. (1979) 'The working-class family as an economic unit', in Sociological Review Monograph No. 28, *The Sociology of the Family: New Directions for Britain*, Sociological Review, Keele, 186–213.

Grevet, P. (1976) *Besoins Populaires et Financement Public*, Editions Sociales, Paris.

Griffiths, L. (1952) 'Margam reconstruction'. *Iron and Coal Trades Review*, special issue, 13–22; 34.

Harris, C. C. (1969) *The Family*, Allen and Unwin, London.

Harris, C. C. (1982) 'The geographical definition of the labour market of west Industrial South Wales', Department of Sociology, University College of Swansea.

Harris, C. C. (1983) 'Social transitions and the deconstruction of the family: reflections on research into the domestic circumstances of the victims of social change'. *Tocqueville Review*, V (ii) 365–81.

Harris, C. C. (1984) 'The idea of a labour market'. *School of Social Studies Occasional Papers No. 4*, University College of Swansea.

Harris, C. C. and Lee, R. M. (1988) 'Conceptualising the place of redundant steelworkers in the class tructure', in D. Rose (ed.) *Social Stratification and Economic Decline*, Hutchinson, London.

Harris, C. C. and Morris, L. D. (1986) 'Labour markets and the position of women', in R. Crompton and M. Mann (eds) *Gender and Stratification*, Polity Press, Cambridge, 86–96.

Heal, D. W. (1974) *The Steel Industry in Post War Britain*, David and Charles, Newton Abbot.

Herron, F. (1975) *Labour Market in Crisis*, Macmillan, London.

Hill, M. J., Harrison, R. M., Sargeant, A. V. and Talbot, V. (1973) *Men Out of Work*, Cambridge University Press, Cambridge.

Humphrys, G. (1971a) 'Manufacturing and service industries', in W. G. V. Balchin (ed.) *Swansea and its Region*, British Association for the Advancement of Science, Swansea, pp. 255–72.

Humphrys, G. (1971b) 'Extractive industry: coal mining', in W. G. V. Balchin (ed.) *Swansea and Its Region*, British Association for the Advancement of Science, Swansea, pp. 225–40.

Humphrys, G. (1971c) 'Swansea Bay City joins the top twenty', *Geographical Magazine*, 43(12), 848–52.

Institute of Manpower Studies (1986) *Changing Working Patterns*, National Economic Development Office, London.

*Iron and Coal Trades Review* (1952) Special Issue: a Technical Survey of the Abbey, Margam, Trostre and Newport Plants of the Steel Company of Wales.

Jeffrys, M. with Moss, W. (1954) *Mobility in the Labour Market*, Routledge and Kegan Paul, London.

Jenkins, Richard (1986) *Racism and Recruitment*, Cambridge University Press, Cambridge.

Jenkins, Richard, Bryman, Alan, Ford, Janet, Keil, Teresa and Beardsworth, Alan (1983) 'Information in the labour market: the impact of the recession'. *Sociology*, 17(2) 260-7.

Jewson, N. and Mason, D. (1986) 'Modes of discrimination in the recruitment process: formalisation, fairness and efficiency'. *Sociology*, 20(1) 43-63.

John, A. H. (1980) 'Glamorgan, 1700-1750', in A. H. John and G. Williams (eds), *Industrial Glamorgan*, Glamorgan County History Trust, Cardiff, pp 1-46.

John, A. H. and Williams, G. (eds) (1980) *Industrial Glamorgan*, Glamorgan County History Trust, Cardiff.

Jolly, S., Creigh, C. and Mungay, A. (1980) *Age as a Factor in Employment*, Department of Employment, Research Paper No. 11, HMSO, London.

Jones, D. R. (1984) 'Redundancy and turnover in the labour force', Institute of Economic Research Working Paper, University College of North Wales, Bangor.

Jones, M. (1972) *Life on the Dole*, Davis Poynter, London.

Joshi, H. (1984) *Women's Participation in Paid Work*, Department of Employment, Research Paper No. 45, HMSO, London.

Kahn, H. (1964) *Repercussions of Redundancy*, Allen and Unwin, London.

Kent, R. A. (1981) *The History of British Empirical Sociology*, Gower, Aldershot.

Klein, R. and O'Higgins, M. (1985) *The Future of Welfare*, Basil Blackwell, Oxford.

Laslett, P. (1965) *The World We Have Lost*, Macmillan, London. 3rd edition 1984.

Lee, R. M. (1983) *Post Redundancy Employment Histories: Preliminary Results*, Department of Sociology and Anthropology, University College of Swansea.

Lee, R. M. (1985a) 'Retraining following redundancy in steel'. *School of Social Studies, Occasional Paper No. 9*, University College of Swansea.

Lee, R. M. (1985b) 'The entry to self-employment of redundant steelworkers'. *Industrial Relations Journal*, 16(2) Summer, 42-9.

Lee, R. M. (ed.) (1986) *Redundancy, Layoffs and Plant Closures: the Social Impact*, Croom Helm, London.

Lee, R. M. and Harris, C. C. (1985) 'Redundancy studies: in Port Talbot and the future'. *Quarterly Journal of Social Affairs*, I (i) 19-27.

Lee, R. M., Morris, L. D. and Harris, C. C. (1983) 'Aspects of the everyday life of the redundant: the role of informal relations'. Paper given at the Fourth SSRC Urban Change and Conflict Conference, Clacton.

Leiss, W. (1978) *The Limits to Satisfaction: On Needs and Commodities*, Marion Boyars, London.

Lippman, J. and McCall, S. (1976) 'The economics of job search: a survey'. *Economic Inquiry*, 14 (June), 155-89.

McIntosh, M. (1981) 'Households, incomes and the politics of needs: problems for the study of poverty and inequality'. Paper presented for the Annual Conference of the British Sociological Association, Aberystwyth, April 1981.

Mackay, D. I. (1972a) 'After the shake out', *Oxford Economic Papers*, 24 (March) 89-110.

Mackay, D. I., (1972b) 'Redundancy and re-engagement; a study of car workers', *Manchester School*, 40 (3) 295–312.

Mackay, D. I. and Reid, G. (1971) *Men Leaving Steel*, BSC Social and Regional Development Department, London.

Mackay, D. I., Boddy, D., Brack, J., Diack, J. A. and Jones, N. (1971) *Labour Markets Under Different Employment Conditions*, Allen and Unwin, London.

Mackay, D. I., Mackay, R., McVean, P. and Edwards, R. (1980) *Redundancy and Displacement*, Department of Employment, Research Paper No. 16, HMSO, London.

McKee, L. and Bell, C. (1985) 'Marital and family relationships in times of male unemployment', in B. Roberts, R. Finnegan and D. Gallie (eds) *New Approaches to Economic Life*, Manchester University Press, Manchester, 387–99.

Manners, G. (1964) *South Wales in the Sixties*, Pergamon, Oxford.

MSC (1982) *The Ford Bridgend Report*, Manpower Intelligence and Planning, MSC, London.

Marsden, D. and Duff, E. (1975) *Workless*, Penguin, Harmondsworth.

Marshall, A. (1925) 'Letter to Percy Alden', in A. C. Pigou (ed.) *Memorials of Alfred Marshall*, Macmillan, London, 446–7.

Marshall, T. H. (1950) *Citizenship and Social Class*, Cambridge University Press, Cambridge.

Martin, R. and Fryer, R. H. (1973) *Redundancy and Paternalist Capitalism*, Allen and Unwin, London.

Martin, R. L., (1982) 'Job loss and the regional incidence of redundancy'. *Cambridge Journal of Economics*, 6, 375–95.

Martin, R. L., (1984) 'Redundancies, labour turnover and employment contraction in the recession'. *Regional Studies*, 18(6) 445–58.

Marx, K. H., (1846) *The German Ideology*, Lawrence and Wishart, London 1965.

Massey, D. and Meagan, R. (1985) *Politics and Method*, Methuen, London.

Meager, N. (1984) 'Job loss and the regions: how important is redundancy?'. *Regional Studies*, 18(6) 459–68.

Meager, N. (1985) *Temporary Work in Britain*, IMS Report No. 6, September, Institute of Manpower Studies, Falmer, Brighton.

Meager, N. (1986) 'Temporary work in Britain'. *Employment Gazette*, January 1986, 7–15.

*Ministry of Labour Gazette* (1963) 50–5.

Molyneux, M. (1979) 'Beyond the domestic labour debate'. *New Left Review*, 116, 3–24.

Morgan, K. (1983) 'Restructuring steel: the crisis of labour and locality in Britain'. *International Journal of Urban and Regional Research*, 7(2) 175–201.

Morris, L. D. (1983) 'Renegotiation of the domestic division of labour', paper presented at BSA Conference, The Periphery of Industrial Society, Cardiff, 1983. Appears in B. Roberts, R. Finnegan and D. Gallie (eds) *New Approaches to Economic Life*, Manchester University Press, Manchester, 400–16 and in H. Newby (eds) *Restructuring Capital*, Macmillan, London 221–43.

Morris, L. D. (1984a) 'Patterns of social activity and post redundancy labour-market experience'. *Sociology*, 18(3) 339–52.

Morris, L. D. (1984b) 'Redundancy and patterns of household finance'. *Sociological Review*, 33(2) 492–522.

Morris, L. D. (1985a) 'Local social networks and domestic organisation'. *Sociological Review*, 33(2) 327–42.

Morris, L. D. (1985b) 'Responses to redundancy: labour market experience, domestic organisation and male social networks'. *International Journal of Social Economics*, 12(2) 5–16.

Newby, H., Bujra, J., Littlewood, P., G. and T. Rees. (eds) (1986) *Restructuring Capital*, Macmillan, London.

Noble, F. (1981) 'Redundancy statistics'. *Employment Gazette*, June 1981, 260–2.

Oakley, A. (1974) *The Sociology of Housework*, Martin Robertson, Oxford.

Office of Population, Censuses and Surveys (1984) *General Household Survey 1982*, HMSO, London.

Pahl, J. (1980) 'Patterns of money management within marriage'. *Journal of Social Policy*, 9, 313–35.

Pahl, J. (1983) 'The allocation of money and the structuring of inequality within marriage'. *Sociological Review*, 31(2), 237–62.

Pahl, R. E. (1980) 'Employment, work and the domestic division of labour'. *International Journal of Urban and Regional Research*, 4(1) 1–20.

Pahl, R. E. (1984) *Divisions of Labour*, Basil Blackwell, Oxford.

Parker, S. R., Thomas, C., Ellis, N, and McCarthy, W. E. (1971) *The Effects of the Redundancy Payments Act*, OPCS, London, HMSO.

Parnes, H. S. (1954) *Research on Labour Mobility*, Social Science Research Council, New York.

Parsons, T. and Smelser, N. (1956) *Economy and Society*, Routledge and Kegan Paul, London.

Payne, D. (1984) *Closure at Linwood: a Follow-up Survey of Redundant Workers*, MSC, Edinburgh.

Pearson, R. and Greenwood, J. (1977) *Redundancy and Displacement: a Study of the Maidstone Labour Market*, Institute of Manpower Studies, Falmer, Brighton.

Phillipson, C., Bernard, M. and Strang, P. (1986) *Dependency and Interdependency in Old Age: Theoretical Perspectives and Policy Alternatives*, Croom Helm, London.

Piore, M. J. (1975) 'Notes for a theory of labour market stratification', in R. C. Edwards, M. Reich and D. M. Gordon (eds) *Labour Market Segmentation*, D. C. Heath, Lexington, Mass, 125–50.

Reid, Graham L. (1972) 'Job search and the effectiveness of job finding methods'. *Industrial and Labor Relations Review*, 25(4) 479–95.

Reynolds, L. G. (1951) *The Structure of the Labour Market*, Harper and Row, New York.

Roberts, R. O. (1980) 'The smelting of non-ferrous metals since 1750', in A. H. John and G. Williams (eds) *Industrial Glamorgan*, Glamorgan County History Trust, Cardiff, 47–96.

Rose, D. (ed.) (1986) *Social Stratification and Economic Decline*, Hutchinson, London.

Rosser, C. and Harris, C. C. (1965) *The Family and Social Change*, Routledge and Kegan Paul, London. Abridged edition 1983.

Safilios-Rothschild, C. (1970) 'The study of family power structure: a review 1960–1969'. *Journal of Marriage and the Family*, 32, 539–51.

Safilios-Rothschild, C. (1976) 'A macro and micro examination of family power and love: an exchange model'. *Journal of Marriage and the Family*, 38, 355–62.

Scanzoni, J. (1979) 'Social processes and power in families', in W. Burr, R. Hill, I. Nye and I. Reiss (eds) *Contemporary Theories About the Family*, Free press, Glencoe.

Scanzoni, J. and Polanko, K. (1980) 'A conceptual approach to explicit marital negotiation'. *Journal of Marriage and the Family*, 42, 315–44.

Scanzoni, J. and Szinovacz, M. (1980) *Family Decision Making: a Developmental Sex Role Model*, Sage, London.

Sengenberger, Werner (1981) 'Labour market segmentation and the business cycle', in Frank Wilkinson (ed.) *The Dynamics of Labour Market Segmentation*, Academic Press, London, 243–60.

Sennett, R. and Cobb, J. (1972) *The Hidden Injuries of Class*, Cambridge University Press, Cambridge.

Smits, M., Simmons, S., Burrows, R., Lloyd, P. and Martin T. (no date). 'Unemployed discourse: some notes towards a sociological analysis of accounts of unemployment', *Occasional Papers in Sociology and Social Policy, No. 8*, Department of Sociology, University of Surrey, Guildford.

Spence, S. (1964) 'Towards a new regional economic policy for South West Wales', in G. Manners *South Wales in the Sixties*, Pergamon, Oxford, 185–98.

Stigler, G. (1961) 'The economics of information'. *Journal of Political Economy*, 69, 213–25.

Stigler, G. (1962) 'Information in the labor market'. *Journal of Political Economy*, 70 (Supplement: October), S94–105.

Straus, A. (1978) *Negotiations: Varieties, Contexts, Processes and Social Order*, Jossey-Bass, San Francisco.

Townsend, A. R. (1982) 'Recession and the regions of Great Britain, 1976–1980: analyses of redundancy data'. *Environmental Planning*, 14(10A) 1389–404.

Towsend, A. R. and Peck, F. (1985) 'An approach to the analysis of redundancies in the UK (post 1976): some methodological problems of policy implications', in D. Massey and R. Meagan *Politics and Method*, Methuen, London, 61–87.

Upham, M. (1980) 'British Steel: retropsect and prospect'. *Industrial Relations Journal*, 11(3) 5–21.

Vaisey, J. (1974) *The History of British Steel*, Weidenfeld and Nicholson, London.

Weber, Max (1978) *Economy and Society*, edited and translated by Guenther Roth and Claus Wittich, University of California Press, Berkeley. Originally published 1915.

Wedderburn, D. (1964) *White Collar Redundancy*, Cambridge University Press, Cambridge.

Wedderburn, D. (1965) 'Redundancy and the railwaymen', Department of Applied Economics, Occasional Paper No. 4, Cambridge University Press, Cambridge.

Wiener, M. J. (1981) *English Culture and the Decline of the Industrial Spirit 1850–1980,* Cambridge University Press, Cambridge.

Williams, J. (1980) 'The coal industry, 1750–1914', in A. H. John and G. Williams, *Industrial Glamorgan*, Glamorgan County History Trust, Cardiff, 155–210.

Wood, S. (1977a) 'A consideration of the study of redundancy'. *Scottish Journal of Sociology*, 51–71.

Wood, S. (1977b) 'Is redundancy a social problem? A comment'. *Personnel Review*, 6(3) 55–9.

Wood, S. and Cohen, S. (1978) 'Approaches to the study of redundancy'. *Industrial Relations Journal*, 8, 19–27.

Wood, S. and Day, I. (1983) *Redundancy*, Gower, Aldershot.

# Name Index

# Subject Index